The Campaign Finance Cases

LANDMARK LAW CASES &AMERICAN SOCIETY

Peter Charles Hoffer
N. E. H. Hull
Williamjames Hull Hoffer
Series Editors

For a complete list of titles in the series go to www.kansaspress.ku.edu.

MELVIN I. UROFSKY

The Campaign Finance Cases

Buckley, McConnell, Citizens United, *and* McCutcheon

UNIVERSITY PRESS OF KANSAS

Published by the University Press of Kansas (Lawrence, Kansas 66045), which was organized by the Kansas Board of Regents and is operated and funded by Emporia State University, Fort Hays State University, Kansas State University, Pittsburg State University, the University of Kansas, and Wichita State University.

Library of Congress Cataloging-in-Publication Data

Names: Urofsky, Melvin I., author.

Title: The campaign finance cases : Buckley, McConnell, Citizens United, and McCutcheon / Melvin I. Urofsky.

Description: Lawrence : University Press of Kansas, 2020. | Series: Landmark law cases and American society | Includes bibliographical references and index.

Identifiers: LCCN 2020006825

ISBN 9780700629879 (cloth)

ISBN 9780700629886 (paperback)

ISBN 9780700629893 (epub)

Subjects: LCSH: Campaign funds—Law and legislation—United States.—Cases.

Classification: LCC KF4920 .U755 2020 | DDC 342.73/078—dc23

LC record available at https://lccn.loc.gov/2020006825.

British Library Cataloguing-in-Publication Data is available.

Printed in the United States of America

10 9 8 7 6 5 4 3 2 1

The paper used in this publication is recycled and contains 30 percent postconsumer waste. It is acid free and meets the minimum requirements of the American National Standard for Permanence of Paper for Printed Library Materials Z39.48-1992.

For my friends in the
Columbia College '61 Lunch and Book Groups

CONTENTS

Rarely does the Supreme Court reverse itself as quickly and profoundly as it did in the campaign finances cases. Law scholars have found the reversal startling and difficult to explain. Now comes a new edition of Melvin Urofsky's classic study of campaign finance law, bringing the study of the statutes and the court cases up to date. Urofsky, one of the leading students of the High Court, has done what readers and students wanted and needed—explain in clear and convincing language what was at stake in the twists and turns of the campaign finances law.

The two principles at issue in the cases are freedom of political speech, the freedom that protects all others, and stewardship of the political process from undue influence. In a time of controversies over political speech in the blogosphere, social media, and cable news, and claims of electoral fraud, no issue could be more important to Americans. In *Buckley v. Valeo* (1976), the Court had decided that campaign contributions could be regulated by Congress. In *McConnell v. Federal Election Commission* (2003), the Court found constitutional the McCain-Feingold Act, limiting the size of campaign advertising by certain groups. Then, in *Citizens United v. Federal Election Commission* (2010), the Court declared portions of the McCain-Feingold Act violated the Free Speech Clause of the First Amendment.

The conventional account of the case law, relying on the 5–4 votes on the Court, concludes that liberals wanted the restrictions and conservatives wanted large corporations to be able to exert disproportionate influence on voters. On its face, this explanation seems to fit a simplistic view of the politics of the Court and the country. Working from a rich store of primary sources, probing the motivations and the ideas of all of the participants in the campaign finance legal story, Urofsky reveals a far more complex picture, and one whose significance is thus far greater than simple political ideologies.

As back and forth the Court went in a bewildering variety of Federal Election Commission case rulings in these pages, we greet a crew of familiar characters. For example, bringing *McConnell* we find Senator Mitch McConnell, as well as Republican congressman Mike Pence, Wayne LaPierre (and the National Rifle Association), fifty-five lawyers (mostly corporate counsel), former solicitor general (and Clinton impeachment special counsel) Kenneth Starr, and then, surprise, some leading First Amendment figures, including Floyd Abrams and Kathleen Sullivan. Strange bedfellows were drawn together in common cause. Then there was the drama of Chief Justice John Roberts scheduling *Citizens United* for reargument, when Justice David Souter's dissenting draft opinion accused the majority of discarding long-settled precedent.

There are gems in the text that readers should not overlook. Urofsky's analysis of the justices' opinions in *Citizens United* is a model of its kind, sophisticated, objective, thoughtful, and persuasive. In these, as in his narrative, Urofsky does not join in the public outcry against the majority, but ably documents how the decision has deconstructed voting patterns and, in the words of President Barack Obama, "opened the floodgates to special interests." The battle goes on, its outcome uncertain, and the combatants' energy unflagging.

The genesis of my interest in campaign finance reform can be traced to a very specific event, lunch in Williamsburg, Virginia, with a dear and now departed friend, Eric Tachau of Louisville. Eric asked me what I thought of the recently enacted Bipartisan Campaign Reform Act (BCRA), also known as McCain-Feingold. I confessed that I did not know all the details, but given the excesses of the 1990s, with the alleged sale of sleepovers in the Lincoln Bedroom, as well as the astounding amounts of money that George W. Bush had raised in the 2000 campaign, I thought that preventing corruption by limiting the amount of money that could be contributed or spent might be a good idea. It might even qualify as the compelling governmental interest that courts require when speech is limited.

Eric disagreed. A true liberal, he believed in the sacredness of free speech, particularly political speech. Then, as befitted a man who was a grandnephew of Louis Brandeis, he reminded me that the justice had always held that the cure for bad speech is more speech, not its restriction. Eric was no knee-jerk theorist of free speech. This was a man who had put his body and his livelihood on the line when he stood up for civil rights in his home city, long before it became fashionable for whites to do so. He and his wife, Mary K., had not just talked about civil rights and civil liberties; they had fought for them.

In our conversation, although I did not recognize it at the time, was the long-standing tension between two worthy goals. On the one hand, there is the desire to protect the integrity of the political system from the impact of large contributions from wealthy donors, unions, or corporations. On the other is the need to protect political speech, which is at the core of First Amendment protection. It is the tension between these two ideals—both necessary in a democratic society—that is at the heart of the story and the crux of the cases decided in our nation's highest court.

Shortly afterward I ran into Mike Briggs, then the editor in chief at University Press of Kansas, and when he asked me if I had anything in mind for a book, I told him about my conversation with Eric. By then, the case of *McConnell v. Federal Elections Commission*, a direct challenge to BCRA, had started working its way through the courts, and everybody knew that it would soon reach the Supreme Court. "Would you be interested in a book on campaign finance, efforts to reform it, and what happened to those efforts in the courts?" I asked. Mike said yes, and the result was *Money and Free Speech*, published by Kansas in 2005, which took the story from the beginnings of our country up through the 2003 *McConnell* decision in the high court.

More recently, David Congdon, now an acquisitions editor for the Press, and Peter Hoffer, an old friend who edits the Landmark Law Cases series, asked if I would be interested in bringing that book up to date. With almost unseemly haste I said yes. At the end of *Money and Free Speech* I did something that historians in general, and I in particular, rarely if ever do—predict the future.

McConnell had been what is known as a "facial" challenge to McCain-Feingold, the type of case where the plaintiff tells the courts that there is a very good chance that this law, on the face of it, will affect me adversely, so won't you please declare it unconstitutional. Courts generally do not like facial challenges; the Constitution says federal courts should only hear real cases and controversies. The high court in *McConnell* had not found any harm to Senator McConnell or any of his coplaintiffs and upheld nearly all of the provisions of the new law. I said that once real cases arose, so-called as-applied challenges where the plaintiffs could demonstrate actual harm, the Court would not look so sympathetically at the law. Since then that is exactly what has happened, with the two major cases being *Citizens United* in 2010 and *McCutcheon* in 2014.

When writing the original book, I found myself conflicted between the poles of free speech and political integrity and wondered if it would be at all possible to reconcile the two. As a historian, I had often regaled my classes with tales of corruption during the post-Reconstruction era known as the Gilded Age, stories of messengers carrying satchels of cash from robber barons to legislators, and the definition of an honest man being a representative who, having accepted the first bribe, did not take another and delivered what had been promised. On the other hand, I have also been a student of the Court in general, and of Louis Brandeis in particular, and have always considered his opinion in *Whitney v. California* (1927) to be the single greatest exposition of why free speech is necessary in a democracy.

The problem is that there is a seeming conflict between two ideals. One is the value of speech unrestricted by any governmental directive, the value embodied in the Speech Clause of the First Amendment. The other is the need for electoral integrity, keeping the political process open to all and not affected by large infusions of cash, the goal of every effort at campaign finance reform since 1907.

My friend Robert Post of the Yale Law School has been teaching First Amendment doctrine there for three decades, and he confesses that he has done his best to avoid addressing the Supreme Court's campaign finance decisions, having been unable to achieve clarity about those opinions in his own mind. "The need for freedom of political speech appears self-evident," he says, "but so also does the need for electoral integrity. Each seems indispensable, and yet in cases like *Citizens United* they appear incompatible."

It is not that politicians and academics have not tried to solve the problem. I am aware of the work of Bruce Ackerman, the Chicago school, and others, but while some of their plans might work in a perfect world, that is one phrase that no one should apply to our politics. In the writings of these people, in the debates in Congress, in the arguments before the courts, and ultimately in the majority and dissenting opinions of the Supreme Court, two themes emerged, the same themes that run through this book.

One is an appeal to the command of the First Amendment that Congress shall make no law abridging freedom of speech, especially political speech, which many scholars believe to be the core value protected by the Speech Clause.

The other is an appeal to facts and common sense, that while political speech is important, if we allow large sums of money to influence who can talk, who can gain access to candidates and officeholders, the political process will be corrupted and the speech will be meaningless.

Much of the confusion over campaign finance law can be laid at the feet of the justices who decided *Buckley v. Valeo* in 1976. In that case the Court drew a distinction between campaign contributions, money given to candidates, and campaign expenses, money spent by candidates. The Court held that the latter, the expenditures, constituted speech, and therefore could not be regulated by the government. Contributions, on the other hand, were not speech, and could be limited. Although technically this distinction still survives, it has drawn withering criticism from judges, politicians, donors, and academics for more than four decades. Why is one of the topics covered in this book.

Most of the campaign finance cases have been decided by a 5–4 vote. Many people make the assumption that since so-called conservative justices often vote to strike down laws like McCain-Feingold, while so-called liberal justices would uphold them, this is simply a case of liberals versus conservatives. It is not. The rationale used to invalidate campaign finance regulations is pure First Amendment rationale, that speech—especially political speech—cannot be regulated in any way by the government. Moreover, in nearly every case from *Buckley* in 1976 to *Citizens United* in 2010, the American Civil Liberties Union, the nation's premier defender of free speech, filed a "friend of the court" brief urging the justices to strike down the law as a violation of the First Amendment. For those opposed to campaign finance regulation, the governing issue is protecting political speech.

For the justices who support these laws, the primary concern has been to protect the integrity of the political system, which they believe is the compelling rationale needed to meet the requirements of the First Amendment. The only case they have "won" is *McConnell*, because it was a facial challenge, and because without a record of real harm, the Court deferred to congressional judgment of the need for such a law. As we shall see, judicial deference did not last long.

It is true, of course, that politicians of all stripes, and especially conservatives, have never wanted anything to get between them and the money they need to run for reelection. The few times that Congress has enacted reform legislation, it has always been in response to a scandal that triggered a public demand for action, such as the revelations of the Armstrong Committee in the early twentieth century, Nixon and Watergate in the 1970s, and Clinton and soft money in the 1990s. In every instance, even without court intervention, politicians and donors managed to get together. As Justice Sandra Day O'Connor put it in *McConnell*, "Money, like water, will always find an outlet."

I am under no illusion that this will be the final word on campaign finance reform. Even as I write, there are cases working their way through state and federal courts attacking different measures that try to contain the vast amounts of money swallowed up by political campaigns. Moreover, a whole new source of funds has become available through the internet. Barack Obama, Bernie Sanders, and Hillary Clinton have shown that in reaching millions of people who cannot make big contributions, they can still raise millions of dollars. In 2016, for example, Sanders raised nearly 60 percent of his money, some $135 million, through small donations. It is not beyond the realm of reality to wonder if at some point this type of fundraising becomes tainted by scandal, and reformers will seek to control it.

While the writing of a book may be an individual effort, to get from my scrawled ideas to the book (or ebook) you hold in your hands has required a small village, and the people at the University Press of Kansas are one of the nicest villages in publishing. My thanks go to Mike Briggs, who invited me to write the original tome; Peter Hoffer, the Landmark Law Cases series editor; and David Congdon, the acquisitions editor, for giving me the opportunity to revise and bring that work up to date. Kelly Chrisman Jacques, the managing editor, saw to it that all went smoothly, and went above and beyond to guide a Luddite author through reading copy-edited manuscript online. Reviewing the copyediting itself was fairly easy, thanks to Susan Ecklund. Thanks also go to Erica Nicholson, a production assistant, and Karl Janssen, who designed the cover.

This book is dedicated to the Washington area guys from Columbia College Class of 1961 who meet each month to discuss anything we want and books that we have read. Who woulda thought!

The Campaign Finance Cases

CHAPTER I

Campaign Finance Reform before 1971

Mark Hanna, the genius behind William McKinley's presidential campaigns, purportedly once said, "There are two things that are important in politics. The first is money, and I can't remember what the second is."

Money is the mother's milk of politics, and this is as true in the twenty-first century as it was in the nineteenth. Both a presidential candidate trying to get his message to more than 325 million people spread out over six million square miles and a soccer parent running for town supervisor in a metropolitan suburb need money to pay for billboards, posters, mailings, television and radio time, and the full-time workers who staff the campaigns. To ignore this truth is to avoid the central issue in campaign finance reform—money is the fuel of political campaigns.

So what rules, if any, can be adopted to ensure fairness, and how do we keep those who have access to large amounts of money from corrupting the political process in which money is a critical necessity? Moreover, does limiting money—who gives it, how much they give, and how it can be spent—actually accomplish what the reformers seek, namely, a political arena in which all candidates vie for office on a level playing field? Beyond that is an even larger question: Do limits on fundraising and expenditures violate the most fundamental of all rights guaranteed by the Constitution, the First Amendment's protection of free speech? As in most public policy debates in a democratic society, the issues are rarely simple, and "truth," if it exists, is not easily seen in stark terms of black and white. In trying to understand where we are at this point in our history, and how we have reached the current state of both legislative efforts at reform and the ensuing judicial responses, we need to turn to our past.

*   *   *

It has always cost money to run for office, although the amount of money spent, as well as the type of expenditures made, have changed considerably over the years. In colonial days and the early years of the republic, campaign finance was not an issue, nor would it be seen as a problem for the better part of the nation's first century. When George Washington first ran for office, a seat in the Virginia House of Burgesses in 1757, he appealed to a rather limited constituency. In the Mount Vernon area, there were 391 eligible voters, all of whom were white and male and owned property. Washington personally knew most of them, and he ran not on a platform of issues but on one of character, reflecting the older British tradition of "standing for office." He also spent money, some thirty-nine pounds to buy refreshments for the voters, including 160 gallons of rum and other alcoholic beverages. The purchase of food and drink remained a staple in US politics well into the twentieth century, and in Washington's time and later, the candidate usually bore the costs himself. This, of course, limited access to office to the affluent, but that did not seem to bother anyone.

In 1776, the year Americans declared their independence from Great Britain, of the approximately 2.5 million men, women, and children—the free and the enslaved—only one in five adult white males met the property requirements needed to cast a ballot. Election campaigns themselves remained fairly simple exercises—some rallies where food and drink would be served, some speeches presented, and perhaps some printed handbills distributed. There appears to have been no vote buying or other fraud, and although this is not to say that election fraud did not exist, it would have been very limited, since the elections involved a relatively small voter base. Moreover, not until Washington's second term in office did the first political parties appear, and they changed the face of US politics forever. Whether one supported the Federalist Party of Washington, Hamilton, and Adams or the Democratic-Republican Party of Jefferson and Madison, one now cast a ballot for issues as well as for the character of the candidate. In fact, as time went on, in some races the person running became less important than the party label he carried.

The existence of parties based on viewpoint changed the nature of politics. Both parties needed ways to get their message across to the people, not only during the actual election campaigns but at other times too. Both the Federalist and Democratic-Republican parties and their successors turned to newspapers as a means of broadcasting their beliefs, and since newspapers reflected the views of the owner-editor, this meant subsidizing him throughout the year. In 1791, Thomas Jefferson asked Philip Freneau to take up residence in Philadelphia, gave him a part-time job as a translator in the State Department, and made him the editor of the *National Gazette*. The Federalists, with money provided by Alexander Hamilton, Rufus King, and others, had already begun subsidizing a paper of their own, the *Gazette of the United States*. At both the national and state levels, whatever party held power could also provide lucrative contracts for government printing work to friendly newspapers. The newspaper owners responded with alacrity, extravagantly praising the candidates and positions of their benefactors, and vilifying with equal fervor those of their opponents. Much of the campaigning before the Civil War relied on newspapers; as late as 1860, Abraham Lincoln secretly bought a small German-language weekly in Illinois for $400 and then gave it to an editor who agreed to support the policies of Lincoln and the Republican Party and to publish in both German and English.

The era of mass politicking began in earnest in the late 1820s with Andrew Jackson and the organization of the Democratic Party, the successor to Jefferson's Democratic-Republicans. Much of the credit goes to Jackson's lieutenant and successor, Martin Van Buren of New York, who organized the first popular mass campaign around the hero of the Battle of New Orleans. By 1829 the electorate had expanded due to immigration into the United States as well as the removal of property and religious qualifications for voting. Van Buren built on the older base of newspapers with rallies, pamphlets, and the appearance of the candidate himself at certain gatherings. Van Buren also oversaw the organization of the Democrats as a mass party, with organizations at the national, state, and local levels. Although the quadrennial campaign for the presidency remained the chief goal of the party, the faithful could now be called on to support candidates in state and local elections, as well as for the House of Representatives. By the late 1830s nearly every political office in the country involved a contest between the two chief parties, the Democrats and the Whigs (a party that arose in opposition to Andrew Jackson). By then congressional races cost $3,000 to $4,000 (more than $107,000 in 2019 dollars), and the 1830 gubernatorial race in Kentucky cost between $10,000 and $15,000, or more than $380,000 in 2019 dollars.

Initially money for these races came from either the candidate's pockets (if he had the resources) or from small contributions by the party faithful. But as the costs rose, party leaders began looking for donors who could make significant gifts to the cause. Prominent New York Whigs such as Philip Hone and Thurlow Weed raised thousands of dollars from fellow merchants, bankers, and well-heeled friends. The Democrats also had their wealthy donors, such as the banker August Belmont. In a development that worried many people, banks and corporations began making donations to one party or the other in an effort to affect policy.

During the Civil War, corporations became an integral part of campaign financing, since government contracts provided so large a source of their income. Abraham Lincoln warned in 1864 that "as a result of the war, corporations have become enthroned, and an era of corruption in high places will follow. The money power of the country will endeavor to prolong its rule by preying upon the prejudices of the people until all wealth is concentrated in a few hands and the Republic is destroyed."

Although there is certainly some hyperbole in Lincoln's comment, he understood that with the growth of large government capable of rewarding its friends with great bounty, US business owners would pour money into politics in order to ensure that they would get their share. In the election of 1864, the Republicans spent more than $125,000 to get Lincoln reelected. That amount doubled by 1872 when the GOP spent $250,000 to reelect Ulysses S. Grant; four years later the two parties spent almost $900,000 apiece in the bitterly contested race between Rutherford B. Hayes and Samuel J. Tilden. Over the next decades, business owners sought land grants to build railroads, tariffs to keep out foreign competition, a sound currency, and freedom from regulatory legislation. To achieve these goals, they freely supplied campaign funds, and in some instances fees and investment opportunities, to ensure friendly government.

Critics of the growing and, as they saw it, pernicious influence of business in politics pointed to the excesses of the Grant administration, especially the Crédit Mobilier scandal, in which members of Congress lined their pockets with stock from a company building the transcontinental railway, and the Whiskey Ring, whose members skimmed off revenue from liquor taxes for the benefit of both parties. But although corruption captured the public attention, in fact most party funds came not from big corporations but from assessments on officeholders and contractors. Andrew Jackson had famously said, "To the victor belong the spoils," by which he meant government offices should be in the hands of the party faithful.

Typically the postmaster general, from Jackson's time through the administration of Harry Truman, handled the awarding of government jobs, and the officeholders showed their loyalty by returning a percentage—usually 2 percent—of their salaries (or, in the case of contractors, a percentage of their price) to the party. This assessment system, first used in the 1830s by the Jacksonian Democrats, grew so much that by 1878 approximately nine out of every ten dollars of the Republican Party's congressional campaign committees' income came from officeholder kickbacks. Not until a disgruntled office seeker assassinated James A. Garfield in 1881 did Congress finally put an end to this practice; in 1883 Congress approved the Pendleton Act, creating the civil service system.

The passage of the Pendleton Act and similar laws at the state level, although sometimes hailed as the first efforts at campaign finance reform, actually sought to protect government employees from party officials. But reliance on the assessment system meant that no one donor had disproportionate influence within the party or on elected officials because of the amount of money he or she gave. In essence, assessments ensured that parties would be free from big money by relying on a large group of small givers. The parties had never, of course, abandoned wealthy backers, but with their main source of revenue at both the federal and state levels now eliminated, both the Democrats and the Republicans had to look elsewhere to cover the costs of ever more expensive campaigns.

* * *

The growing industrialization of the country as well as economic expansion across the continent made a closer relationship between business and government inevitable. The building of the transcontinental railroad, for example, could not have taken place without the federal government financing it through a series of land grants. Sponsors of regional railroads and canals looked to state and local government for needed subsidies. The tariff schedules passed by Congress gave infant US industries protection from European competitors, although the protection continued long after the companies needed it. Wealthy men like August Belmont and his son, August Belmont Jr., Samuel Tilden, John Wanamaker, and Jay Gould continued to be important contributors to the two parties. Gradually, however, the amount collected from corporations, primarily by Republicans but also by Democrats, became the chief source of funding for political campaigns. In the campaign of 1888, for example, Philadelphia department store magnate John Wanamaker contributed $50,000 to the presidential campaign of Republican Benjamin Harrison. Moreover, 40 percent of the party's national campaign expenditures (totaling $1.35 million) came from manufacturing and corporate interests in Pennsylvania alone, collected by that state's party boss, Matthew Quay, who had just assumed the post of national party chair.

By the 1890s campaign costs had risen across the entire political spectrum. The 1892 contest between Republican Benjamin Harrison and Democrat Grover Cleveland cost more than $4 million, with the victorious Cleveland outspending his opponent by almost three to two. That same year Carter Henry Harrison spent $500,000 to become mayor of Chicago, and "Hinky Dink" Kenna raised $100,000 in his race for alderman. Kenna lost, however, when someone stole his campaign funds. No one, however, had a greater gift for getting corporations to give money to politics than Marcus Alonzo Hanna of Ohio.

Hanna had made his fortune in coal, iron, and oil, and from the 1880s on had dabbled in Ohio Republican politics. He retired from business completely in 1895 to devote himself to the election to the presidency of his good friend William McKinley. He financed McKinley's primary campaign practically out of his own pocket with a donation of $100,000 and then, as national chair of the Republican Party, turned to the greater task of raising money for the presidential campaign. The Democrats and the Populists nominated William Jennings Bryan on a platform of silver currency and other "radical" ideas, all of which played directly into Hanna's plan.

He contacted bankers and businessmen all over the country with a simple message—election of the radical Bryan would be bad for business, but the victory of McKinley would assure the continuation of the gold standard in currency and prosperity for big industries. He then went on to tell them how much they should give. He assessed banks one-quarter of 1 percent of their capital and assigned other businesses flat amounts based on their ability to pay. He reportedly raised $3,350,000 for McKinley's campaign, twice the amount spent by Harrison in 1892. No presidential hopeful had ever spent that much, and the sum would not be exceeded until the Harding campaign of 1920. Unofficial estimates, however, put the amount at well over $10 million. Hanna collected $250,000 from Standard Oil alone, an amount almost as large as Bryan's entire campaign fund, and a similar amount from J. P. Morgan. The Chicago meatpacking houses combined to give $400,000.

Interestingly, Hanna made it quite clear to those whom he tapped that the only thing they could expect would be a pro-business attitude from a Republican administration. He insulated McKinley from donors and returned money from contributors who in any way implied that they expected special favors. He even refunded money to corporations that, for one reason or another, sent in more than their assessed rate. Hanna had no difficulty raising money because the nation's business community, including well-to-do Democrats, feared the consequences of a Bryan victory. The fact that the depression that had begun in 1893 lifted soon after McKinley took office—an event that had nothing to do with the Republican victory—helped to embed the idea in the minds of business leaders that the Republicans stood for prosperity and the interests of the banking and corporate community. That idea, in large part, has survived to this day.

The Democrats, although often outspent by the Republicans, also had their corporate sponsors and deep pockets. In 1896 the owners of silver mines in the western states contributed a hefty part of Bryan's campaign chest, and both parties relied on wealthy donors. In the 1904 election, for example, the Democratic candidate, Alton B. Parker, received more than $700,000 from August Belmont Jr. and Thomas Fortune Ryan. The Democratic vice presidential candidate, Henry Davis, owned silver mines and made a large contribution. Although the parties continued to solicit money from small donors, in fact the amount of money raised this way did little more than augment the crucial contributions of large givers. As late as 1928, both parties relied on contributors of $1,000 or more for 70 percent of their expenses; to put that figure in perspective, that year a new car cost $500.

* * *

Around the turn of the century some states began, for the first time, to regulate campaign finance. In 1897 Nebraska, Missouri, Tennessee, and Florida banned corporate contributions. All four states had voted for Bryan the year before, and the statutes were enacted in retaliation against the corporate sponsors of McKinley. These laws, passed partly out of political pique and partly out of democratic idealism, foreshadowed a problem to which I will return later in this study. Corporations gave money to advance positions they believed would be of benefit to them, the same reason that individual donors made contributions. These donations constituted then, as now, a form of expression, or of speech. Moreover, this speech, by either a company or a person, involved political issues, and political speech has always been considered the form of expression most protected by the First Amendment. In 1886 the courts determined that a corporation had some of those rights accruing to "persons" mentioned in the Fourteenth Amendment (*Santa Clara County v. Southern Pacific Railroad Co.*). If natural persons could make contributions to further their interests, then could corporate persons be denied their rights of expression? This basic issue—whether some expression can be silenced in the name of reform—is a leitmotif in the debate on campaign finance.

On the federal level, Congress did not act until a major scandal revealed the extent to which corporations had become involved in the political process. In 1905 the big three life insurance companies—the New York, the Mutual, and the Equitable—came under investigation by the state of New York. The Armstrong Committee and its counsel, Charles Evans Hughes, relentlessly exposed how officers of the companies had abused their trust by using assets belonging to the policyholders as their private piggy banks, which they raided for a variety of personal purposes. On September 15, Hughes called to the stand the treasurer of New York Life and asked him to explain a nonledger check for $48,702.50 issued at the order of the company's president, John A. McCall. The treasurer confessed that he knew nothing about it. Hughes then called George W. Perkins, a partner of J. P. Morgan, a power in the Republican Party, and a vice president of New York Life. Perkins quite openly acknowledged that the check represented money paid to the Republican National Committee. He added that the company had paid similar amounts to the Republican presidential campaigns of 1896 and 1900 and defended the payments as "an absolutely legitimate thing for us to do to protect the securities of these hundreds and thousands of [policyholders] everywhere."

Although everyone knew that corporations gave money to political campaigns, the investigation detailed how much had gone to the Republican Party, and suddenly the idea of corporate contributions became scandalous and a menace to democracy. The *New York Tribune*, one of the nation's leading Republican newspapers, reported the following day that the testimony "caused a profound sensation as it furnished the first tangible evidence of connections between the insurance company and a political party."

Shortly afterward, President Theodore Roosevelt met with some of his leading advisers at his home at Sagamore Hill on Long Island. Although the meeting had been planned before the Perkins testimony, there is little question that the Republican leaders discussed ways to control the damage. In Roosevelt's annual message to Congress in December 1905, he repeated an earlier call for greater publicity about campaign finance and declared, "All contributions by corporations to any political committee or for any political purpose should be forbidden by law; directors should not be permitted to use stockholders' money for such purposes; and, moreover, a prohibition of this kind would be, as far as it went, an effective method of stopping the evils aimed at in corrupt practices acts."

In fact, a bill to that effect had been introduced into Congress five years earlier by one of the founders of the Republican Party, Senator William E. Chandler of New Hampshire. At the time no one paid any attention to the Chandler bill, but the revelations of the Armstrong Committee and Roosevelt's message to Congress breathed new life into the measure. Chandler by then had retired from the Senate, and he could not get another Republican senator to sponsor it, so he turned to Senator Benjamin R. Tillman, the populist and racist Democrat from South Carolina. The onetime radical Republican from the North and the unreconstructed Confederate had become friends nearly a decade earlier, when Tillman had backed Chandler in a battle over the cost of armor plating for navy vessels.

It took Tillman the better part of two years to move the bill through Congress. He managed to get the Senate to pass it without debate in June

1906, a result many attributed to fear that the GOP would be branded as a party of corporate corruption in the upcoming midterm election. Then the bill went to the House of Representatives, where it died when the House adjourned without bringing it to the floor. The Republicans kept control of Congress and decided that they could afford to appease public opinion. The House passed the bill in its original form, but the Senate Elections Committee weakened it because the chair, Joseph Foraker of Ohio, did not believe that Congress had the power to regulate state-chartered corporations. Chandler's original proposal rested primarily on congressional authority to regulate interstate commerce, and only secondarily on the power to regulate elections to the House, and he would have barred political contributions from all corporations but the smallest.

In the eyes of many, the final version of the Tillman Act was but a pale shadow of the original proposal. It banned contributions only by federally chartered corporations, a group that represented only a small percentage of companies. How effective it proved is hard to determine. According to one analysis, although it dried up actual cash, the companies soon found ways around it by donating other items, such as office space, typewriters, and even travel (many of the federally chartered companies were railroads). Another way around the law involved keeping company officers on the payroll even when they devoted all of their time to working for a candidate. Since enforcement proved nonexistent, within a few years money from corporate coffers again flowed into campaigns. A half century after passage of the Tillman Act, one board chair, Duncan Norton Taylor, told a reporter that "a lot of corporate presidents just reach in the till and get $25,000 to contribute to political campaigns." The first federal effort at campaign finance reform, in short, had little practical effect.

A second bill passed a few years later had a more lasting effect. In 1910 Congress passed the Publicity Act, sometimes called the first Federal Corrupt Practices Act. The new law required the postelection disclosure in House races of each donor of more than $100, a sum equal to $2,675 in 2019 dollars. The following year Congress passed amendments also requiring disclosure to be made ten days before the election and extended the coverage to include Senate races. Although at that time state legislators still chose senators, a great deal of politicking went on that in most ways resembled political campaigns. The amendments also limited the amount that could be spent in Senate races to $10,000, and in House races to $5,000.

Like the Tillman Act, the new law failed to do what its sponsors had hoped for: to shine a bright light on campaign financing. Although it did set a precedent for making contributor lists public, the bill failed for four reasons. First, Congress doubted its constitutional power to regulate state and local committees, so the disclosure rules applied only to party committees operating in two or more states, or, in other words, only to the national committees, which at that time played a minor role in congressional elections. Second, the law on its face seemed to apply only to candidates, so committees, nominally without the candidate's knowledge or involvement, soon sprouted to assist in the campaigns, and they completely ignored the reporting rules. Third, a decade later the Supreme Court held in *United States v. Newberry* (1921) that Congress had no power to regulate primaries, and in practically the entire South, whoever won the Democratic primary faced only token opposition in the general election. Finally, the bill had no enforcement provisions and did not assign responsibility for monitoring and enforcement to any federal agency. Although the disclosure requirements would later be expanded and would become an important part of campaign finance reform, in the short term the Publicity Act and its amendments, like the Tillman Act before it, did little to curb abuses in campaign fundraising.

* * *

Technically, the Teapot Dome Scandal of the Harding administration had nothing to do with campaign contributions; it involved, instead, simple old-fashioned bribery of public officials, especially Secretary of the Interior Albert B. Fall, who awarded oil leases on federal land in return for kickbacks from the oil companies. Harding himself had not been the choice of the big corporations, and the majority of his money in both the primaries and the campaign came from small contributors or from wealthy friends. But in the investigation it emerged that oil magnate Harry Sinclair had made large, albeit legal, contributions to the Republican Party in nonelection years, thus escaping the provisions of the Publicity Act, which required disclosure of money received only in an election year.

Congress, after dithering about for more than a year, finally passed the Federal Corrupt Practices Act of 1925, and President Coolidge promptly signed it into law. The new measure closed the loophole Sinclair had exploited by requiring disclosures regardless of when donors gave their money. It raised the spending ceiling for Senate races to $25,000 and required disclosure of all receipts by candidates for either the House or the Senate and by political committees acting in two or more states.

The bill had a number of flaws. It required reporting only those expenditures made with a candidate's "knowledge or consent." Since most office seekers interpreted this as applying only to their personal outlays, they did not report expenditures made by committees. As political scientist Louise Overacker commented, evasion of the law only required that "the astute candidate be discreetly ignorant of what his friends are doing." Passed on the eve of the great expansion of radio in the 1920s, leading to the purchase of airtime for political advertisements, the act specified spending limits that were out-of-date before Coolidge even signed the bill.

Nearly all payments for airtime went through committees, which routinely ignored both the limit and the reporting provisions. National party committees, the only ones affected by the measure, evaded the provisions applying to them by routing funds through state or local groups. The reports they did file tended to be vague and incomplete. Other committees claimed the law did not apply to them, and House clerk William Tyler Page, the officer designated in the law to receive the reports, could do little about it. "It is not for me to say," he said, "whether an organization, politically active, comes within the purview of the law or not. That was for the officers of such associations [themselves] to determine." If any other sign were needed that Congress really did not intend this bill to be very effective, one merely had to note that it lacked any enforcement provisions. There would not be a single successful prosecution under the act for the forty-six years that it remained on the statute books.

In addition, Congress did not challenge the Supreme Court's ruling that it had no authority over primaries, even though many in the legislature believed that *Newberry* did not provide a clear precedent. Even after the Supreme Court rejected this holding and held that Congress had authority over primaries in *United States v. Classic* (1941), Congress did not act. A coalition of Republicans and southern Democrats opposed federal regulation of primaries, and although Congress attempted further regulation of elections in the two decades following World War II, it did not reassert the authority first claimed in 1911 until the Federal Election Campaign Act of 1971.

* * *

The 1928 campaign took place at the height of the decade's prosperity; four years later, both parties spent far less—a total of $5.1 million by the national committees—but they still relied on large donors, who in each case gave more than 40 percent of the totals raised. By 1936, though, the amount contributed by donors of $5,000 or more had shrunk to 26 percent for the Democrats and 24.2 percent for the Republicans. Although the GOP continued to rely on business contributions, the Democrats had successfully tapped into a new source not only of revenue but also of campaign workers—the labor unions.

The Republicans had been no friends of labor unions, and conservative judges—usually Republicans—had consistently struck down laws that helped workers and had issued injunctions preventing strikes or pickets. With the New Deal, labor for the first time found an administration in Washington sympathetic to its goals. The National Industrial Recovery Act of 1933 guaranteed labor unions' right to bargain collectively, required industrial codes to adopt fair labor standards of minimum wages and maximum hours, and appropriated $3.3 billion to put unemployed workers on the payrolls of federal projects. After the Supreme Court invalidated the act, Congress passed the Wagner Labor Relations Act of 1935, reaffirming labor unions' right to organize and bargain collectively, and established the powerful National Labor Relations Board to enforce this policy. The 1935 Social Security Act created a fund to provide supplemental benefits to older Americans, and in 1938 Congress passed the Fair Labor Standards Act, establishing maximum hours, minimum wages, and safety conditions for workers employed in interstate commerce. Overseeing all these developments were prominent Democrats like Harold Ickes and Frances Perkins, whom organized labor recognized as friends.

Years earlier, Samuel Gompers had established the political policy for the American Federation of Labor (AFL): it would reward its friends and punish its enemies, but it would neither take overt political stands nor endorse particular parties or candidates. All that changed in the 1930s as both the more conservative AFL and the newer and more liberal unions in the Congress of Industrial Organizations (CIO) rushed to reward Roosevelt and the Democrats not only with their votes but also with dollars. Although in 1936 Roosevelt rejected a $250,000 check hand-delivered by CIO president John L. Lewis because he feared being too closely associated with unions, the Democratic National Committee had no problem accepting the money and in fact got an additional half million from labor unions for that election. Organized labor had contributed nothing to either party in 1928 or 1932, but roughly 10 percent of all Democratic campaign funds came from unions in 1936 and 16 percent in 1940.

By the late 1930s, however, both Republicans and conservative southern Democrats suspected that Roosevelt was using New Deal programs—especially those benefiting labor—to build a powerful new political base for himself. The various government employment projects such as the Public Works Administration, the Civilian Conservation Corps, the Tennessee Valley Authority, and the Works Progress Administration had put millions of men and women to work on the government payroll, but outside the civil service restrictions of the Pendleton Act. After Roosevelt failed to purge the Democratic Party of its more conservative members in the 1938 election, a coalition of Republicans and conservative Democrats united to push through the Hatch Act in 1939.

Named for its chief sponsor, Senator Carl Hatch of New Mexico, the measure extended the ban on political contributions and participation in campaigns beyond the civil service (covered under the Pendleton Act) to include all government employees. Although supposedly a reform measure, the bill had no other purpose than to strike at what its sponsors feared was Franklin Roosevelt's growing political power. The following year, Congress amended the Hatch Act to ban donations by federal contractors, or by employees of state agencies, financed in whole or in part by federal funds. The amendment also limited contributions to national committees to $5,000 and placed a spending limit on national committees of $3 million per campaign. The Hatch Act amendments proved as futile as previous measures. The $5,000 limit on contributions only meant that people wishing to give more than that amount would funnel their money into other committees, a practice the act did not cover. Then, in the midst of World War II, Republicans capitalized on the negative reactions to a bitter strike by John L. Lewis's United Mine Workers to push through, over a presidential veto, the Smith-Connally Act, also known as the War Labor Disputes Act. Section 9 of the act prohibited labor unions from contributing to political campaigns for the duration of the war. The unions circumvented §9 with a device that would come to play a key role in the debate over campaign finance reform a half century later, the political action committee (PAC). Union members contributed to labor-organized PACs through automatic payroll checkoffs, and then the PACs, supposedly independent entities, contributed that money to candidates. Lawyers for the CIO also interpreted §9 as prohibiting donations going directly to candidates, but not for expenditures made independently. The CIO, therefore, freely engaged in a whole variety of activities and supported particular Democratic candidates. Once again, an effort at supposed campaign finance reform—although in truth an attack on the political activities of labor unions—produced results opposite to those intended. In the 1944 presidential campaign, organized labor participated more fully than it had ever done before, and the CIO's PAC alone spent almost $2 million in support of Democratic candidates.

* * *

Well before the end of the war, organized labor had become a major ally of the Democratic Party, and when the Republicans gained control of both houses of Congress in 1946, for the first time in sixteen years, they did not delay in going after the unions. The Taft-Hartley Act, passed over Harry Truman's veto, made permanent the Smith-Connally ban on union contributions. It also banned all union expenditures on political activity, including communications with union members that related to politics. As the House report accompanying the bill noted, the wording "making any contribution" was to be interpreted broadly, to include not just direct contributions to candidates but the indirect expenditure of funds to help candidates. Unions could not use money from their general treasury for political purposes, even, under §304, to fund a newsletter for members in which the union endorsed a candidate. Taft-Hartley not only attempted to regulate the use of money but for the first time overtly tried to limit the political speech of a particular group.

The unions immediately challenged this latter section, and the *CIO News* published an editorial backing a Democratic candidate in Maryland. The government brought suit, and eventually the case reached the Supreme Court, which, in a rather convoluted opinion by Justice Stanley Reed, totally twisted the legislative history of the act to hold that the ban did not apply to internal communications. None of the justices wanted to support a ban on unions' communications with their members, but only Justice Wiley Rutledge, joined by Hugo Black, William O. Douglas, and Frank Murphy, believed that §304 violated the First Amendment because it limited free speech (*United States v. Congress of Industrial Organizations* [1948]).

In 1957 the Justice Department indicted the United Auto Workers for violating Taft-Hartley's ban on external communications—that is, sending political messages to the public at large. The union defended itself by claiming that this ban, like that on internal communications, violated the First Amendment. The Warren Court, under attack because of its rulings on segregation and the free speech rights of communists, ducked the issue on procedural grounds and sent the case back to a district court, where a jury trial acquitted the union (*United States v. International Union of United Automobile, Aircraft, and Agricultural Implement Workers of America*). The case marked the first time that any group had been indicted for speaking to the public about political issues, and in some ways it foreshadowed the future debate about "issue advocacy" and whether groups can spend money that helps a candidate through "education" of the public about particular issues.

Despite this victory, unions for the most part did cease direct communication with the public, because they really had no need for it. Workers, at that time still heavily Democratic, continued to send money to the union PACs through payroll checkoffs, and the PACs not only made contributions to candidates but also financed messages to the public. Moreover, internal communications through union newspapers and newsletters reached millions of members, urging them to support particular candidates, usually Democratic. Truman's surprise victory over Thomas Dewey in the 1948 election is often credited to the support he received from labor unions angry at the Republicans and grateful to

Truman for his effort to block Taft-Hartley through a veto. Truman benefited not only from the money unions spent on his behalf but also from the tens of thousands of union members who worked on campaigns, staffed phone banks, registered voters, and helped Democrats in a myriad of other ways.

Ironically, very few corporations at this time set up PACs to evade the restrictions placed on them by the Corrupt Practices Act, in part because corporate leaders doubted that they could legally use company funds to establish a PAC. Moreover, company officials felt no need to do so. As noted earlier, well after the passage of the Tillman Act, corporate executives made large contributions for which their companies reimbursed them, or just simply ignored the ban by reaching into the corporate till and sending in money to a campaign committee. The lack of enforcement of the Tillman Law made the chance of indictment practically nil.

* * *

By the late 1950s, the United States financed its campaigns through a system that, according to Frank Sorauf, a political scientist at the University of Minnesota, had several features that would in effect determine the course of future campaign finance reform. To begin with, campaigns at the national level, including congressional races, depended primarily on large contributors consisting of wealthy individuals, corporations (which funneled their money through their officers' supposedly "personal" donations), and labor unions. In 1952 about two-thirds of all money spent on federal elections came from donations of $500 or more (a little under $5,000 in current dollars). In state and local politics, patronage and payments remained a significant source of funds, with large contributors often rewarded after a victorious campaign with plum appointments.

Political parties also played an important role in campaigns as the intermediaries between contributors and candidates. Although federal rules may have limited expenditures by the national committees, members of the Democratic National Committee and the Republican National Committee knew and, directly or indirectly, helped guide other committees and PACs in spending money beyond what federal law allowed. Very often the solicitations for funds, an important part of raising money for campaigns, came from party officials.

Finally, federal and state laws aimed at regulating campaign finance all added up to nothing more than an exercise in futility. Although some of the more blatant and corrupt practices had been eliminated or at least marginalized, no mechanism existed to enforce the laws, nor, if truth be told, did government officials really want to do so. Both Democrats and Republicans wanted and needed money to run their campaigns.

All this began to change in the 1960s, with the development of new campaign technologies unlinked to print media, and a concomitant change in the nature of political parties. Although there had been public opinion polls since the 1930s, and politicians had begun using them in the 1940s, John F. Kennedy's campaign in 1960 used polls in a way that had not been done before, essentially relying on them to shape campaign strategy. At the same time, radio and television became the new media, and the costs of buying airtime and producing sophisticated commercials drove up the expenses of campaigning far beyond what they had been. In 1948 the Democratic National Committee spent $2.7 million on the Truman campaign. In the two races in which Dwight Eisenhower ran for president, the Republican National Committee spent $6.6 million in 1952 and $7.8 million in 1956. In 1960 the national Nixon campaign spent $10.1 million, and the Democrats paid out $9.8 million for Kennedy. When Nixon ran again in 1968, his campaign exceeded $25.4 million, and four years later the Nixon reelection campaign spent $61.4 million. Although not all of this money went to radio and television, much of the increase can be attributed to the costs associated with these media. Later, new technologies such as direct mailing and the use of computers for a variety of purposes would add to the skyrocketing costs.

Related to this development, the nature of political parties and their relationships to candidates and campaigns changed. Through the 1940s and into the 1950s, there had been close ties between the candidate and party leaders. Originally, the parties had existed for the sole purpose of getting their candidates elected, and candidates in turn recognized their obligations to party officials and workers for their own success in attaining office. Franklin Roosevelt and Harry Truman worked hand in glove with the national Democratic leadership, not only during campaign years but between elections as well. Voters often went Democratic or Republican regardless of the candidate because they understood that the candidates shared and represented the basic values of the party.

The new technologies, however, placed greater emphasis on

candidates than on their parties. In print advertising, campaign managers could spell out party platforms and positions. Television and radio demanded sound bites, and the former also required candidates who could project to the viewers. Many people credit John F. Kennedy's photogenic appearance in his first debate with Richard Nixon as the single most important factor that led to his eking out victory in 1960. Suddenly candidates had to have sex appeal and be able to use the new media. Throughout the nineteenth century, it is likely that no more than a few thousand people at a time actually saw or heard the candidates. Even with all the campaigning that Woodrow Wilson or Herbert Hoover or Franklin Roosevelt did, no more than 2 or 3 percent of the electorate—if that much—actually saw the men.

In 1960 nobody who owned a television set could avoid images and advertisements for Kennedy or Nixon, and that pattern has only intensified. As a result, political parties, although still important, became to some extent secondary in the crucial matter of raising funds. Candidates and their own advisers now did the soliciting, and in 1972 Richard Nixon had so little use for the Republican National Committee that he established his own group, the Committee to Re-elect the President (CREEP), that operated wholly independently from the Republican National Committee.

Few people welcomed this development. Fundraising, which had been cyclical and tied to national races, now became constant. The results of an election had barely been certified before fundraising began for the next one. The traditional start of the presidential campaign, Labor Day, disappeared as candidates began declaring their availability two or even three years earlier. Although some candidates, such as Barry Goldwater (who in 1964 stood far to the right of the mainstream Republican Party) and George McGovern (who in 1972 stood far to the left of the mainstream Democratic Party) raised a relatively high percentage of their campaign funds from small contributors, the role of the big givers—either directly to the candidates or to the national party committees, PACs, or other groups—became more and more important in funding campaigns.

A number of commissions sought to establish guidelines for campaign finance reform during the 1950s and 1960s, including one that President Kennedy set up, which unsuccessfully called for matching federal funds in presidential races. But little actually happened. In 1966 Congress passed the Long Act, designed to lessen the influence of wealthy contributors on presidential races. The measure also called for public funding of political parties to pay for presidential campaigns, but ensuing acts of Congress permanently postponed implementation of that section.

Looking back, one needed only seven fingers to count the acts of Congress that tried to impose some order and reform on campaign finance practices—the Tillman Act (1907), the Publicity Act (1910), the Federal Corrupt Practices Act (1925), the Hatch Act (1939), the Smith-Connally Act (1943), the Taft-Hartley Act (1947), and the Long Act (1966). In addition, by 1959, forty-three states had some requirements for reporting campaign finance expenditures by candidates, their committees, or committees run by the parties; thirty-one states had some limits on expenditures, although in most cases the limits applied only to the candidate or those expenditures made with his or her knowledge or consent. Only four states had limits on individual contributions, and these ranged from $1,000 to $5,000 per person and could be easily bypassed through contributions to party committees.

The effects of these laws, at both the federal and state levels, could be described as negligible at best. As quickly as legislatures enacted new laws and restrictions, candidates and parties found means around them. Moreover, as one commentator noted, "Many state and federal laws are unenforced because they are unenforceable; the statutes themselves are vague and riddled with loopholes." Then, in 1971, Congress passed the first serious attempt to reform campaign finance.

Reform and Response

The Federal Election Campaign Act and *Buckley*

Shortly after John F. Kennedy became president in 1961, he appointed a commission on campaign costs in presidential elections. The total cost of the presidential campaign in 1960 had been nearly $20 million, almost twice as much as the $11.6 million spent in 1952. Aside from the escalating costs involved in running for public office (even the 1960 figures would soon seem like small potatoes), there had been increasing concern that the injection of large sums of money from private donors would corrupt not only candidates and elected officials but also the integrity of the political process itself. The regulatory system then in effect had proven both ineffective and unworkable. Representative Jim Wright (D-TX) noted that "there is not a member of Congress, myself included, who has not knowingly evaded its purpose in one way or another." Over the next decade Congress struggled fitfully with the issue, finally passing, in 1971, the first significant campaign finance reform measure in decades. Following the revelations of the Watergate scandal, Congress then toughened the law, only to see much of its work undone by the Supreme Court in the landmark decision of *Buckley v. Valeo* (1976).

Both the provisions that the Court left standing and the First Amendment rationale of Buckley would color efforts at campaign finance reform for the next quarter century.

* * *

John Kennedy had been interested in campaign financing for a long time. While in the Senate he had been a member of the Special Committee to Investigate Political Activities, Lobbying, and Campaign Contributions. As a wealthy man, he knew the importance of money in politics and had often heard accusations that his family fortune had bought public offices for him. But as the nominal leader of the Democratic Party, Kennedy also knew about the $3.8 million deficit from the 1960 campaign that the party now had to cover. Kennedy named Alexander Heard to chair a presidential commission on campaign costs in presidential elections.

The committee submitted its report the following year and made some limited, albeit innovative, recommendations. The proposals offered by the committee included the following:

- Individuals, businesses, labor unions, and private organizations should be encouraged to participate in and underwrite voluntary nonpartisan political activities such as voter registration and fundraising drives, and expenses related to these activities should be tax deductible.
- Tax incentives should be tried for an experimental period, covering at least two presidential campaigns, allowing individual contributors to take a credit against their federal income taxes for a certain percentage of their donations or to take a deduction of up to $1,000 in any given tax year.
- The unrealistic and unenforceable ceilings on individual contributions and on total expenditures by political committees should be abolished, and an effective system of public disclosure should be put into place.
- Congress should provide funds for the reasonable and necessary transition costs that a newly elected president would have in preparing to take over the office.
- Section 315 of the Federal Communications Act should be suspended, as it had been in 1960, to permit broadcasters to make the airwaves available to the nominees of the major political parties on an equal basis (such as for debates) without having to do so for the candidates of the dozens of fringe parties.

Only one of the commission's recommendations became effective during Kennedy's time. The Internal Revenue Service (IRS) authorized taxpayers to deduct expenditures in connection with local, state, and federal elections, if the money went to advertising designed to encourage voter registration, the sponsorship of debates among candidates, or giving employees paid time off to register and vote. The IRS ruling remained in effect for many years, and few people realized that the costs associated with joint appearances of candidates on radio or television, or "battle pages" in newspapers could be sponsored by corporations and counted as business expenses.

Very little else happened regarding campaign finance for the rest of the decade. President Lyndon Johnson in his 1966 State of the Union address announced that campaign finance reform would be a high priority of his administration. He derided the laws then on the books: "Inadequate in their scope when enacted, they are now obsolete. More loophole than law, they invite evasion and circumvention." He promised to send Congress comprehensive legislation, but it took Johnson four months before he sent a bill up to the Capitol. The measure he recommended consisted primarily of proposals that reformers had been making for more than two decades—primary elections would be brought under the law, contribution limits would be tightened, there would be greater disclosure and publicity of campaign finances, and all restrictions on expenditures would be repealed.

*   *   *

It would be easy to dismiss congressional—and presidential—inaction by cynically noting that the system of campaign finance regulation in place, if it can be called a system, apparently worked. Candidates could raise as much money as possible, they could rely on wealthy contributors, and the reporting requirements could best be described as meaningless. When Richard Nixon became president in 1969, W. Pat Jennings, the clerk of the House of Representatives, sent to the Justice Department a list of twenty Nixon fundraising committees that had failed to file a single report for the campaign, along with the names of 107 congressional candidates who had also violated the disclosure law. A year later the Justice Department announced that none of the violators would be prosecuted because, given the history of the act and its enforcement, it would be unfair to do so. However, the department declared it would prosecute violators in the future.

Although there is undoubtedly some truth in that response, the fact is that campaigning had become more and more expensive, and many House members and senators had come to believe that they spent far too much time chasing after political contributions. The biggest campaign, that for the presidency, cost the most, and every four years the sums expended by both parties leaped upward. When Thomas Dewey had run against Harry Truman in 1948, their combined expenditures had been a little under $5 million, or about the same amount that had been spent in the 1944 race between Dewey and Franklin Roosevelt. In the two races between Dwight Eisenhower and Adlai Stevenson, the totals rose to $12 million, then $20 million in 1960, $24.7 million in 1964, and $37 million in the race between Nixon and Humphrey in 1968. These numbers would be eclipsed by the $91 million spent in the 1972 election, with Richard Nixon outspending George McGovern by a two-to-one margin.

Although both parties tried to appeal to all income levels, during the 1960s the Republicans actually had success attracting small, so-called nickel-and-dime givers as well as big donors. Republican fund drives in 1968 produced $6.6 million in gifts, averaging $15 from each of 450,000 individual contributors. Although Barry Goldwater in 1964 and George McGovern in 1972 raised large sums from a broad base of small donors, for the most part the GOP relied primarily on big givers, especially corporate donors, to finance its presidential campaigns; and the Democrats, who began to rebuild their small-donor base at the end of the decade, looked primarily to labor unions and their political arms for money. If one adds in the costs of primary campaigns, fought out in at least one party each year except 1956, the totals are significantly higher.

Nor did the costs of running for the House or Senate remain stable. According to a study by the Citizens' Research Foundation, the total cost of campaigning for all federal offices in presidential election years tripled between 1952 (the first year for which dependable figures are available) and 1972.

The big change in the 1960s, of course, involved the growing use of television in campaigns. In 1952 the government freeze on new stations ended, and in the following years television stations and, more important, household sets, proliferated. Television became an important—and expensive—part of campaigning. In 1952, the first year both parties used the new medium, they spent $3.7 million to purchase time; twenty years later that number had tripled. Abraham Lincoln's entire campaign in 1860 had cost $100,000; in 1960 it took that much to buy thirty minutes of airtime.

The problem did not abate; if anything it worsened as the years passed. To give but one example, in 1988 former Florida governor Reuben Askew sought the Democratic nomination for the US Senate. One of his aides recalled a primary campaign rally in northern Florida: "A hunched-over, withered dirt farmer approached the governor with a $100 check. 'I want you to have this,' said the man, trembling with awe. 'I've supported you for years, and I'm behind you now.' With a 30-second television spot in Tampa costing around $6,000, the farmer's contribution paid for about a half-second of television. I didn't have the heart to tell him."

Television may have been the single greatest factor in increasing overall campaign costs by 50 percent between 1964 and 1968. As Senator Edward Kennedy (D-MA) later testified, "Like a colossus of the ancient world, television stands astride our political system, demanding tribute from every candidate for public office, incumbent or challenger. Its appetite is insatiable, its impact unique."

Although some studies indicate that television ads are not very effective in House district races, their impact grows in statewide Senate races and, of course, in the nationwide presidential campaign. A survey taken of twenty-three senators and ninety-one representatives after the 1968 election found that nearly three-fourths of the Senate candidates had used television extensively, 18 percent had used "some" television, and only 9 percent had used none. By contrast, only a quarter of the House races had depended heavily on television, and nearly half had not used the medium at all. Politicians, and especially members of the Senate, began to look more favorably on spending and contribution restrictions as radio and television advertising became a bottomless pit swallowing up millions of dollars.

The ever-increasing costs of campaigning, and the resulting reliance on corporate and union contributions, raised fears that the end result would be corruption not only of individuals but of the entire political system and the faith of the citizenry in its integrity. Although there are plenty of stories about corporate donations leading to favorable legislation, many political analysts note that there are so many issues confronting members of Congress it would be almost impossible for them to pay back every contributor by voting for each one's interests, especially since some of those interests no doubt conflicted. Senators and representatives, who are keenly aware of what the main economic interests are in their home state or district, realize that if they hope to keep their seats, they have to vote in a way that will benefit their constituents. If a senator comes from a dairy state, she will not require a contribution from the dairy industry in order to support legislation favoring dairy farmers. While one may not agree with Charles Wilson's aphorism "What's good for General Motors is good for the country," a congressman from Detroit is certainly aware that a healthy GM means jobs for his constituents and prosperity for his district.

The worry that the system might be corrupted, or even appear that way, did not provide sufficient impetus to move Congress to action in the 1960s. Just as Sam Rayburn had buried earlier legislation to reform campaigns, so too did Wayne Hays (D-OH), chair of the House Administration Committee and an unapologetic opponent of any change in the campaign finance system, now kill any bill that would endanger what he saw as a vested right—the ability of incumbents to secure more funds than their challengers. Moreover, he had allies on his committee: northern Democrats who did not want anything to get in the way of labor support for their party, and southern Democrats who wanted to keep the financing of party primaries as veiled as possible. But pressure built, and if a reform package could get past the obstructionists, like Hays, it stood a good chance of passage. Finally, Congress acted not once but several times in the 1970s.

* * *

A variety of reform proposals had been batted around during the 1960s, following the report of the presidential commission. Some emphasized full disclosure of contributions and expenses, and a broadening of the parties' financial bases (by limiting contributions of big donors) to provide a fairer and more stable finance system. Other groups, such as the Citizens' Research Foundation, recognized the need for greater campaign resources, to be kept in check by stringent reporting requirements and the spotlight of publicity. Such publicity, they believed, would keep the candidates, the parties, and the system honest. A third approach, championed by public interest lobbies such as Common Cause, a citizens' lobby headed by former cabinet secretary John Gardner, introduced a new idea—limit campaign resources by imposing ceilings on both campaign contributions and expenditures. The tight limits on individual contributions would be offset with public funds. The ideas of this third group, although quite different from the traditional reforms that had been pushed since the end of World War II, nonetheless caught the attention of key members of Congress. Aware of the escalating costs of campaigning and the ever more difficult and time-consuming task of fundraising, they found the idea of limitations on both income and expenditures very attractive.

In 1970, both houses of Congress passed a relatively limited campaign finance reform bill. Among other things, the measure would have suspended §315 of the Communications Act (the equal-time provision) for presidential and vice presidential candidates, and required stations to sell airtime to all legally qualified candidates at a price not to exceed "the lowest unit charge of the station for the same amount of time in the same time period." Another feature limited the amount that candidates could spend for the use of broadcasting time to either seven cents for each vote cast for all candidates for that office in the previous election or $20,000, whichever was greater. This part applied to president and vice president, senators and representatives at the national level, and governors and lieutenant governors at the state level. For primary campaigns, candidates (with the exception of those seeking the presidency) could spend no more than one-half of the limit for the general election. To enforce this provision, each candidate or a representative had to certify in writing to the station that buying the requested time would not exceed the legal limits. Stations could not sell time to candidates who refused to submit such affidavits.

Despite the limited nature of the bill, President Richard M. Nixon vetoed it, on grounds that it did not go far enough. He described the measure as a "good aim, gone amiss." The problem with campaign spending, he declared, "is not radio and television; the problem is spending. This bill plugs only one hole in a sieve." Nixon also disapproved of the fact that, as he saw it, the bill discriminated against broadcasters. Since the expenditure ceilings applied only to radio and television, the broadcast media would be at a disadvantage. Candidates could spend their quotas, and then spend as much as they wanted in other venues, such as newspapers, billboards, and mailings. As a result, Nixon claimed, overall campaign spending would not be curtailed. The president had a number of other objections, and although critics might discount them as self-serving, since at the time his reelection committee had already begun amassing the biggest campaign finance war chest hitherto seen in US politics, he made a number of valid points. The bill would favor incumbents and discriminate against broadcasters, and the formula did not take into account differing costs in different markets. Although defenders of the bill believed that one step in the right direction would be a good start, Nixon in essence said that if Congress really wanted to reform campaign finance, then it should do so.

Shortly after the Nixon veto, Common Cause filed a suit challenging the nonenforcement of the Federal Corrupt Practices Act (FCPA), the 1925 act that still governed campaign expenses. The suit sought to enjoin the Republican National Committee and Democratic National Committee as well as the Conservative Party of New York from violating two sections of the FCPA. Common Cause alleged that the committees had encouraged the formation of multiple committees on behalf of individual candidates in order to get around the law's limit of $5,000 on an individual contribution to a committee and the expenditure by any one committee of more than $3 million in one year.

The courts eventually dismissed the suit, but it served a useful purpose in focusing attention on the shortcomings of the FCPA and showing how easily the major parties circumvented its restrictions. Moreover, Common Cause may well have wanted to prod Congress to act quickly, aware that with the 1972 presidential campaign just around the corner, the potential for even greater abuse could not be ignored.

* * *

To everyone's surprise, Congress did in fact completely overhaul federal campaign law by passing two measures, the Revenue Act of 1971 and the Federal Election Campaign Act (FECA) of 1971. The Revenue Act finally put into effect the Long Amendment of 1966 by creating a general fund for presidential and vice presidential campaigns, and permitting taxpayers to check off a dollar of their taxes to underwrite the fund. To get Nixon's approval, Congress agreed to delay implementation until the 1976 presidential election. The FECA had two main goals—tightening reporting requirements and limiting expenditures for media advertising. But it also looked at other aspects of modern campaign finance and brought many of the provisions of the old 1925 law up-to-date. The law broadened the definitions of both "contributions" and "expenditures" to include almost any donation and cost associated with a political campaign. In a clear effort to reduce the advantage of wealthy candidates, the law imposed a ceiling on what candidates for federal offices could spend out of their own pockets or those of their immediate families—$50,000 for president or vice president, $35,000 for senators, and $25,000 for representatives.

The FECA set up fairly specific rules for reporting contributions and expenditures, which made the law far more effective than its predecessor. On the contribution side, the names of all donors or lenders who gave $100 or more had to be reported, and the names of all committee officials had to be listed. The drafters of the measure had such great confidence in the reporting provisions that the bill repealed the largely unenforceable prior limits on contributions and expenditures. Only the old prohibition against direct contributions by corporations and labor unions remained intact.

The media provisions to some extent addressed some of the problems Nixon had pointed out in his veto of the earlier bill. Candidates now had limits on all media spending, both broadcast and print, with a maximum of $50,000 for the smallest district and up to $1.4 million for the senatorial candidates in California. Of this amount, no more than 60 percent could go to radio and television. Recognizing that inflation could make these limits meaningless and therefore susceptible to evasion, the bill indexed the ceilings to adjust to changes in the cost-of-living index.

Only time would have told if the FECA regulations would do what its sponsors had hoped—shed the bright light of publicity on the abuses and excesses of campaign finance, restrict both large contributions and large expenditures, and provide a more level playing field for challengers and incumbents by having them both operate under the same rules. The bill, signed into law by President Nixon in January 1972, seemed to meet some of its goals in the 1972 election. As Frank Sorauf noted, it "brought the fullest disclosure of campaign transactions in American history; and while it did not curb the growth of campaign spending generally, it did limit the use of media advertising." Moreover, its provisions may have helped unravel one of the largest scandals in US history—Watergate.

* * *

The break-in at the Democratic National Committee headquarters in the Watergate complex in Washington, DC, by a group funded by the

Committee to Re-elect the President (CREEP), proved to have been the first step in a chain of events that eventually led to the resignation of Richard Nixon in August 1974. But Watergate is far more than a botched burglary. The stories uncovered by investigative journalists and in House and Senate hearings detailed an unparalleled abuse of executive power. For the purposes of our story, however, Watergate stands for the worst-case scenario of a badly flawed campaign finance system that failed to forestall corruption or prevent out-and-out criminal activity. That in the end constitutional safeguards worked to save the political system and forced Nixon from power provided little comfort to those seeking to reform the system of financing elections.

Nixon had decided to bypass the Republican National Committee as much as possible, in part because he and his top aides assumed that the committee would play by the rules, which would prevent them from raising and spending the massive amounts of money Nixon believed necessary to win in 1972. His campaign created an independent body, the Committee to Re-elect the President, and the money flowed in. Financier Robert Vesco (who later fled the country after embezzling millions of dollars from his companies) delivered $200,000 in cash in an attaché case. Billionaire aviation manufacturer and movie producer Howard Hughes put $100,000 into a safe deposit box belonging to Nixon's friend Bebe Rebozo. Clement Stone reported giving $73,000, but later investigations showed that he had provided more than $2 million secretly. At least thirteen corporations and their foreign subsidiaries made more than $780,000 in clearly illegal contributions. All told, the committee received an estimated $5 million in large individual and corporate donations, most of them illegal. To hide these donations, the committee kept a great deal of the money in cash on hand, allowing for payouts of $250,000 to Herb Kalmbach, the president's lawyer; $350,000 to Gordon Strachan, H. R. Haldeman's aide; and $83,000 to G. Gordon Liddy, this last money going to finance the Watergate break-in.

How did sophisticated and wealthy men become dupes of the Nixon committee? After all, they had made donations, perhaps even large ones, before, but not since the days of the Tweed Ring in the late nineteenth century had there been stories of fat cats turning up at party headquarters with satchels stuffed with bills. In part Nixon turned the primary fear of the reformers on its head. They had worried that big corporations, eager

{ *Chapter Two* }

to get the government to act for their advantage, would offer money and essentially "buy" legislators and their votes. Nixon did the opposite. His lieutenants went to corporations and told them that if they hoped to be treated well, they had better pony up.

The disclosures of Watergate fed the demand for reform. In the late 1960s there had been, as Seymour Martin Lipset and William Schneider noted from their study of public opinion polls, "a virtual explosion in anti-government sentiment." Although the Vietnam War may have been the "catalytic event" in creating this mistrust, Watergate heightened popular distrust of both government and its leaders.

Common Cause attracted 100,000 members within six months of its founding; by the beginning of 1972 that number had increased to a quarter million. Common Cause and other groups dedicated to electoral and governmental reform played an important role in campaign finance reform over the next three decades. When the Federal Election Commission (FEC) proved slow or unwilling to enforce the law, these groups stepped in and generated publicity as well as lawsuits. Common Cause filed its first lawsuit within months of its creation, challenging the efforts of both the Democratic National Committee and the Republican National Committee to evade the 1971 FECA contribution and expenditure limits by setting up multiple committees. A key issue in the suit was whether or not the law gave nongovernmental groups standing to seek a right of private enforcement. Common Cause won a significant victory when the federal district court ruled that it had standing to bring class action suits on behalf of all voters. The suit did more than just put the major political parties on notice that Common Cause intended to serve a watchdog function; it also gave the new group immediate legitimacy and a seat at the table in the discussion of future campaign reform measures (*Common Cause v. Democratic National Committee et al.* [1971]).

The Watergate hearings did for campaign finance reform in the 1970s what the Armstrong hearings had done for the 1907 and 1911 laws. Not only Common Cause but also other groups signed on to the issue. To take but one example, Sears, Roebuck and Company heir Philip M. Stern, a liberal philanthropist and author, established the Center for Public Financing of Elections. The executive director, Susan B. King, had been the Washington, DC, director of the National Committee for an Effective Congress, a liberal political action committee (PAC), and she proved extremely adept at building a coalition of church, labor, and professional organizations, all committed to campaign finance reform. King, Gardner, and other reformers, all veterans of politics, knew how to lobby, and they knew how to get their side of the story into the media. On some days, as one scholar dryly noted, "members of Congress might well have felt that the morning newspapers, nightly television news, constituent mail, and pro-reform lobbyists all over the Capitol had created pressure for new legislation that was too great to resist."

*   *   *

Most of the crimes related to Watergate had little or nothing to do with campaign financing, such as the break-in at Democratic Party headquarters, obstruction of justice, or use of the IRS to try to punish "enemies." Nixon had not been forced to resign because of violation of the 1971 FECA, nor did the trials and convictions of many of his associates deal with campaign finance. But as the facts of how Nixon had raised and used money became public, they fed a growing public outrage. Gardner noted that many of the illegal activities committed by the administration and its hirelings had been financed by money paid to CREEP, and that Watergate was "a particularly malodorous chapter in the annals of campaign financing." The public outcry grew so powerful that it enabled reformers in Congress to push through substantial changes to FECA that in fact dwarfed the reforms of the 1971 act. Although known as amendments, the 1974 measures not only addressed the perceived shortcomings of the 1971 FECA but also tackled just about every item on the reformers' agenda.

To begin with, Congress finally created a mechanism to police the candidates and the parties in their adherence to the campaign finance laws. The FEC would be composed of six members, three Democrats and three Republicans, serving staggered six-year terms. The president, the Speaker of the House, and the president pro tem of the Senate would each appoint two members, one from each party, and all six members would be subject to confirmation not just by the Senate but also by the House of Representatives. In addition, the secretary of the Senate and the clerk of the House would serve as ex officio members.

The 1971 law set no limits on either contributions or expenditures, except for what wealthy candidates could give to their own campaigns.

The amendments set a $1,000 contribution limit to any one candidate for each primary, runoff, or general election, with a maximum of $25,000 to all candidates for federal office in any election cycle. No contributor could give more than $5,000 to any political organization or committee, but there were no limits on the aggregate amount a person could give through multiple committee donations. A private person could not expend more than $1,000 on behalf of a single candidate. Contributions of more than $100 had to be paid by check or money order, a clear response to people carrying envelopes stuffed with money into the Nixon campaign headquarters. Foreign contributions were barred completely.

On the expenditure side, candidates for president could not spend more than $10 million in the primaries. In any specific state primary, they could not spend more than twice what a senatorial candidate would be allowed to spend. For the general elections the law capped presidential expenditures at $20 million. Candidates for the House had a $70,000 limit in both the primary and the general election, and candidates running for the Senate faced limits determined by the population of the state, but no more than $100,000 in the primary and $150,000 in the general election.

In an important step the new law finally implemented public funding of at least part of the presidential campaign, through a voluntary check-off on a taxpayer's return. A formula determined how much a candidate would get once he or she had raised a minimum of $100,000 in amounts of at least $5,000 in each of twenty states or more. In addition, the law tightened the reporting requirements and directed that periodic reports be delivered in a timely manner to the FEC. In other areas as well, the law attempted to strengthen the rules set out in 1971.

To call these changes simply "amendments" to the 1971 FECA is clearly erroneous. This law went well beyond the 1971 regulations, attempted to avoid the problems revealed by the Watergate scandals, and in many ways fulfilled the agenda that many reformers had been advocating for more than two decades. In some of its goals the 1974 law was in fact a great advance over all previous measures. By extending public financing to all levels of the presidential campaign, it acknowledged the importance of both the primaries and the general election in choosing the nation's chief executive. But reformers could not get public funding for congressional campaigns, primarily because of the intransigence of Wayne Hays, now the powerful chair of the Ways and Means Committee, and other representatives from essentially one-party districts who did not care to see their challengers paid for by tax dollars.

The question of whether spending limits would increase the advantage enjoyed by incumbents played a major role in the debates in both houses of Congress. In the House, William E. Frenzel (R-MN) had noted in the 1971 debate that "when you establish a spending limitation you literally insure that incumbents are not going to be defeated because the only weapon the non-incumbent has . . . is [money to] get his name known." By the time Congress debated the 1974 measures, it had figures from the 1972 elections showing that challengers to incumbents did well only if they spent a great deal of money, usually more than would be allowed under the new limits. Several representatives and senators said plainly that they would never have been elected if the proposed spending limits had been in place when they first ran for office.

Part of the problem in setting a viable limit arose from the different experiences of those involved. Proposed limits for the expenditures for House races ranged from $30,000 to $190,000. Representative Frenzel thought that $150,000 made sense because "that is what it cost me to get elected the first time." Wayne Hays and John Herman Dent (D-PA) thought that $35,000 to $40,000 would be enough, but both men ran in districts where they normally had weak opposition. In the end the House set a limit of $70,000 on the primary and an equal amount on the general election, with another 20 percent allowed to cover the costs of raising these funds. A single number, applying to all races, made sense for the House, since all districts are by law roughly equal in population.

Candidates for the Senate, however, faced a far different situation. Running in California or Texas meant covering more ground and persuading more voters than running in Rhode Island or New Hampshire. Thus the bill allowed senatorial candidates to spend the larger of two amounts—$100,000 or eight cents per eligible voter in a primary, and then $150,000 or twelve cents per voter in the general election.

Those who predicted that the 1974 limits would favor incumbents were proven right, and one need not be cynical to assert that the drafters of those limits recognized that such would in fact be the consequence. To begin with, the regulations embodied in the bill made it that much more difficult to raise money, and would-be donors tended to give to incumbents, who had not only the name recognition but also the power of an office they already occupied. Various studies showed that incumbents on the average raised twice as much as challengers, and that challengers had a difficult time (unless they had personal wealth) getting the start-up money to run a campaign. The regulations for contributions also made it more difficult for both challengers and incumbents to raise money, with the result that much more time went into the effort to fund a campaign than went into the actual campaigning itself. Sixty-one percent of Senate candidates and more than half of the House candidates—both incumbents and challengers—responded in the affirmative to a survey taken after the 1976 election: that the new FECA rules made it more difficult to raise campaign funds.

Perhaps some reformers considered this good news, but even before the bill had gone into effect some politicians began warning that no bill, no matter how comprehensive, could free campaign finance from the influence of money. Senator Edward Kennedy asked: "Who really owns America? Is it the people or is it a little group of big campaign contributors?" According to Kennedy, Congress had failed to solve the energy crisis because of the campaign gifts of the oil industry. National health insurance had been sabotaged by the American Medical Association and private insurers, while the National Rifle Association blocked meaningful gun control laws. Failing to provide for public financing of Senate and House elections, Kennedy warned, guaranteed that the influence of powerful interests would continue. As if in response, Senator Lowell Weicker (R-CT), one of the heroes of the Watergate investigation, urged the public not to place too great a faith in public financing, which, he declared, "is not a magical Clorox guaranteed to end forever the dirty laundry of Watergate. It does not cut the cost of campaigns; it just shifts the cost." Senator Howard Baker (R-TN), another popular figure during Watergate, worried about the constitutionality of a law that used taxpayers' money to fund candidates they did not support. Public subsidies, he warned, could "abridge the individual's First Amendment right of freedom of political expression."

As it turned out, the 1974 FECA amendments did abridge the First Amendment, but not quite in the way that Senator Baker had worried about.

* * *

The first challenge in the courts to FECA began in the spring of 1972, when three old-line liberal activists walked into the offices of the American Civil Liberties Union (ACLU) with an incredible story. On May 31, they and others had sponsored a two-page advertisement in the *New York Times* calling for the impeachment of Richard Nixon following the bombing of Cambodia, and praising those few members of Congress who had voted against the bombing. The ad included two coupons that readers could use to send in contributions to the National Committee for Impeachment. Almost immediately afterward, Nixon's Justice Department filed a lawsuit in federal court demanding to know how the group had been organized and who had paid for the ad. In addition, government lawyers threatened the dissidents with injunctions and ordered them not to engage in further political speech unless they filed reports and disclosures with the government and otherwise obeyed a whole host of rules and regulations they had never heard about. All they had done, they told the ACLU, was sponsor an ad critical of the president. Wasn't this the very type of political speech protected by the First Amendment?

The irony, if one can call it that, is that the rules and regulations used by the Nixon Justice Department to threaten the committee had just been passed by Congress—the Federal Election Campaign Act of 1971. The government argued that, even though it spoke only about issues, the advertisement mentioned, criticized, or praised people who would be running for public office that year, and thus might affect the results of those elections. This constituted not political speech but political activity by a "committee" of the type Congress had intended to include within the limitations imposed by FECA. The Justice Department managed to get an injunction from a friendly district judge, only to be slapped down and reversed by a unanimous three-judge panel of the Second Circuit in October. In 1972, the panel ruled that campaign finance laws could not be used against nonpartisan, issue-oriented committees engaged in commenting on or even advocating policies related to important public issues (*United States v. National Committee for Impeachment*).

In one way the government had been right. Speech such as that in the newspaper ad might influence people's opinions about members of Congress and the president, and thus influence their vote at the next election. Even if that had not been the primary purpose of the ad, its sponsors must surely have hoped to influence those who read it. Moreover, the ad cost about $18,000, or $113,000 in current dollars, an amount that is clearly "serious money." If one is to be consistent about campaign finance reform, one would indeed have to include any type of paid speech that, directly or indirectly, might affect the electorate. Such controls, whether in FECA or in later legislation, have one thing in common: they penalize people for exercising their First Amendment right to speak out on important issues.

The ACLU not only won that case but also managed to get another provision of the 1971 bill nullified in court. The law placed a limit on media spending, and if every issue ad, or even an ad placed by a private citizen, came within the legal limits of $50,000 or ten cents a voter, that limit would soon be met, causing great harm to candidates seeking to place their own ads. The ACLU argued that just because a privately placed advertisement praised—or damned—a candidate, it did not make that ad part of campaign advertising. Once again the courts agreed and held that FECA did not apply to groups like the ACLU, whose major purpose involved issue discussion, not the election of candidates. Suddenly the warnings of those who had said campaign finance reform might run afoul of the First Amendment took on new life.

Whereas proponents of campaign finance reform saw FECA and its 1974 amendments as cleansing the political process of potentially corrupting influences, opponents saw it as restricting the free exchange of ideas and treading on that most precious of American rights, free speech to criticize the government. The most telling of the criticisms might be summed up as follows:

- The law restricted the right of candidates to expend money, even if it all came from small contributors. The claim that big business or special interest groups could "buy" candidates through big contributions made no sense if the money all came from small donors.
- The amounts set by Congress were, even by the standards of the time, much too low. The $70,000 limit on House races came to less than House members on the average spent on the free mail privilege and other constituent services. These limits clearly favored incumbents, who already had the name recognition and could bypass limits by

flooding their districts with materials sent out under the free postage privilege.

- The act limited what candidates could contribute to their own campaigns. If the idea had been to prevent corruption, how could candidates corrupt themselves? Under this rule, the campaign of John Heinz for the Senate from Pennsylvania in 1976, or later presidential bids by Ross Perot and Steve Forbes, would have been illegal.

- The law silenced independent speakers by limiting how much any person could give in so-called political expenditures. The $1,000 limit at that time would have barely purchased a quarter-page ad in the *New York Times*. (This was, of course, the provision the Justice Department had attempted to use in *National Committee for Impeachment*, although the actual constitutionality of that provision would not be tested until later.)

- The law invaded one's privacy, because even the smallest contributor would have his or her name disclosed publicly and then put on file by the government.

- Under the terms of the 1974 act, issue-oriented groups that reported on the voting records of members of Congress and then drew up "box scores" indicating how House members and senators had voted would have to file reports as "political committees." What did political speech mean other than the right to evaluate and judge the performance of elected officials?

Given the fact that the 1974 act severely curtailed the amount of money that a candidate could raise and expend, it is not surprising that there would be a court challenge. But to make that challenge, there had to be a constitutional basis, and that is where the advocates of free speech came in. FECA would be challenged on the grounds that limiting how much money a person could donate to a political candidate, or how much a person could spend in running for public office, violated the First Amendment.

By 1975, moreover, even with the addition of more conservative justices appointed by Richard Nixon, the Supreme Court had adopted a highly speech-protective view of the First Amendment. The majority of the Court adopted the position that in order for the state to curb expression, it had to show a compelling governmental interest. If it could meet this heavy evidentiary burden, it then had to show that the means adopted were the least restrictive in manner.

Free expression can take many forms, and although the Court's record over the years has been erratic in some areas, since the 1950s it has adhered to the notion that political speech is at the very core of First Amendment protection. While drawing on theorists such as Zechariah Chafee Jr., Alexander Meiklejohn, and Thomas Emerson to develop the notion of protected free expression, one can also point to one of the most influential opinions in the Court's history, the concurrence of Justice Louis D. Brandeis in *Whitney v. California* (1927). In that opinion Brandeis provided what has become the root rationale for the protection of speech. The First Amendment, he explained, protects both the speaker's right to expound unpopular ideas and the listener's right to hear and evaluate such ideas. In a democracy each person, to be a good citizen, needs to be informed about public issues in order to make intelligent choices through the political system. The protection of political speech is thus crucial to each citizen's ability to perform civic obligations, and although the content of that speech may at times be offensive, in the final analysis the people in their collective wisdom will choose the better ideas and discard the less useful. Rather than stifle "bad" or unpopular speech, Brandeis declared, the remedy is more speech; the result will be an informed citizenry and a vibrant democratic society.

In order to overturn the campaign finance laws, then, challengers would have to prove that the government had not shown any compelling interest in limiting the purest form of political speech, campaigning for office. Opponents of FECA believed they had a good chance at doing so, and on January 2, 1975, a coalition of conservatives and liberals filed suit attacking key parts of FECA. The litigants included James Buckley (brother of conservative columnist and icon William F. Buckley Jr.), then a Conservative Party senator from New York; former senator and liberal presidential candidate Eugene McCarthy; financier and liberal activist Stewart Mott; the conservative journal *Human Events*; the ACLU; the New York Conservative Party; and the American Conservative Union. The coalition had been put together by David Keene, an assistant to Senator Buckley, who realized that opposition to the law ran across the political spectrum, and that it would be expedient if all these individuals and groups could pool their resources to cover the costs of the suit.

The coalition attacked the law on several grounds. It opposed the public financing of presidential campaigns because, in accepting public money, candidates had to agree to abide by spending and contribution limits. It alleged that such limits, whether tied to the public financing provisions of the presidential campaign, or freestanding in regard to House and Senate races, violated the candidates' First Amendment rights. Similarly, contribution limits invaded private citizens' rights of political expression. In essence, money, whether given by a willing contributor to a campaign, or expended by a candidate seeking office, constituted speech. Moreover, as political speech, it stood at the apex of the type of expression protected by the First Amendment.

The case, *Buckley v. Valeo*, began in the US District Court for the District of Columbia, which upheld the act; from there, it was certified for appeal to the Court of Appeals for the District of Columbia, which, sitting en banc, upheld all but one provision of the act. That provision, §437a, required issue advocacy groups, including those that rated members of Congress on their voting records, to file detailed reports with the government disclosing contributors and the amounts they had given. All of the circuit court judges, ranging from the liberal David Bazelon and J. Skelly Wright to the conservative Edward Tamm and Malcolm Wilkey, upheld the law.

* * *

Buckley did not mark the first time that the High Court had heard cases involving political corruption (but these had usually involved corruption in office rather than questions of campaign finance). As recently as 1972 the Court had decided a case in which a senator had accepted a bribe and claimed legislative immunity from prosecution, a claim the Court rebuffed (*United States v. Brewster* [1972]). In three cases there had been First Amendment issues involved. First, the Court had dismissed an indictment under the FCPA against the Congress of Industrial Organizations for publishing an internal newsletter that endorsed political candidates (*United States v. Congress of Industrial Organizations* [1948]). Second, in 1957 the Court had sustained the indictment and conviction of a union for illegally using union dues to sponsor television commercials supporting pro-labor candidates (*United States v. International Union of United Automobile, Aircraft, and Agricultural Implement Workers of America*).

Third, the Court had held that the 1971 FECA did not prevent unions from making political contributions if the money had been given voluntarily and through a segregated fund (*Pipefitters Local Union No. 562 v. United States* [1972]).

In none of these cases, however, had the Court actually reached the First Amendment issue, and it had always based its conclusions on other grounds. The Court had not hitherto directly addressed the question raised by the plaintiffs in *Buckley.* Did limitations on campaign contributions and expenditures, without any evidence of wrongdoing, violate the First Amendment?

The Court heard oral arguments on November 10, 1975, and handed down its decision fairly quickly, on January 30, 1976, no doubt wanting to clear up any questions about the validity of portions of the act before campaigning for the 1976 elections began in earnest. The opinion is somewhat complicated and came down in per curiam form—that is, as the opinion of the Court with no justice listed as the author. Only three members of the Court, William Brennan, Potter Stewart, and Lewis Powell, joined in all parts of the opinion. In addition, there were separate opinions by Chief Justice Warren Burger and Justices Byron White, Thurgood Marshall, Harry Blackmun, and William Rehnquist, all joining the opinion in part and dissenting in part. Justice John Paul Stevens, who had recently joined the Court, did not participate in the decision.

In essence, the Court in *Buckley* upheld the limits on individual contributions, the reporting provisions, and the public financing scheme for presidential elections. But it struck down on First Amendment grounds all limits on campaign expenditures by candidates or by PACs. According to the Court, spending money in a campaign constitutes a form of expression, since it buys time or space in public forums to get across ideas; limiting expenditures, therefore, limits speech. The Court rejected a similar argument against contribution limits, even though they also imposed some restrictions on expression, because it accepted the government's argument of a compelling governmental interest in preventing corruption and maintaining the integrity of the political process. In addition, the Court invalidated the means of appointing FEC members and ruled that appointments could be made only by the president, by and with the concurrence of the Senate.

The Court ruled that FECA restricted "the voices of people and interest groups who have money to spend and reduce[d] the overall scope of federal election campaigns . . . [since] the alleged 'conduct' of giving or spending money 'arises in some measure because the communication allegedly integral to the conduct is itself thought to be harmful.'" In other words, the only reason one would want to restrict contributions and expenditures would be to restrict the message being circulated, and this could not be done without violating the First Amendment. The Court also noted that, unlike earlier cases in which it had approved content-neutral time, place, and manner restrictions, this action, although technically content-neutral, in fact aimed at squelching the message completely.

Recognizing the realities of current campaigning, the Court noted that restrictions on money spent in political communication necessarily reduced the amount of that expression and the number and variety of issues discussed "because virtually every means of communicating ideas in today's mass society requires the expenditure of money." In particular, the Court singled out the $1,000 ceiling on spending by interest groups, which "would appear to exclude all citizens and groups except candidates, political parties, and the institutional press from any significant use of the most effective means of [communication]." In terms of preserving the right to expression, the Court held that so long as a political advertisement did not use certain words, later called "magic words"—such as "vote for," "elect," "defeat," or "reject"—the ads did not come within the definition of political advertising. Although no one recognized it at the time, this was the first step in what would eventually become the avalanche of "issue advertising." The Court did, however, approve the reporting requirements, holding that by themselves such requirements did not limit free expression, and served the legitimate purpose of public scrutiny of campaign finance and expenditures.

The opinion then drew a distinction between limits on expenses, which would restrict expression, and limits on contributions, which the Court said would not have that great an effect:

A limitation upon the amount that any one person or group may contribute [entails] only a marginal restriction upon the contributor's ability to engage in free communication. A contribution serves as a general expression of support for the candidate and his views, but does not communicate the underlying basis of the support. [At most], the size of the contribution provides a very rough index of the intensity of the contributor's support for the candidate. A limitation on [contributions] thus involves little direct restraint on political communication.

Although admitting that greater contributions would allow the candidate greater expression, the Court noted that it was not the contributor's free expression, but that of the candidate, that reached the public. Moreover, the Court found that no evidence showed that contribution limits would have any dramatic effect on the ability of political campaigns to raise the money they needed.

As for the First Amendment issues, the decision brushed them aside almost casually: "It is unnecessary to look beyond the Act's primary purpose—to limit the actuality and appearance of corruption resulting from large individual financial contributions—in order to find a constitutionally sufficient justification for the $1,000 contribution limitation. . . . The deeply disturbing examples surfacing after the 1972 election demonstrate that the problem is not an illusory one." Clearly the Court, like the Congress that passed the 1974 FECA amendments, had Watergate on its mind and used that example to undergird its constitutional argument that the necessity of avoiding corruption or its appearance provided the compelling interest to justify the act.

The Court's reasoning is confusing. If spending money is expression, then the amount of money one has in hand clearly enables or limits candidates or parties in sending out their message. The more money, the greater the capacity for expression; the less money, the less the ability to express. The Court seemed to assume that if candidates could no longer count on the big givers, they would still raise the money they needed by tapping larger numbers of small givers. If, however, a rich person strongly believed in an idea or program championed by a candidate, then it is plausible to assume that by financing that candidate, the donor is also making an expression. In our society there are many instances in which a person expresses his or her ideas through others. This contradiction becomes even more puzzling when we note that the Court struck down the limits on amounts that a candidate could give to his or her own campaign. Individuals such as Nelson Rockefeller or John Heinz could pour millions of their own money into their own campaigns. Rich candidates, in other words, had unlimited expression rights, but rich donors did not. The Court ignored the claim that contributors were also expressing their views. And, as we shall see in chapter 3, this forced the political system to create alternative means by which those with deep pockets could give vent to their expressions, devices that within a short time would change the landscape of US political campaigning.

In the third major part of the opinion, the Court upheld the provisions providing for public financing of presidential campaigns: "Subtitle H is a congressional effort, not to abridge, restrict, or censor speech, but rather to use public money to facilitate and enlarge public discussion and participation in the electoral process, goals vital to a self-governing people. Thus, Subtitle H furthers, not abridges, pertinent First Amendment values."

Buckley has had its supporters and detractors ever since. The decision lifted the limits on expenditures by candidates and by groups operating independently of candidates, and the bar on how much candidates could give to their own campaigns. The limits on contributions remained in effect, restricting how much PACs, individuals, and political parties could give to specific campaigns; the public funding of presidential elections through a voluntary tax checkoff remained untouched; and the FEC would now be the official federal agency overseeing campaign finance. But although the Court apparently equated the expenditure of money by candidates with free expression, the lack of rigorous analysis in the opinion would cloud the issue of campaign finance reform for the next quarter century.

* * *

Even after *Buckley*, the 1974 amendments still marked a significant improvement over the nearly useless scheme that had been in effect before 1971 The new regulatory plan did include one very familiar element, a ban on corporate and union contributions and expenditures in federal elections, and the law now put a little bite into these prohibitions by making it unlawful for anyone—a candidate or a committee member—to accept such contributions. But the law did allow for a PAC, whose administrative and fundraising expenses could be paid for by a parent corporation or union, so long as the actual funds expended politically

{ *Chapter Two* }

came from voluntary contributions. One wonders if the drafters of this provision realized that, far from reining in campaign finance abuses, PACs would be the proverbial camel's nose in the tent.

The 1974 law also treated political party committees as a type of political entity that had to register with the FEC, and it subjected them to fairly specific limits on donations they could receive and expenditures they could make. But party committees, as part of the official political party structure at national, state, and local levels, did in fact receive special treatment as well. Individuals could contribute up to $20,000 a year to national party committees and an additional $5,000 to a state party committee. These committees could then transfer unlimited sums to other party committees without the transfer being treated as a contribution. A national party committee could also transfer $17,500 during an election cycle to a senatorial candidate, and both national and state parties could make limited "coordinated" expenditures on behalf of their candidates for federal offices. These amounts varied by office (representative, senator, president) and by state population (more in New York and California than in Nevada and Mississippi), and they were indexed to the rate of inflation.

In what would prove the greatest flaw in the new plan, the law made no distinctions between various types of party accounts, some subject to federal law and others not. The statute makes no mention of "federal" or "nonfederal" accounts, and this created the first problem that arose after the law went into effect in 1976. The limits set on coordinated party spending clearly had a harmful effect on traditional grassroots party activity, leading Congress to amend the law in 1979 to correct this problem. Neither did the 1974 law distinguish between what we now call "hard" and "soft" moneys. The 1974 law and the 1979 revision created what would become the bane of reformers for the next two decades; the difficulty resulted, as we shall see, from the response of the FEC to concerns related to the federal system—how best to facilitate the work of party organizations that have roles in both federal and nonfederal election campaigns. The internal inconsistencies in the Supreme Court's decision in *Buckley v. Valeo* boded poorly for the future.

CHAPTER 3

Soft Money, PACs, and the Failure of Campaign Finance Reform after 1976

Shortly after Richard M. Nixon resigned the presidency in the wake of Watergate, Senator Edward M. Kennedy (D-MA) noted that "abuses of campaign spending and private campaign financing do not stop at the other end of Pennsylvania Avenue. They dominate congressional elections as well." Kennedy's comment pointed to one of the major problems that would confront campaign finance reform over the next quarter century. The quadrennial presidential election, the largest, the most expensive, and the most visible of all campaigns, captures the public's attention, and abuses in the Nixon years epitomized for many people the corruption inherent in the campaign financing system. But 100 senators and 435 members of the House of Representatives also have to stand before their constituents. In addition, there are gubernatorial, legislative, and local elections in all fifty states, the District of Columbia, and the territories.

That most astute of political commentators, former Speaker of the House Tip O'Neill (D-MA), once famously declared that "all politics is local." It stands to reason, therefore, that people wishing to influence political decision-making have to target those elected officials whose actions will most directly affect their interests. Developers will be more interested in the decisions of local zoning boards and county supervisors than in the deliberations of members of Congress and will direct their political contributions toward local campaigns. Policies that affect many businesses are enacted by the states, and businesses with large stores in specific states will try to shape state laws on sales taxes, labor regulations, and the like. Although the president of the United States has enormous power to affect the implementation of regulations, those rules flow from statutes enacted by Congress, and large national and multinational corporations prefer to have Congress act in their favor. Of course, some groups like the National Rifle Association, the National Organization for Women, and the Sierra Club operate at all political levels—local, state, and national—since policies affecting them may be implemented at all these levels.

To view campaign finance reform, therefore, just as a question of cleaning up presidential politics is to look at the tip of the iceberg and fail to realize that most campaigning goes on below that level. Reforming the system, therefore, required that members of Congress place limits on themselves; yet the variety of districts and states represented in Congress precluded any simple one-size-fits-all solution. Although some of the limits imposed on presidential candidates would make sense in congressional and senatorial campaigns, others would not. In terms of state and local politics, Congress does not have the constitutional authority to impose regulations.

The reforms enacted in the 1974 Federal Election Campaign Act (FECA) amendments would not have greatly affected the vast majority of campaigns in the country. Congress responded to the *Buckley* decision by amending FECA in both 1976 and 1979, but these changes had little impact on campaign financing. In fact, in the opinion of many, the problems only grew worse in the next twenty-five years as party officials and professional fundraisers found ways, some of them ingenious, to get around FECA proscriptions. Reformers pointed to ever-worsening scenarios, Congress held hearing after hearing, and nothing happened. The costs of running for office, however, kept rising, and candidates became ever more dependent on campaign contributions.

* * *

Following *Buckley*, Congress moved to correct some of the FECA deficiencies struck down by the Court. It reconstituted the Federal Election Commission (FEC), this time providing that its members be nominated by the president and confirmed by the Senate. To maintain its influence over the FEC, Congress gave itself a veto power over any rules proposed by the commission. The drafters also took the opportunity to fine-tune some of the regulations, such as raising the limit on individual contributions from $1,000 to $5,000. But although it allowed larger donations to campaigns, Congress also tightened the reporting requirements and limited solicitations by political action committees (PACs) to members or defined constituent groups. The 1974 law, modified by the 1976 amendments and indexed for inflation, remained the basic law governing campaign finance until the passage of the Bipartisan Campaign Reform Act (McCain-Feingold) in 2002.

In 1979 Congress passed a series of noncontroversial amendments that supposedly tightened federal election law but—with one important exception—had little effect. The main provisions made no significant changes in federal election law, but a seemingly innocent provision on party building within a few years mushroomed into the bête noire of campaign finance reformers—soft money.

Two main trends emerged in campaign financing between 1974 and the early 1990s. First, there was growth in the total amount expended, much of it supplied through PACs, with the rate of increase greatest not at the presidential level but in congressional races. The second trend was that a large percentage of the money raised went to incumbents. Scholars who follow campaign spending trends note that the large growth in spending took place mostly in the late 1970s and 1980s, and then leveled off or even decreased slightly (in terms of constant dollars) in the early 1990s.

Much of the jump in expenses can be traced to the ever-increasing role that media played in campaigns. As Larry Makinson of the Center for Responsive Politics noted, it takes a multimillion-dollar campaign to run for the presidency: "But in the four decades since the first 'I Like Ike' TV commercials hit the air, the business of political advertising and consulting has penetrated to nearly every level of office-seekers." To raise that money, candidates and parties have tapped into three main sources: soft money, PACs, and personal wealth.

*   *   *

Soft money is the result of a provision in the 1979 FECA amendments that eliminated any limits on donations to political committees providing that (1) they are not placed in the budget of any particular candidate's campaign, and (2) they are at least nominally directed toward so-called party-building activities, such as get-out-the-vote efforts, polling, and state campaign coordinating efforts. One may wonder whether the sponsors of this legislation ever intended or even imagined that it would create the greatest single device for evading both the letter and the intent of the FECA. As Mr. Dooley remarked of antitrust legislation in another era, lawyers could take what had been erected as a solid wall and turn it into a triumphal arch. By the mid-1990s, total soft money contributions rivaled the amount raised by the campaigns themselves, even in presidential elections where the federal government put in nearly $100 million in funding. According to some analysts, the soft money frenzy drove the costs of campaigning for the presidency from $325 million in 1984 to $500 million in 1988, and to more than $600 million four years later, of which less than one-sixth constituted the federal funding designed to place a cap on campaign costs.

When the Court in *Buckley* upheld the FECA's limits on contributions, it assumed that "contributions" included any "funds provided to a candidate or political party or campaign committee either directly or indirectly through an intermediary," in addition to "dollars given to another person or organization that are earmarked for political purposes." Congress in the FECA defined contributions and expenditures as the donation of and use of money or anything of value "for the purpose of influencing an election for federal office." The statute did not go into any greater detail, leaving clarification of particulars to the FEC, which issued formal regulations in 1977. In those rules and in several advisory opinions, the FEC seemed to take a tough stance on how political committees could use money for party organization building or voter registration drives. At the time, however, the FEC only addressed the issue of money raised under FECA provisions, and not "nonfederal funds," or what we now call "soft money." In subsequent rulings and advisory opinions, the FEC moved to the position that registration and get-out-the-vote drives could be financed by a combination of federal and nonfederal funds. Although for audit purposes they could maintain separate accounts of federal and nonfederal moneys, it seemed that both would be subject to the same regulations. By 1979, however, the FEC ruled that both national and state parties could solicit and accept donations that would not be subject to FECA source and amount limits, so long as the parties maintained these funds in separate accounts, and that these funds could be used to influence elections for nonfederal offices. The only restriction the FEC imposed involved auditing practices, whereby the committees had to allocate administrative and certain other costs between federal and nonfederal funds.

Then, in 1979, Congress amended the FECA to relieve state and local party organizations from many of the law's strictures, on the grounds that federal requirements interfered too greatly with traditional grass-roots and volunteer activities. The new law exempted activities such as state party expenses for campaign materials (buttons, bumper stickers, lawn signs, and the like) used to support candidates, but the exemption rested on the use of "hard money"—that is, money raised under FECA guidelines for the support of a candidate. In other words, if Mr. Jones gave $1,000 to the Republican Party to elect Representative Smith, and the party allocated that money to Smith's local campaign committee specifically for the use of campaign materials, that money would not count against the expenditure limits imposed on Smith's campaign by FECA. Similarly, party expenses for voter registration and get-out-the-vote drives, if paid for by hard money, also would not count against the FECA expenditure limits. But money given by Mr. Jones directly to a committee—either an established political committee or a special com-mittee—specifically for these purposes would not count in any manner against FECA limits; as a result, by the following year, such money had become an important part of national party campaign finance.

Professor Thomas Mann of the Brookings Institution, a well-known student of campaign finance, noted that the 1979 amendments did not create soft money, and in fact Congress had no venal motives at the time. The amendments simply grew out of the recognition that political parties at the local, state, and national levels had roles to play in both federal and nonfederal elections, and that the limits established by the 1974 FECA amendments hampered what most people considered valu-able work of these committees in motivating voters and getting them registered and to the polls. By 1979, the FEC had significantly relaxed its rules regarding what state and local committees could do with non-federal funds, so long as the expenditures did not violate state laws. The Democratic National Committee and Republican National Committee then argued to the FEC that they, too, should have the flexibility that the FEC allowed to state and local committees. The 1979 amendments did not authorize national committees to accept unlimited donations from individuals or from corporate or union treasuries. Instead, they expanded the uses state and local parties could make of hard money.

Once Congress permitted state and local committees to spend

unlimited funds on grassroots activities that benefited federal as well as state and local candidates, the FEC permitted national party committees and the campaign committees of federal candidates to pay for a portion of these activities with funds outside the FECA limits. Beginning in the 1980 election cycle, soft money—that is, funds not subject to FECA limits and outside the scrutiny of the FEC—could be used by all political groups to finance certain activities. National parties could thus approach corporations and unions for direct contributions to these separate funds that ostensibly would be used solely for grassroots, voter registration, and get-out-the-vote drives. In addition, soft money could be used for so-called party-building activities; the only limitation would be applicable state law, which in many states was either nonexistent or ineffective. Therefore, reports of soft money were notoriously unreliable, since there were practically no required filings for the amounts raised or spent.

The best estimate we have was done by Anthony Corrado, and from his work we can get an idea of how important soft money became in the two decades following 1980.

In 1980, the first year that the national committees could raise and spend soft money, it accounted for only 8 percent of their total outlay; by the 2000 election, soft money accounted for 42 percent of the total expenditures of the national committees. Even in off-year cycles, the national committees raised and spent millions in soft money—$98.8 million in 1994 ($1 in $5 of the total), and $220.7 million in 1998 ($1 in $3). By 1988, parties raised much of their soft money through gifts from large contributors, with more than 400 persons, corporations, or unions each giving $100,000 or more. In that year the Republican National Committee set up "Team 100," a roster of contributors who donated at least $100,000 to the party, most of it in soft money. After the election the Republicans announced that they had received gifts of at least $100,000 from 267 donors; the Democrats that year received gifts of similar sizes from 130 donors. Four years later, the top category went to donors who gave $200,000 or more.

Throughout the 1980s and early 1990s, party organizations used soft money to finance a wide range of party expenses and activities. Both national party committees and their Senate and House campaign committees paid for administrative expenses, staff salaries, fundraising costs, and general advertising (ads not expressly directed to favor a candidate). Of course, some of the money actually went for buttons, bumper stickers, and yard signs.

Technically, soft money could not go to financing the campaigns of federal candidates, but in fact that is exactly where it went. The process began with the national party raising soft money, primarily through large donors, who made out their checks to nonfederal party accounts. The parties then transferred the money to state and local parties in districts and states where competitive elections were expected to occur. This transfer then allowed the state or local party to cover administrative costs or to make contributions to state or local candidates, freeing up hard money that had been raised to cover such purposes, which could then legally be given to federal campaigns. State and local committees simply could not transfer national party soft money to federal candidates, but by exploiting the wording of the law—and with careful accounting procedures—soft money could be used to cover costs normally associated with hard money expenditures. The transfer allowed state parties to help federal candidates by essentially "washing" the soft money.

Campaigns have open and hidden costs, both of which are necessary. The general public sees the television ads, billboards, bumper stickers, and yard signs and may hear the voice of a staff member calling to urge support for the candidate. What is not seen are the overhead costs—rental of office space, purchases of computers and other office equipment, staffing for phone banks, telephone charges, costs of polling, transportation, the ad agencies that create the media spots, and the like—all of which are every bit as essential to a successful campaign as the appearances by the candidate and the constant mention of his or her name in the press, on billboards, on bumper stickers, and so on. One may read about the amount of money raised at a $1,000-a-plate dinner for a candidate, but how much did it cost to rent the hall; pay for the catering, flowers, and liquor; solicit the contributors; and make sure that the committee sold all the seats?

If a candidate had $300,000 to pay for the overt costs, and did not have to worry about the hidden expenses, then in fact she had far more than $300,000 on which to campaign. Although the FECA had been amended in part to support the election of nonfederal candidates, the bulk of the money went to helping federal candidates. In the 1992 election, barely

$2 million of the $80 million in nonfederal funds went to state and local candidates. The two national parties transferred $15 million to state party committees, nearly all of which they had to use in support of federal candidates. Approximately two-thirds of the soft money transfers of each party went to ten states considered up for grabs in the presidential election. The bulk of the money, it is true, did go to financing voter identification and get-out-the-vote activities, the latter through large phone banks in which voters received not only the message to get out and vote but also information on the candidates responsible for their getting that call: for example, "William Jackson, the Republican candidate for Congress in the Tenth District, urges you to go out on election day and cast your vote." These campaigns also admittedly benefited state and local candidates, but only incidentally. The extra people hired, the phone banks created, the computerized voting lists—all of these had one aim: to elect federal candidates. The people who raised the soft money—the national committees—wanted state and local candidates of their party to win, of course, but they raised and spent the money to benefit candidates for the Senate, the House, and of course the White House.

The parties also used soft money for so-called generic advertising. Mostly television ads run in key states, this advertising reinforced the message of the presidential candidates. The two parties spent about $14 million on this effort in 1992, using funds generated by the FEC rule that allowed for joint federal-nonfederal activities. The ads never mentioned the candidates' names, since both parties believed that only hard money could be used for candidate-specific ads. Rather, the ads urged the citizenry to "Vote Democratic" or "Vote Republican" and stressed the major themes of the presidential campaigns.

For people with large amounts of money that they wanted to invest in candidates and campaigns, soft money opened a door that had supposedly been shut in 1974. An individual under the FECA could give a candidate only $1,000 per election (primary and general), $5,000 to a PAC, and a total of $20,000 in a year to political parties. But there were no limits at all on independent expenditures for or against a candidate, or on how much could be given to an interest group or a political party for issue advocacy or to a political party's soft money accounts. Before long the amounts solicited from, and given by, wealthy contributors easily rose above the old pre-Watergate levels.

Although the growth of soft money increased at an exponential pace, the FEC did essentially nothing to control it or even to have the amounts spent reported in a meaningful manner. Since much of the soft money supposedly went to state and local activities, the FEC reasoned, state and local governments ought to have the responsibility of policing their expenditures. This led Common Cause to request the FEC to issue new allocation laws on how the national parties could spend soft money, and to charge that the Democrats and the Republicans had improperly used nonfederal funds to influence federal elections by taking advantage of the FEC's loose guidelines. When the FEC refused to act, Common Cause took the agency to court, and the federal district court ordered the FEC to revise its regulations, give party committees more specific guidelines on how moneys could be allocated and spent, and also to keep records of how much soft money the committees expended. *Common Cause v. FEC*, decided in 1987, had little impact on the growth of soft money spending. In 1988, the soft money total for both parties reached $45 million; four years later it went to $80 million, then to $271 million in 1996, and nearly half a billion in 2000. From a little over 10 percent of the total expenditures by the national party committees, soft money had gone up to 42 percent by the time George Bush faced Al Gore in 2000.

By the end of the 1992 campaign, it had become clear that soft money and its use directly contravened the purposes of the FECA. The FEC, whose initial rulings had treated soft and hard money similarly, had essentially abandoned the field and had to be dragged into court and forced to issue minimal regulations. State and local candidates, the object of congressional intent in permitting nonfederal funds, had been marginalized as national committees used soft money everywhere to help federal candidates. Soft money had become a means of financing federal elections, not funding grassroots state and local activities.

*   *   *

Prior to the 1996 election, most people assumed that one could not run candidate-specific ads except with hard money. Then President Bill Clinton and Dick Morris, his political consultant, devised a method to get around this limitation, through what they called "issue advocacy." Starting in the fall of 1995, the Democrats spent some $34 million of soft money on television ads to promote Clinton's reelection. Although the spots featured Clinton, the party did not charge them against the Clinton campaign committee. Instead, the party paid for them with soft money and utilized a totally new legal argument—namely, that party communications that did not explicitly advocate the election or defeat of a federal candidate should be treated as generic party advertising and, according to FEC rules, be financed by a mixture of hard and soft money (although in practice the greatest percentage came out of the soft money pocket). Such "communications," the Democrats claimed, constituted issue advocacy, a form of political speech subject neither to campaign spending limits nor to the source or size of contributions to political parties for this purpose.

The argument could be traced directly back to *Buckley*, in which the Court used an express advocacy test as a means of narrowing disclosure requirements and contribution limits. Political communications consisted of those messages that "in express terms advocate the election or defeat of a clearly identified candidate for federal office." The Court then elaborated in a footnote examples of such "express advocacy," which soon became known as the "magic words" test. The Clinton ads, by carefully avoiding the magic words, sidestepped the intent of the FECA, the FEC regulations, and the *Buckley* test. Moreover, no limits existed on what donors could give to this issue advocacy campaign, a fact that Clinton, a champion fundraiser, put to good advantage.

Of the $34 million expended on such ads in 1996, the Democratic National Committee paid $12 million in hard money and $22 million in soft money. It accomplished this feat by transferring most of the soft money directly to state committees, which operated under more favorable FEC rules regarding the allocation ratios of hard and soft money, and the state committees purchased the airtime.

The Republicans soon realized that the FEC would not oppose issue advocacy and launched their own campaign. In May 1996 the Republican National Committee announced a $20 million issue advocacy campaign to show "the differences between Dole and Clinton and between Republicans and Democrats on the issues facing our country, so we can engage full-time in one of the most consequential elections in our history." Like the Democrats, the Republicans financed the campaign with a mixture of hard and soft moneys, funneled most of the soft money through the state committees, and targeted what they expected to be the key battleground states in the upcoming election.

One might suggest that issue advocacy, at least in the abstract, ought to have been welcomed, if it in fact gave voters greater information on where candidates stood on issues and explained those issues to the people. If President Clinton, for example, had spent some time explaining why health insurance mattered to the nation, and then simply said, "And that's why I fought for it," the message would have been clear. If Robert Dole had tried to make clear why integrity constituted the one indispensable character trait of a president, and then said, "That's why I am in this race," many people would have preferred that to a three-second sound bite. Such ads would also have passed the "magic words" test of *Buckley*. But neither party wanted to operate on that plane. Before long issue advocacy ads appeared that barely, if at all, passed the *Buckley* test, and that in many cases proved virtually indistinguishable from regular campaign ads. Moreover, the practice soon spread into the congressional and Senate races, providing a golden opportunity for individual interest groups to support candidates who passed the litmus test on their issue and oppose those who did not. None of the following ads, under the rules then in effect, were considered to be election advertisements:

- "Working families are struggling, but Congressman [. . .] voted with Newt Gingrich to cut college loans, while giving tax breaks to the wealthy. Tell him his priorities are all wrong." (AFL-CIO, for use in many districts)
- "Congresswoman Andrea Seastrand has voted to make it easier to dump pollutants and sewage into our water. . . . Fact is, it's time to dump Seastrand, before she dumps anything else on us." (Sierra Club)
- "Tell President Clinton: You can't afford higher taxes for more wasteful spending." (Republican National Committee)
- "Who is Bill Yellowtail? He preaches family values, but he took a swing at his wife. And Yellowtail's explanation? He 'only slapped her.' But her nose was broken." (Citizens for Reform)

According to the Annenberg Public Policy Center, issue advocacy ads cost between $135 million and $150 million in the 1996 election cycle, about one-third as much as all federal candidates combined spent on direct candidate ads. Political parties spent about half this money, and interest groups spent the other half. The AFL-CIO by itself accounted for half the sum spent by interest groups. Because these ads stood outside the contribution limits of FECA, corporations and labor unions could tap their own treasuries to run the spots, either under their own names or through an anonymous intermediary. Although some candidates began to complain that they could no longer set their own campaign agenda, by the late 1990s most candidates, especially challengers, realized that large issue advocacy promotions had become critical to their chances of success.

* * *

Reformers saw soft money and its abuses as one of the two great villains of the campaign finance system; they saw PACs as the other culprit. Such committees had been in existence well before Congress enacted the Federal Election Campaign Act. But the act, and especially the 1974 amendments, completely transformed the role of PACs in the political process. As one reformer noted, "That's not what we meant to do."

Prior to 1974, PACs had, with few exceptions, been relatively minor players in campaign finance. The leading PAC, the AFL-CIO's Committee on Political Education (COPE), had by the early 1970s emerged as an effective and powerful body that not only raised and distributed funds but also led highly regarded voter registration and get-out-the-vote drives. The AFL-CIO had been forced to create COPE because of the Taft-Hartley Act restrictions on the use of regular union funds for political action. Corporations, on the other hand, had eschewed PACs, even though the Corrupt Practices Act also forbade the use of corporate treasuries to fund political activity. Corporate officials, however, had not been restricted in how much they personally could give to campaigns, and although company money, after suitable laundering, may have made its way into the campaign chests of some candidates, business owners personally faced no barriers in giving large amounts of money to candidates.

During the 1960s no questions had been raised about the legality of PACs, but in 1970 a court ruled a union PAC in St. Louis illegal. Although no one mounted a challenge to COPE itself, labor leaders worried about the possibility and worked closely with the Democrat-controlled Congress to put language into FECA that explicitly allowed unions and corporations to establish "separate segregated funds" to create and operate PACs. The clause gave corporations a legal basis to establish PACs, and a few did. Then Common Cause filed a lawsuit against several companies that had set up PACs, on the basis that FECA prohibited campaign contributions by firms or other groups that had contracts with the government. The suit, although aimed at business, also worried labor leaders. A number of unions had secured contracts from the government to train workers under Lyndon Johnson's War on Poverty programs. Once again the AFL-CIO went to Congress, and in the 1974 FECA amendments it responded by protecting not only unions with government contracts but corporations as well, and permitted companies that had large defense and other government contracts to use corporate funds to establish and administer PACs and to fundraise for them.

Between 1974 and 1982, the number of PACs organized by business and labor unions more than quadrupled from 608 to 2,601. By 1999, 3,835 PACs had registered with the FEC, most of them corporate. In 2000, 43 percent of all PACs represented businesses, and 8 percent labor; the rest spoke for a variety of interests that ranged from religious and social conservatives to the National Rifle Association and environmental groups like the Sierra Club. PACs not only helped to fund presidential campaign committees but over the years came to play an ever-increasing role in congressional campaigns. In 1978 PACs accounted for 13 percent of all contributions to senatorial candidates; ten years later that amount had increased to 22 percent. In the same period of time the percentage of funds provided to House candidates by PACs went from 24 to 40 percent. Common Cause, which had championed the provision legitimizing PACs, noted that despite the economic stagnation of the early 1980s, "PACs have become a truly remarkable growth industry." The Center for Responsive Politics declared the 1974 legislation a partial failure. Although ending the era of "unregulated, free-wheeling, under-the-table campaign finance," and instituting a system of reporting that provided fairly accurate information, the reforms "only served to sanitize, rationalize, and legitimize the same old system of privately financed federal elections dominated by wealthy individual and corporate contributors."

It is hardly surprising that corporate America seized the opportunity provided by the 1974 amendments. Critics of corporate PACs charge them with legalized corruption, undermining the democratic process, buying undue access to government decision-makers, and using the PAC device to bypass federal laws prohibiting the use of company funds for political purposes. The PACs have their defenders as well, and each of these points carries with it at least some truth:

- Corporate and other PACs represent individuals who subscribe to a common set of beliefs, and can therefore find greater expression in the political arena through collective action. PACs thus provide legitimate interest representation for individuals.
- The money provided by PACs enables candidates without personal wealth to seek office and have a chance of winning. The admission of these new voices into politics enriches the democratic process and opens it to greater diversity of participation.
- The rules that govern corporate PACs, such as disclosure requirements, have brought corporate political involvement, which always existed, out of the shadows and into the sunlight where it can be scrutinized. Instead of backdoor exchanges of money satchels, corporations now operate in the open, and must do so according to the rules.
- PACs foster debate and competition in politics by emphasizing issues that might otherwise be ignored.
- Corporate PACs have helped to balance what had hitherto been the overwhelming political influence of organized labor.

It is possible to quibble with each of these points, but the fact remains that corporations have interests that are affected by political decisions, and the Supreme Court has since the early nineteenth century held that corporations enjoy some of the rights accorded "natural persons." If so, then they ought to be able to defend their interests just as natural persons do. Moreover, although government policy has always had an impact on the business community (through tariffs, land grants to build the transcontinental railroads, and protective labor legislation in the nineteenth and early twentieth centuries), the increase in government regulations in recent decades has made business even more sensitive to protecting itself in the political arena.

PACs derived at least part of their influence from the mushrooming rise in campaign costs. Congress in the FECA amendments had put limits on campaign contributions at the same time that television and the new computer technology needed to manage campaigns and voter databases drove up the cost of running for office. By 1996 the average campaign for the Senate cost $4 million, and a House seat required half a million. A typical senator, therefore, needed to raise $15,000 a week, every week, for six years, in order to finance a reelection bid. Even the indexing provisions of FECA, which adjusted campaign limits on the basis of inflation, did not help because the costs associated with running for office grew at a far faster rate than the overall inflation index. Television costs in particular skyrocketed, as the medium played an ever more crucial role in office seeking, and by 1990 the two parties spent nearly $1 billion on media advertising.

PACs provided candidates with the most accessible means of money to pay for advertising, polling, and the other accoutrements of a modern campaign. In 1980 PACs gave $55.2 million to congressional candidates, a figure that almost quadrupled to $206.8 million by 1998. The reason PACs became such an important source in campaign financing could be found in FECA and its amendments. PACs could give no more than $5,000 per election directly to a candidate, up to $15,000 per year to a national party committee, and no more than $5,000 in combined contributions to state and local committees. But because PACs had no aggregate annual limit, they could give money to multiple candidates, to state and local committees that would support those candidates, and to various independent committees for activities such as issue advocacy. Moreover, individuals could give up to $5,000 to each of several PACs. The American Petroleum Institute, an organization of petroleum producers and refiners, could not give $100,000 to a single candidate, but it could create ten different PACs and then give $10,000 to each one for transfer to a candidate. It is little wonder that PACs became so important.

Another aspect of PAC activity that drew the attention of critics lay in the fact that PACs fostered the advantage that incumbents had over challengers. Common sense tells us that unless he or she has displeased a good part of the constituency, an incumbent enjoys an advantage in fundraising. By 1998 House incumbents on the average outspent challengers by a ratio of four to one, and nine out of ten incumbents won reelection. PACs, as a result, saw an incumbent as a good investment, one that would increase over time as a member gained seniority and, with it, plum committee appointments and chairmanships. From the beginning, then, PACs not only supported incumbents but did so in a lopsided manner. In 1974, PACs gave 72 percent of their donations to incumbents, and only 28 percent to challengers. By 1998, congressional challengers received only 8 percent of PAC donations; the rest went to incumbents.

*　*　*

What did the Federal Election Commission do during these years? The answer is, "Not much." Ten years after the creation of the FEC, the *Congressional Quarterly* described it as an agency "with no constituency, little money, and few friends, . . . an agency whose administrative decisions are vilified by politicians, ridiculed by lawyers, and overturned by courts."

The FEC behaved pretty much as Congress intended it to, and in fact the rules make it almost impossible to secure any truly effective action. Most agencies, such as the Securities and Exchange Commission (SEC), the Federal Trade Commission (FTC), and the Interstate Commerce Commission (ICC), have five voting members, but the FEC has six. The agency is supposed to be politically neutral, with three of its members Democrats and the other three Republicans. But for the agency to agree on anything requires four votes, which means that either the proposed measure is so innocuous that it will not offend anyone or so egregious that it cannot be ignored. Although ideally the FEC should be nonpartisan or at the most bipartisan, in fact Congress has demanded partisanship, and presidents have acquiesced by nominating people who will act in a partisan manner to protect the interests of the parties.

Most of the work of the FEC during the 1980s and 1990s was noncontroversial and involved questions of campaign housekeeping and reporting; by some estimates, only one in ten cases aroused any type of partisan controversy. The reason for this may be that the parties and the candidates held the FEC—and the laws it supposedly enforced—in such low regard that in many instances they just ignored the agency. The candidates and their parties appeared willing to take potentially illegal or controversial actions without seeking an advisory opinion from the FEC. They operated on the assumption that even if there should be an investigation, it probably would not take place until after the election had been held, and then the FEC vote would split three to three along party lines, negating any action at all. One political operative claimed that most candidates and their advisers take the view that "the Commission is never going to get four votes, so they can do anything they want. It is undercutting what was anyway a rather weak enforcement system and making it even more toothless."

To give an idea of how little regard candidates and campaign committees had for the FEC, and how little they feared its enforcement powers, one might look at a *Harper's* magazine simulation from 1987 regarding how the 1988 presidential campaign would run. Robert Beckel, who had been Walter Mondale's 1984 campaign manager, and Harrison Hickman, a Washington-based pollster, agreed that their candidates would ignore state spending limits if necessary in order to win primaries and delegates. At worst, the FEC would take months to get around to investigating, and then, even if it managed to overcome its squabbling, all that would happen would be a slap on the wrist and a small fine.

Even when the FEC agreed to investigate, the process could drag on indefinitely, and for the most part, the agency acted only on minor issues and in a manner that was, at the least, embarrassing. It failed to act on claims that millions of dollars had been wrongly unreported. However, when the Central Long Island Tax Reform Immediately Committee raised $135 to print a pamphlet that outlined a congress member's voting record on tax reform, the FEC found "reason to believe" that the committee had violated the law by not filing the appropriate financial disclosure report. The commission then spent thousands of dollars and four years in court in a battle against the committee, being slapped down by one judge after another. Judge Irving Kaufman of the US Court of Appeals for the Second Circuit tongue-lashed the FEC, declaring that it had "failed abysmally" in carrying out "its obligation to exercise its powers in . . . harmony with a system of free expression."

Yet this is exactly how the two parties and Congress wanted it. Mark Braden, the former general counsel for the Republican National Committee, admitted this in an amazingly candid comment: "If we had an efficient commission, then we might have them having an impact on elections, which I don't think, at least from my perspective . . . I would be real happy with. In some ways I sort of like the snail's pace that you have now, so that they never get anything done, so it does not affect any election." The responsibility for enforcing campaign finance laws rested in an agency created by Congress, with closer ties to Congress than any other federal agency had, and that had the responsibility for overseeing campaign laws without offending members of Congress who had to campaign under those laws.

In fairness, the FEC did carry out its statutory obligations on rulemaking and other matters. It also kept making recommendations to Congress on ways that it could become more effective, and it asked for more money so that even within its crippling structure it might handle more complaints in an expeditious manner. It also recommended changes in the election law from time to time. All came to nothing, as Congress consistently turned a deaf ear. As Mark Braden said, "No one is really sure that they want [a commission] that works. Because they are afraid of what would happen if it works."

* * *

Just as Congress attempted to deal with what it saw as the problems of financing federal elections, states also tried to keep themselves free of the corrosive influence of money and other inducements that might affect the ballot. State laws focused primarily on disclosure and limitations, although a few established some public financing of state campaigns. Nearly every state required reports on contributions and expenditures, although the laws varied enormously with respect to what candidates had to report and in how much detail, and how often. Often these laws constituted sections of larger statutes regulating lobbyists, the type and value of gifts that state officials could accept, or, in some instance, so-called sunshine laws designed to ensure that the activities of elected officials would not be hidden from the public.

For the most part, state laws proved no more effective than FECA—supposedly rigorous laws on the books violated or ignored by candidates, especially incumbents. As reformers in general despaired, *Washington Post* correspondent David S. Broder found a silver lining in the state situation. The very fact that so much could be reported, he declared, "is in itself a direct by-product of the legislative reforms that preceded the 1974 campaign." Before then there would have been no reports of how much money had been raised or where it had come from. If corruption had not been eliminated—and it had not—at least the reporting system made it easier for the press and the public to see what was going on.

* * *

Herbert Alexander, a noted scholar of campaign finance, has commented that the effort to reconcile the concept of "one person, one vote" in a democracy and the inequities of financial resources is the core issue of money in politics. Critics of soft money and PACs believe that the two cannot be reconciled, and that since money translates into political power, those who have the resources to give to PACs and to candidates will have an undue voice in political decision-making. Judge J. Skelly Wright of the Court of Appeals for the District of Columbia eloquently summed up this view:

> As individuals are squeezed out, as the behemoths of concentrated wealth dwarf the individual and bid fair to dominate the political field, the very purpose of direct democracy is defeated, and voters are bound to become disillusioned and apathetic. This picture might not trouble a convinced pluralist who sees democratic government as nothing more than the results of the pull and tug of aggregated interests in a field of political vectors and partisan forces of greater or lesser intensity. But I believe in the role of equal individuals in the process of American self-government, and I am convinced that this role cannot be snuffed out without at the same time destroying the integrity of our electoral process and the essence of our political faith.

This problem—how to resolve the inherent tension between democratic equality and economic disparity—is at the core of congressional efforts to reform the campaign finance laws, an effort that eventually culminated in the McCain-Feingold bill. The second issue, how to resolve the potential conflict between the demands of the First Amendment and efforts to regulate the political process, would confront the Supreme Court as it moved from *Buckley* to challenges of McCain-Feingold.

CHAPTER 4

The Road to McCain-Feingold

The normally staid Association of the Bar of the City of New York began its special report on campaign finance reform in early 2000 with the alarmist cry that "our federal campaign finance system is in a state of disarray." This idea, however, had by then become common parlance among those writing or talking about the financing of the US electoral system. Thomas Mann of the Brookings Institution, who would be an expert witness in the case testing McCain-Feingold, called it a "regulatory regime in disarray." Regardless of where they put the blame—on the courts, on political action committees (PACs), on soft money, on the Federal Election Commission (FEC), or on corrupt and greedy politicians—most people agreed that the 1974 Federal Election Campaign Act (FECA) had been a dismal failure. Although providing better reporting of the dollars raised and spent, FECA had imposed no real controls on campaign finance.

If everyone accepted the fact of a broken system, little agreement could be found on how to fix it. Moreover, even if the system were in fact broken, that did not mean that everybody wanted it repaired. Soft money and PACs, the bugaboos of the reformers, benefited incumbents greatly, although few members of the House or Senate would admit this openly. Special interest groups also had no real incentive to push for reform, since they could spend almost unlimited amounts of money advancing their cause or supporting friendly candidates. Presidential candidates had such little difficulty raising money that some turned down the federal match, since accepting those dollars would have limited what they could raise and spend.

The journalist Elizabeth Drew wrote that the questions and answers about campaign finance could not have been more obvious: "Why is all this money floating about? What do investors expect? At a minimum they expect access, but access is only the required entry ticket for getting something done."

Not everyone thought that way. Senator Mitch McConnell (R-KY) denied that any corruption existed, because when you looked at the big picture, not all that much money was involved. "Federal campaign spending," he explained following the 1996 election, "amounted to $3.89 per eligible voter, about the price of a McDonald's value meal." McConnell has a point, and although people differ about the actual sums involved, some scholars have suggested that for $10 per person per year, all levels of elections—federal, state, and local—could be publicly funded.

Whether the public believed that money corrupted the political process, or that corruption did not exist, events beginning in the 1980s and continuing through the Clinton administration led many people to call for something—indeed anything—to fix the mess. As one scandal after another broke on the political scene and as the amount of money spent in successive elections skyrocketed, the pressure for reform increased, until it finally succeeded in the passage of the Bipartisan Campaign Reform Act (BCRA) of 2002, commonly known as the McCain-Feingold Act. But whether that law would pass constitutional muster, or if in fact it could actually fix the system, remained to be seen.

*   *   *

In 1980 Republican John Connally became the first major party presidential candidate to decline partial federal funding of his campaign. The idea behind federal funding had been to offer candidates a fairly substantial sum of money, to be paid for by a checkoff on individual tax returns, if the candidates agreed to limit their spending. Connally, a wealthy Texas businessman, intended to use his wealth and that of his backers to far outspend the Democratic candidate that year, President Jimmy Carter. Connally, however, never got to test this plan because he lost to Ronald Reagan in the GOP primary. Twenty years later, however, another Texan, George W. Bush, revived that strategy and announced that he would forgo partial federal funding. Bush raised a record $100 million and became the first major party candidate to win the nomination without following the Watergate-era limits. His huge war chest played a key role in his victory, as one would-be challenger after another dropped out of the race. In announcing her withdrawal, former secretary of labor Elizabeth Dole put it quite bluntly: "The bottom line is money."

In the 2000 campaign, total spending for the presidential race reached a record $607 million (covering primaries and the general election). The major political parties spent an additional $693 million, with soft money accounting for $498 million. Although these categories cannot be accurately divided between presidential and congressional races, it is fair to say that the Bush-Gore contest alone cost in excess of $1.3 billion.

At the congressional level, spending increased from $666.2 million in 1988 to $1.05 billion in 2000. The average cost of running for a seat in the House of Representatives rose in those twelve years from $697,757 to $1.31 million, and the average Senate race increased in cost from $8.88 million to $13.17 million. The range for any election would have been very broad, with representatives in safe seats spending far less, and candidates in highly contested elections expending a great deal more. Rick Lazio and Hillary Clinton, vying for the New York seat in the Senate that had been vacated by Daniel Patrick Moynihan, between them spent $70 million, and across the Hudson River in neighboring New Jersey, Jon Corzine spent $63 million, nearly all of it his own money, in a successful bid for the Senate.

*　*　*

The increase in campaign costs would have been enough for most reformers to urge a change in the system, but the numbers by themselves would have been insufficient to arouse public ire to the point where Congress finally felt it had to do something. One scandal after another reinforced the charges of reformers that the current system of campaign finance corrupted the political process.

The savings and loan collapse in the 1980s remains the most expensive regulatory scandal in US history, with the ultimate cost to American taxpayers running into the hundreds of billions of dollars. Among the various horror stories emerging from that debacle, one is of particular relevance to campaign finance reform. A California savings institution, Lincoln Savings and Loan, received special attention because its president, Charles H. Keating Jr., his family, and his associates contributed $1.3 million to influential legislators, a group eventually tarred by the epithet "the Keating Five."

Lincoln's questionable financial practices, especially large loans made to favored customers with minimal collateral, had begun drawing the attention of state and federal regulators in 1988. Keating either made or arranged direct contributions from others to five US senators—$34,000 to John Glenn (D-OH), $47,000 to Alan Cranston (D-CA), $112,000 to John McCain (R-AZ), $55,000 to Dennis DeConcini (D-AZ), and $76,000 to Donald Reigle (D-MI). In addition to the $324,000 in hard money that went to senatorial campaigns, Keating also arranged for $200,000 in soft money to go to a committee run by Senator Glenn, the National Council on Public Policy, and for an additional $850,000 in soft money to go to committees working on voter registration and turnout, one of them a tax-exempt group managed by Cranston's son. Keating gave $85,000 to the California Democratic State Central Committee for voter activities, and the American Continental Corporation, a company that Keating also headed, gave $90,000 to the California Republican Party in 1988. Lincoln Savings and Loan, despite laws to the contrary, gave $5,000 to California Republicans in 1987.

Although defenders of the system claimed that large donations made little difference in voting records and purchased little more than access to an official, in this instance Keating's money secured far more than "face time" with the senators. All of the Keating Five summoned the chair and key officials of the Federal Home Loan Bank Board, the agency responsible for savings and loan oversight, to discuss what the board intended to do about Lincoln and the possibilities of taking milder measures.

When information about the donations to the Keating Five—and their subsequent efforts to help Keating—became public, all of the senators denied doing any favors because of political donations. McCain, DeConcini, and Cranston explained that they had done no more than provide simple constituent services, since Keating was an Arizona resident with his holdings primarily in Arizona and California. However, at a news conference Keating said: "One question, among many, has to do with whether my financial support in any way influenced several political figures to take up my cause. I want to say in the most forceful way I can: I certainly hope so."

In September 1990 a grand jury indicted Keating and three associates for violating California securities laws by misleading investors about the nature of Lincoln's assets, many of which turned out to be worthless junk bonds. All told, the grand jury returned an indictment of forty-two separate counts (of which Judge Lance Ito dismissed twenty-five), and Keating went to jail until he could post bond, originally set at $5 million and later reduced to $300,000. At his trial a jury found Keating guilty, and while awaiting sentencing he learned that he would be indicted for other fraudulent actions by the Securities and Exchange Commission (SEC).

During the 1996 election, the most serious campaign finance violations since Watergate took place. Anthony Corrado, one of the leading political scientists studying campaign finance, declared that the election "was nothing less than the breakdown of the campaign finance system. The system we created in the early 1970s essentially collapsed. It's the Wild West out there. It's anything goes." Bill Clinton had been attacked by Republicans early in his first term for his aggressive fundraising, but in 1996 he and Al Gore showed not only how easily candidates could circumvent the laws on the books but also that they could just plain ignore many of them. First came allegations that the Chinese government, in order to maintain the friendly trade regulations promulgated by the Clinton administration, had made major donations to the Democrats through figurehead Chinese business owners in the United States. If true, this would have constituted a clear violation of the ban against foreign governments and nationals contributing to US campaigns.

In 1997 the Senate Governmental Affairs Committee, headed by Fred Dalton Thompson (R-TN)—rumored to be a potential candidate in 2000, but who became an actor on the television series *Law and Order*—called a number of witnesses to testify about this so-called Asian connection. The cast included John Huang (who visited the White House ninety-four times and met with the president fifteen times in Clinton's first term) and Charlie Trie, both friends of the Clintons from their Little Rock, Arkansas, days. Trie is remembered for turning in two manila envelopes containing $460,000 in cash allegedly collected from penniless Buddhists, and Huang's donors included those with untraceable addresses or with identical handwriting, and a few who, reminiscent of Tammany Hall and Chicago politics, were dead! Veteran Democratic fundraiser Johnny Chung, who raised money for Clinton, charmingly explained that the "White House is like a subway: You have to put in coins to open the gates." A group of Buddhist nuns testified about Vice

President Gore's alleged fundraising activities in a Buddhist temple. Although the election was over, the hearings proved embarrassing to Clinton and Gore, and the Democratic National Committee returned $1.6 million of the $3.4 million Huang had raised, as well as $645,000 raised by Trie.

Clinton and Gore well understood the mystique of the White House. Again, in seeming violation of laws against soliciting campaign money on federal property, they raised tens of millions of dollars from those attending "coffee" sessions in the White House, where the president and/ or vice president would stop in and chat. Then there were the infamous sleepovers in the Lincoln bedroom. Michael McCurry, speaking for the administration, declared that "the question is whether the president directly solicited funds during these occasions, and he did not." Although this statement was perhaps technically true, 90 percent of the people who attended the sessions had either made donations before being invited or sent them in within a month after sharing coffee and pastries with the chief executive.

In addition, both Clinton and Gore solicited funds by telephone from the White House, although the White House counsel in 1995, Abner J. Mikva, believed these calls to be clearly illegal and issued a directive that "no fund-raising phone calls or mail may emanate from the White House or any other federal building." Clinton and Gore ignored him, and his successor, Lanny Davis, in 1997 issued a new memorandum approving such calls. In public comments defending his fundraising calls from the White House, Al Gore repeatedly asserted, "My counsel tells me there is no controlling legal authority that says there was any violation of the law." If Gore had stopped there he might not have received the ridicule and suspicion that arose when he tried to explain that the money had not been raised "directly." But he added, "I never asked for a campaign contribution from anyone who was in a government office." No matter where he called from, the real transaction—the offer of a contribution—took place at the receiving end of the line.

Although later impeached but not convicted for lying about his relationship with White House intern Monica Lewinsky, Clinton faced no legal problems regarding his fundraising practices, and neither did Al Gore. In October 1997 the Republican-controlled Congress voted down all efforts to reform campaign finance, and in December Attorney

General Janet Reno announced that no grounds existed to warrant appointing a special prosecutor to investigate charges of impropriety. Republicans predictably responded with outrage, but had they been serious about correcting the defects of the system, they could have acted in the one way that would have made a difference, passing campaign finance legislation (because they controlled Congress, they could control the agenda of committee hearings).

Moreover, the Republicans did not exactly come into the debate with clean hands. The GOP had its Asian connections as well. Haley Barbour, the chair of the Republican National Committee (RNC), had solicited a $2.2 million loan guarantee from Ambrous Tung Young, a wealthy Hong Kong businessman, in the last weeks of the 1994 congressional campaign. Theoretically, the loan went to National Policy Forum, a Republican-sponsored think tank, but according to its former president, Michael Baroody, any separation between the forum and the RNC was little more than a "fiction." In his resignation letter, Baroody told Barbour, "I told you . . . that you were right about the possibility foreign money could be raised, but thought it would be wrong to do so." The forum used $1.6 million of the Young loan to pay back money it owed to the RNC, which in turn immediately funneled it into some twenty Republican committees in key states around the country. Two years later the forum defaulted on the loan, leaving Young with a $700,000 loss, but the Republican Party went into the 1996 campaign free of that debt.

The Republicans had other campaign finance irregularities that needed explanation. The FBI investigated Dan Burton (R-IN)—who had at times vociferously called for campaign finance reform—for allegedly threatening to deny a lobbyist for the government of Pakistan access to key government officials if a $5,000 donation to his campaign did not materialize. A Department of Education official claimed that Burton pressured him to delay eligibility standards for foreign medical schools involved in a US government student loan program, and that the meeting took place only one week after Burton received the second of two campaign contributions from the president of a Caribbean medical school. In addition, Burton asked the school to admit his daughter and to help his son-in-law get a job.

Simon Fireman, a vice-chair of Robert Dole's 1996 campaign finance committee, had to pay a $6 million fine (half of which was assessed against his company) for evading the $1,000 limit on individual contributions by persuading his employees to make gifts with the understanding that they would be reimbursed from an overseas fund. Fireman thus had managed to raise $120,000 for the 1992 Bush-Quayle ticket. As some commentators noted, this constituted the largest penalty ever imposed by the FEC, and it might just as well have been for stupidity, since Fireman could have legally given that amount or more in soft money.

If Clinton and the Democrats raised large amounts of money through utilization of the White House and the presidential mystique, at least they never explicitly detailed just what particular contributions would buy. Not so the Republicans, who, at the same time they were publicly bemoaning the "selling" of the Lincoln bedroom, put out a price sheet on what certain contributions might purchase. For a quarter million dollars, a "season ticket holder" would receive "the best access to Congress," meet with "the party's inner circle," and have private meetings with GOP leaders and key support personnel. One could become a member of "Team 100" by giving $175,000 over four years; this would earn meetings with high-ranking Republican leaders as well as invitations for "international Team 100 business missions." A $10,000 check secured admission into the "Senatorial trust," where one would have "intimacy" and "one-on-one interaction with Republican senators." If a person could not afford the higher levels, no need to despair. According to a fundraising letter sent out by Senate majority leader Trent Lott (R-MS), $5,000 put the donor into the "presidential roundtable," with "plenty of opportunities to share your personal ideas and vision with some of our top Republican leaders."

This ought not to be seen as a contest over who abused the system more, Democrats or Republicans, because they both acted in gross disregard of the law. Candidates from both parties engaged in sloppy bookkeeping, accepted questionable contributions, looked the other way when donors funneled money through third parties (such as children or grandchildren), and, in general, simply ignored the laws. After all, what did anyone have to worry about? A cynical public expected politicians to act this way. Wealthy donors, whether for ideological or simple business reasons, rushed to write checks. The FEC did practically nothing and blandly presided over the collapse of what had been intended, in the wake of Watergate, as a system to rein in campaign finance abuses.

*   *   *

The pattern of campaign finance reform appears to be that of cause and effect—the cause being a major scandal highlighting either the weaknesses in the system or out-and-out corruption, and the response being legislation addressing the perceived evils. Just as Watergate led to the Federal Election Campaign Act of 1974 and its strengthening amendments, so the Keating Five aroused Congress to consider new campaign finance regulations, although one suspects that it did so while fully aware that no matter how strong the measure, it would not matter. And so it happened.

Every year some House members and senators proposed legislation to reform the system, but with Republicans in control of the White House and the Senate following the 1980 election, there seemed little hope that a new bill would secure approval. In 1986 Senators David L. Boren (D-OK) and Barry M. Goldwater (R-AZ) proposed limits on the total amount of PAC money that a candidate could receive in any election cycle. Although the measure gained favorable notice both in and out of Congress, it never made it out of committee. When the Democrats regained control of the Senate after the 1986 election, Boren (after Goldwater had retired in 1986) reintroduced a strengthened proposal as Senate Bill 2. This time it looked as if something might happen, as Boren secured cosponsorship from an enthusiastic majority leader, Robert Byrd (D-WV), and all but ten of the Democratic senators. A strengthened bill passed the Senate Committee on Rules and Administration with a vote, along strictly party lines, of 8 to 3, on April 29, 1987.

The Boren bill provided for, among other things, public financing of senatorial candidates, who, like presidential candidates receiving public funds, agreed to observe spending limits in both the primary and general elections. To receive the public funding, they had to raise a minimum amount from individual contributors, the level depending on the voting-age population of the state. Candidates also had to agree to limit the money they received from PACs to no more than 20 percent of their total expenditure. Even if a candidate decided to forgo public funding, the Byrd-Boren bill imposed a limit of 30 percent of the state's allowable expenditures that could be raised from PACs. Other provisions included aggregate limits on how much national party committees could receive from PACs, prohibition of PAC bundling of contributions through related organizations, and expanded reporting requirements to cover more soft money expenditures.

The Byrd-Boren bill aimed primarily at reducing the influence of PACs and candidate dependence on PAC money. Had the bill passed, however, it might have run once again into the law of unanticipated consequences. One result would have been that candidates and parties would have focused their attention on the wealthiest PACs, since the easiest way to raise PAC funds up to the prescribed limit would have been to concentrate on those able to give the largest amounts. Smaller PACs, representing a variety of less affluent interests, would have been noncompetitive and ignored by all except the most desperate candidates. Moreover, the aggregate-limit provision, a new concept, would have undoubtedly raised constitutional issues under the then-prevailing *Buckley* precedents.

The bill elicited near-universal opposition from Senate Republicans, who derided it as still another Democratic raid on the federal Treasury. Senator Robert Packwood (R-OR) called Senate Bill 2 a Democratic effort "to take three or four hundred million dollars from taxpayers . . . to perpetuate their majority in the U.S. Congress." Moreover, the facts of the 1986 election seemed to undercut any urgency for reform. A majority of the fifteen biggest-spending senatorial candidates lost, and five challengers beat incumbents who had outspent them by two to one or more in the campaigns. In June the Republican caucus voted not to accept any public financing or spending limits, even though Senate minority leader Robert Dole (R-KS) had accepted public financing in his failed presidential bid a year earlier, and Senator Ted Stephens (R-AK), who would lead a filibuster against the bill, had cosponsored a constitutional amendment providing for mandatory limits on campaign expenditures. Despite efforts to modify the bill to win some Republican support, party lines held firm, with only two Republicans defecting to support the bill and only two Democrats lining up against it. Although more than 430 newspapers and seventy-three organizations, such as Common Cause, endorsed the bill, the Republicans would not budge. They believed that since the GOP had greater access to PACs and other forms of financing, the bill would only work against their interests.

Then came disclosures that some contributors had given more than

$100,000 during the 1988 presidential campaign—a figure reformers believed had been prohibited by the post-Watergate legislation and the revelations related to the Keating Five. The multibillion-dollar bailout of the savings and loan industry also spilled over into the campaign finance debate. Although no other scandals proved as titillating as that of the Keating Five, apparently many other legislators had attempted to help out constituents and had accepted money from PACs associated with the thrift industry. In addition, a public uproar over an alleged "salary grab" by Congress (the House voted itself a 25 percent pay raise) led the new Bush administration to seize the moment and propose a campaign finance scheme of its own, one that so blatantly favored the GOP over the Democrats that it had little chance of passage.

Presented in June 1989, the Bush proposal called for the near elimination of PACs (which had given three out of every five of their dollars to the Democrats in the 1988 election cycle), and strengthening the role of party committees (since Republican committees had raised three times as much money as their Democratic counterparts). Although the Bush plan sought to curtail or even shut off some sources of campaign funding, it made no provisions for raising money from other sources. It seemed a strange plan, with supposedly less money to spend, yet no limits on expenditures.

The Congress now found itself confronted with two very different campaign finance reform bills and a public clamor that it do something. Party leaders in both houses recognized this and believed they had little choice but to put campaign finance reform at the top of the legislative agenda.

Over the next few years, proposals would arise and be greeted by reform advocates as the long-awaited breakthrough, only to disappear from sight as soon as someone zeroed in on one or more of their features. As a disgusted Herbert Alexander wrote, members of both houses of Congress had little interest in actually reforming the system; they essentially postured for public relations purposes, so they could tell the folks back home that they had really tried to secure campaign finance reform. Both parties, he complained, "sought to maximize their partisan advantages and minimize the resources of their adversaries, appealing to popular notions of reform whenever possible—even when such notions were plainly misconceived or impossible to attain. And the role of

President Bush and the White House staff was prominent throughout but mainly because of a premature announcement in July that the president would veto any legislation containing public funding or spending limits."

On August 1, 1990, the Senate, by a vote of 59 to 40, agreed on a revised Boren bill, labeled Senate Bill 137, and two days later the House passed a similar bill by a vote of 255 to 155. The margins in both houses—60 percent in the Senate and slightly more in the House—masked the fact that the leadership in both houses did not really care for the measure. They took their time setting up a conference committee to iron out the relatively minor differences, and in fact the committee never met; the 101st Congress adjourned without passage of a campaign finance reform law.

On May 23, 1991, the newly elected Senate adopted the Boren proposal by a vote of 56 to 42. The House took much longer, with intra- and interparty wrangling lasting more than six months. The full House passed its version of the measure in November, and this time a conference committee did meet and iron out the differences between the two versions, but not until April 1992. The House of Representatives approved the committee's reconciliation by a vote of 259 to 165, and the Senate followed on April 30 by a vote of 58 to 42.

The main provisions of the Campaign Spending Limit and Election Reform Act included increased spending limits for Senate races, ranging from $950,000 to $5.5 million depending on the size of the state, with up to an additional $2.75 million for primaries (again, depending on the state's size). The limit on House races went to $600,000 for the entire two-year cycle, with another $250,000 permitted if there was a primary fight. Although these limits were voluntary, candidates who abided by them would reap additional benefits. Senate candidates who raised money primarily in donations of $250 or less would get vouchers for broadcast time and would also be allowed to buy additional time at 50 percent of the regular rate. House candidates could get up to an additional $200,000 in public money matching contributions of $200 or less, but they would have to agree not to take any more than $200,000 in contributions greater than $250.

The bill made no changes in the existing $1,000 limit on individual contributions, but it did reduce the amount a PAC could give to any one candidate from $5,000 to $2,500 for Senate candidates; the limit would remain at $5,000 for House candidates. PAC money could account for no more than 20 percent of a Senate campaign, and for House candidates it could be no more than $200,000, a figure that few congressional candidates then exceeded. The bill prohibited the national committees from using soft money in federal elections but otherwise put no limits on the amount of soft money that could be raised or spent by other entities.

Because the White House the previous year had indicated that the president would not sign any measure that limited campaign expenses, it is little wonder that George Bush, who in his one term used the veto more than many presidents have in two, refused to approve the measure.

One suspects, perhaps a bit cynically, that a good many of the votes for the revised Boren bill were cast in the full knowledge that the measure would not become law, thus allowing the lawmakers to have their cake and eat it too. They could tell their constituents that they had supported and voted for campaign finance reform, without having to worry about the proposed reforms actually affecting their own campaigns. Neither house, even on the initial vote, had the necessary votes to override the promised presidential veto. Although the Boren bill had gone further than any other reform proposal in more than a decade, it, too, died, and the truth be told, few members in Congress mourned the passing.

*   *   *

Bill Clinton, aware that campaign finance reform played well with the voters, tried to capitalize on the Bush veto, and in the 1992 campaign promised to end big-money domination of politics. In fact, in his first inaugural he proclaimed: "Let us resolve to reform our politics so that power and privilege no longer shout down the voice of the people." In his first address to Congress he challenged the legislators to reenact the Boren bill, promising to sign it if they were to do so. Whether Clinton really wanted a campaign finance reform bill or not is open to question, but he certainly pushed for one in his first year in office and even proposed a modification of the Boren bill, focusing on limits that PACs could give to presidential ($1,000) and senatorial ($2,500) campaigns, as well as shutting off soft money. He also proposed that the tax laws be changed so that companies could not deduct lobbying costs as a business expense, and individual citizens could raise the amount of their voluntary checkoffs for elections from $1 to $5. Whether Clinton really meant what he said or not, he soon got caught up in the fight to reform health care insurance, and campaign finance wound up on a back burner, moving to the front every now and then for the rest of his administration.

After the Republicans won control of both houses of Congress in the 1994 midterm election, Clinton and Speaker of the House Newt Gingrich (R-GA) found themselves at a joint appearance at a senior center in New Hampshire in June 1995. The president declared that he would love to have a bipartisan commission look at meaningful campaign finance reform. Gingrich immediately joined in and said: "Let's shake hands right here in front of everybody. How's that? Is that a pretty good deal?" In the year that followed, Clinton, Gingrich, and Senate majority leader Robert Dole failed to name a commission; in fact, they hardly ever mentioned it again. In that same period various representatives and senators introduced hundreds of proposals, not a single one of which ever made it out of committee.

In his 1997 State of the Union address, Clinton again challenged Congress to give him a campaign finance reform measure that he could sign by July 4. In the meantime, whenever appointments opened on the FEC, Clinton nominated the same sorts of Democrats and Republicans to the vacancies, partisan political types who would never rock the status quo by attempting to enforce the law seriously. In September, after Congress failed to send him a bill to sign, Clinton threatened to keep the legislature in session until it acted. Dozens of House members and senators introduced bills, knowing the proposals would never get out of committee, but the claim for sponsoring campaign reform would be very useful for reelection purposes. Then, suddenly, a fluke occurred—in late September, reform legislation somehow came straight to the floor of the House without going to the committee. Despite this surprise, congressional leaders made it very clear that they intended to kill the measure, which they did. As for Clinton, once again his priorities had changed— he wanted Congress to pass the North American Free Trade Agreement (NAFTA). With the full cooperation of Republican congressional leaders, he once again buried campaign finance reform.

*　*　*

The fundraising scandals of the Clinton administration and the massive amounts of money raised and spent by both sides in the 2000 presidential election constitute the immediate backdrop to the BCRA of 2002, commonly known as the McCain-Feingold bill. In many ways, however, BCRA is just one more step in a century-long effort to divorce the influence of money from federal elections, and although its supporters hailed it as a major step forward, detractors claimed it would eventually fail, as had earlier efforts.

Despite the veto of the 1992 law by President George H. W. Bush, reformers kept plugging away in the House and Senate throughout the 1990s, trying in vain to impose some limits on both soft money and PACs. Although President Clinton on several occasions indicated that he favored such legislation, with the Congress being controlled by the Republicans for six of his eight years in office, he could do little more than stop enactment of measures he did not like; he never had the votes to put through important legislative reforms of his own. Nor, one can assume, did campaign finance reform figure high on his agenda, despite the lip service he gave to it. Clinton's greatest contribution to reform may have been his highly successful efforts to raise money, efforts that displayed all the weaknesses in the moribund system in effect. In the 2000 election, national and congressional party committees broke all previous records in raising soft money. The RNC raised $249.5 million, and the Democrats lagged only slightly behind at $245.2 million. The national committees transferred more than half of this money to state party committees, primarily to pay for television advertisements.

The original version of the BCRA had been introduced as Senate Bill 1219 in the 104th Congress in September 1995. The bill not only provided restrictions on soft money but also called for voluntary spending ceilings in congressional races and free airtime and reduced-rate mailing privileges for candidates who abided by these ceilings (both provisions were taken from the 1992 measure). It also placed limits on what candidates could spend out of their own pockets, a response to several recent races in which wealthy candidates had spent millions of dollars of their own money. The bill never made it out of committee, but at each succeeding session of Congress, Senators John McCain (R-AZ) and Russell D. Feingold (D-WI) reintroduced a version of their bipartisan campaign proposal.

The McCain-Feingold bill died due to a filibuster in the 104th Congress. During the following session, the House of Representatives passed a companion measure, H.R. 2183, known as the Shays-Meehan bill, after its sponsors, Representatives Christopher H. Shays (R-CT) and Martin T. Meehan (D-MA). Senate sponsors of the bill tried and failed three times in the 105th Congress to break a filibuster, but the reformers would not give up. In the 106th Congress, the House again passed the Shays-Meehan bill (H.R. 417), only to see their work thwarted once again by a Senate filibuster. Even a scaled-down version of McCain-Feingold, consisting of nothing more than a ban on soft money (S. 1593), fell before another filibuster.

Finally, in the 107th Congress, the sponsors of the latest version of McCain-Feingold (S. 27) not only gained majority approval but beat back thirty-eight amendments designed to cripple the measure. On April 2, 2001, the full Senate passed an amended but still potent McCain-Feingold bill by a vote of 59 to 41.

Now the spotlight shifted to the House, which in previous sessions had passed the Shays-Meehan bill. But now, with a Senate-passed version on their desks and no indication from the White House that President George W. Bush would veto the measure, representatives had to deal with the very real possibility that a campaign finance bill would actually clear Congress. The House Administration Committee held hearings that lasted from April 2001 until March 2002. The committee then reported favorably to the full House on the Ney-Wynn bill (H.R. 2360), a much-watered-down version of the Senate measure, and reported unfavorably on the Shays-Meehan bill (H.R. 2356), which more closely tracked the provisions of McCain-Feingold. On July 12, showing how many of the members did not really want to deal with the issue, the House rejected by a vote of 228 to 203 a proposed rule that would have brought discussion of campaign finance reform to the floor.

One week later, a group of so-called Blue Dog Democrats began circulating a discharge petition to force the House leadership to resume debate on the bills. The petition needed 218 signatures (a bare majority of the 435 members) to force a floor vote, and on January 24, 2002, the last 4 members signed on. The House approved the stronger Shays-Meehan proposal on February 7, 2002, by a vote of 240 to 189. Normally at this point House and Senate leaders would appoint a conference committee to iron out the differences between the two versions. When it became clear that such a committee would probably be stacked with opponents of campaign finance reform, Senate proponents decided to vote directly on the House version. On March 20, 2002, the Senate voted 68 to 32 to end debate on the bill, proving that supporters had the necessary votes to cut off a filibuster. Later in the day the Senate approved the measure by a vote of 60 to 40 and sent it on to President Bush.

The president reluctantly signed the bill into law one week later. During the 2000 presidential primary season, John McCain had run a strong race against the ultimately successful George W. Bush, and a key feature of the Arizona senator's platform had been campaign finance reform. After his election, Bush put forth a counterproposal, which allowed individuals to give as much soft money as they wanted. Bush decided to sign the bill, but without the usual ceremony where sponsors received signing pens. A legislative aide—not the president—called McCain at his home in Arizona to inform him that the bill had become law. Bush issued a written statement in which he essentially gave the back of his hand to the legislation. This bill, he wrote, "is the culmination of more than six years of debate among a vast array of legislators, citizens, and groups. Accordingly, it does not represent the full ideals of any one point of view. But it does represent progress in this often contentious area of public policy debate. Taken as a whole, this bill improves the current system of financing for federal campaigns, and therefore I have signed it into law." When asked why there had been no formal ceremony, White House spokesperson Claire Buchan said, "The manner in which the president signed the campaign finance reform into law was consistent with his views on the legislation."

Bush thereupon left on a two-day fundraising trip, where he hoped to raise more than $3.5 million for Republican senatorial candidates. Asked if he saw any irony in signing the bill and then embarking on such a trip, Bush said he saw no reason to stop his money-raising efforts. "I'm not going to lay down my arms. The Senate races are very important to me."

* * *

Although BCRA had numerous provisions, some key objectives in the legislation are discernible—an effort to do away with soft money, a redefinition of what constitutes campaign advertising, limits on contribution amounts and sources, and tougher disclosure and reporting requirements.

The act banned soft money contributions to the national political parties after November 6, 2002, and required the national party committees to dispose of all soft money in their accounts by December 31, 2002. Under a congressional compromise, individuals and groups could contribute up to $10,000 in soft money (known as Levin funds) to each state and local party committee, if permitted by state law, for voter registration and mobilization drives in federal elections (§101). At the same time, the act increased the amount of hard money that could be given, partly to offset the loss of soft money but also because hard money faced tighter reporting and accounting regulations. Individuals could now give $2,000 instead of $1,000 per candidate, per election, and $5,000 to a PAC. The amount that individuals could give to the national party committees went from $20,000 to $25,000, and donation limits for state and local party committees went from $5,000 to $10,000. The limits on PAC contributions to candidates and parties remained unchanged ($5,000 per candidate, per election; $5,000 per outside PAC, per year; $15,000 per national committee, per year; and $5,000 per state or local committee, per year) and were not indexed for inflation; moreover, the law imposed no annual aggregate limits on PACs, so although they faced limits on individual contributions, the wealthier PACs could continue to give hundreds of thousands of dollars a year across the political spectrum from local races on up to presidential candidates (§§102, 308).

In a provision that was sure to be challenged on First Amendment grounds, BCRA prohibited corporations, trade associations, and labor organizations from paying for "electioneering communications" within sixty days of a general election and thirty days of a primary using "treasury money." The law defined an electioneering communication as any sort of advertisement that referred to a clearly defined federal candidate and was targeted to that candidate's district (i.e., a congressional district for a member of the House of Representatives, a state for a senatorial candidate, and the nation for a presidential candidate). Although no corporation, trade association, or union could pay for such ads out of its treasury, its PAC could run and finance such ads because under the law's definitions, such funds would count as hard money and be subject to those regulations (§201). Moreover, individuals who paid for political ads could no longer hide behind either anonymity or some front committee, but would have to identify themselves, and candidates would have to indicate that they had approved ads run by committees they controlled. ("This is John Doe, and I have approved this ad.")

Much to the distress of some reformers, the law kept the FEC as the primary regulatory agency to enforce the law. BCRA required the FEC to issue new regulations to put the law's provisions into effect (§§307, 501, 502). (Within a very short time the FEC did issue regulations that, in effect, undermined the BCRA's ban on soft money, causing one of the law's chief sponsors, Christopher Shays, to file suit against the FEC.) Soon critics began calling for the abolition of the FEC, although some regulatory mechanism would then have to be put in its place to enforce the law and serve as a clearinghouse for reports.

In direct response to the Clinton scandals, the bill prohibited fundraising on federal property, including the White House (§302), and also banned contributions from persons who were not citizens or permanent legal residents of the United States (§303). In response to concerns about millionaires self-financing elections, BCRA allowed opponents of self-financing candidates to raise and expend sums beyond the normal limits (§§304, 318).

One of the provisions of the bill forbade donations made through children and grandchildren (§318), a device that had commonly been used to circumvent the FECA limit on individual contributions. Between 1980 and 2000, contributions of $1,000 from "students" increased fourfold. Senator Edward M. Kennedy apparently holds the record for so-called kiddie cash, collecting more than $65,000 from people eighteen and under in his 1994 campaign for reelection. Senator Fred Dalton Thompson raised more than $25,000 from children, some as young as nine. Business owner Vinod Gupta, for example, managed to give $50,000 to the Democrats, utilizing his seventeen-year-old son's trust fund. According to the FEC's own reports, in the 1996 election between twenty-five and fifty of the top four hundred political donors also had their children and grandchildren—ranging from preteens to graduate students—contributing to their favorite candidates.

* * *

The ink had hardly dried on George Bush's signature before the BCRA came under attack. Senator Mitch McConnell, a leading opponent of campaign finance reform, announced within hours of the signing that he would challenge the law in the courts and that he welcomed other groups that believed the BCRA deprived them of their constitutional rights to join with him. Anticipating the passage of the bill, McConnell had begun lining up his legal team. It included Floyd Abrams, a well-known civil liberties attorney and defender of the First Amendment; former solicitor general, appeals court judge, and special prosecutor Kenneth Starr; First Amendment scholar and Stanford Law School dean Kathleen Sullivan, who had for several years attacked efforts to restrict funding and speech in campaigns; prominent Washington attorney Jan Baran; and James Bopp, the general counsel of the Madison Center for Free Speech. "Today, I filed suit to defend the First Amendment right of all Americans to be able to fully participate in the political process," McConnell declared. "I look forward to being joined by a strong group of co-plaintiffs in the very near future."

McConnell did not have long to wait. The National Rifle Association (NRA), which had used campaign contributions to oppose gun control for years, claimed that it had been the first to file suit after Bush had signed BCRA into law. Wayne LaPierre, the NRA executive vice president, and James Jay Baker, executive director of the NRA's Institute for Legislative Action, in a joint statement, challenged Congress's efforts to quiet the gun lobby. "The First Amendment," they announced, "protects us from such directives from the government. The First Amendment does not allow Congress to make laws which deny us the right to speak out on issues, the right of our members to associate together on public policy issues and the right to petition our government for redress of grievances. This is what this lawsuit is about." Before long other groups joined in, although not necessarily agreeing with the position taken by McConnell and the NRA. The AFL-CIO was upset primarily over the limits placed on PACs. The US Chamber of Commerce and the National Association of Broadcasters, worried about how much the new law would cost in lost revenues, also filed suit. Soon afterward the RNC, the California Democratic Party, the California Republican Party, and other local committees and officials joined the suit.

The American Civil Liberties Union (ACLU), declaring that it had long supported campaign finance reform through public financing, found the BCRA a threat to the First Amendment and used a particularly telling example of how the law could stifle open discussion. "Just last week," the executive director of the ACLU said, it had run "a series of radio and newspaper issue ads that would be outlawed under the new campaign finance legislation." The radio ads went out to more than fifty thousand people in the congressional district of Speaker of the House Dennis Hastert, urging him to allow a floor vote on the Employment Non-discrimination Act, a bill that would prohibit employment discrimination against gays and lesbians. The ad ran within thirty days of a primary election in which Hastert was unopposed. According to the ACLU, this ad would have been prohibited by BCRA, even though it did not urge voters to support or oppose Hastert's reelection.

Defenders of the bill reacted promptly. Immediately after McConnell's statement, the four major sponsors—McCain and Feingold in the Senate, and Shays and Meehan in the House—held a press conference to announce that they would intervene in the suit. Although the Department of Justice has the primary responsibility of defending the constitutionality of laws enacted by Congress, the four acted under a section of the BCRA providing a statutory right for members of Congress to intervene as parties. It is possible they had doubts about the enthusiasm with which the Justice Department would defend the law, and so they too rounded up a legal team to defend the measure. Seth Waxman, a former solicitor general in the Clinton administration and then a partner in the powerhouse Washington law firm of Wilmer, Cutler, and Pickering, led the effort.

In addition, there would be lawyers from both the private and academic worlds, all acting pro bono, as were the lawyers for McConnell. In their statement regarding intervention, the four sponsors, plus Senators Olympia Snowe (R-ME) and James Jeffords (Ind-VT), declared that they would show that the basic provisions of BCRA not only were constitutional but actually protected core First Amendment values: "As the legislative record reflects, the American electorate is losing confidence in the democratic process because of the specter of actual and apparent corruption created by 'soft money' and other campaign finance abuses. . . . By closing loopholes in current law and prohibiting clearly identifiable abuses, the Reform Act encourages renewed citizen confidence and participation in all aspects of our democracy, thereby strengthening First Amendment values."

*   *   *

The bill included a "fast-track" provision: that any challenges would take place in the federal district court of the District of Columbia, and that appeals would go from there directly to the Supreme Court. After more than two decades, Congress had finally acted. Now the action shifted from the legislature to the judiciary.

CHAPTER 5

The Supreme Court and Elections

From *Buckley* to *McConnell*

The drafters of the Bipartisan Campaign Reform Act (BCRA) of 2002 knew that their handiwork would be challenged in the courts, primarily on First Amendment grounds. Although the law would not go into effect until after the 2002 midterm election, they wanted it—assuming it withstood constitutional challenge—to be in place for the 2004 cycle.

In the quarter century after it decided *Buckley v. Valeo*, the Court heard a number of cases relating to both the election process and campaign finance. But although the justices hinted in their various opinions that they might no longer feel constrained to follow the *Buckley* rule, they had not negated it.

* * *

If one were to ask a layperson whether the Supreme Court ever got involved in elections, the answer would probably be, "Oh, yeah, they decided the 2000 election." Although it is true that *Bush v. Gore*, which barred a recount of the Florida vote and thus gave that state's electoral ballots and the election to George W. Bush, may be the best known of the Court's election-related cases, it is far from the only one. It is also far from being the most important in terms of constitutional doctrine. In fact the majority justices went out of their way to claim that their decision had little or no precedential effect, but rather applied to a unique set of facts. Nevertheless, the Supreme Court has played a historic role in shaping modern election law.*

---

* The Court has heard a number of cases involving the Fifteenth Amendment's guarantee of the vote regardless of race, as well as the constitutionality of various provisions of the 1965 Voting Rights Act. In addition, it decided cases requiring states to reapportion their legislatures. Although these issues grabbed headlines, they did not directly implicate questions of campaign financing.

The Supreme Court over the years has also heard a number of cases involving political corruption, allegations of bribery, and the regulation of money in politics, both before and after *Buckley*. Although that case is pivotal in our discussion because it touches directly on the matter of campaign financing, one must keep in mind that the range of cases heard by our nation's highest court reflects all the concerns and problems that affect the democratic process. As historian Jack Rakove points out, corruption in the political system under the Articles of Confederation played a major role in the thinking of the framers of the Constitution, especially that of James Madison. Madison's ideas on federalism and separation of powers, for example, mirrored "his disillusionment with the failings of state legislators and citizens alike." Whereas structural features such as checks and balances and separation of powers worked to ensure that no one part of government could gain ascendancy over the others, they also were intended to serve as a check on corruption.

To take one example, the Court in *United States v. Brewster* (1972) had to decide whether the Speech and Debate Clause (Art. I, Sec. 6) provided immunity to a senator, Daniel B. Brewster (D-MD), for allegedly accepting a bribe and then using his influence to obtain favorable postal rate legislation. In his opinion for the Court, Chief Justice Warren Burger ruled that no immunity existed; the clause only prevents the executive or judicial branches from examining conduct relating to the legislative process as well as from attempting to search out the motivation behind related conduct. As for Brewster, the government had prosecuted him under a narrowly drawn bribery statute; it had shown that he had accepted a bribe, and it had not attempted to determine whether that bribe had led to specific conduct. For Burger, this meant the government could prosecute a senator for wrongdoing and at the same time preserve a basic element of separation of powers. The courts, therefore, would not be asked to adjudicate issues relating specifically to legislative actions.

Until *Buckley*, however, the Court had relatively little to do with campaign finance regulation. It did look at both the Tillman Act and the Taft-Hartley Act in a 1957 case involving political expenditures by a labor union. In a thorough history of both measures, the Court concluded that Congress had had legitimate concerns about the effects on the political system of large contributions from both labor unions and corporations (*United States v. United Auto Workers*). But prior to the Federal

Elections Campaign Act of 1974 and its amendments, Congress had not tried to limit the amounts that individual contributors could give or that individual candidates and political committees could spend. When it heard *Buckley*, the Court had decided only a handful of political corruption cases implicating First Amendment values.

* * *

The Taft-Hartley Act, as noted earlier, attempted to regulate the use of money by labor unions for political purposes, and in §304 prohibited unions from using their internal newsletters to endorse a candidate. The majority of the Court evaded the First Amendment issue by holding that the legislative history of Taft-Hartley indicated that it had not been meant to apply to internal communications. But three justices joined an opinion by Wiley Rutledge that considered that provision a violation of the First Amendment's Free Speech Clause (*United States v. Congress of Industrial Organizations* [1948]).

In 1957 a majority of the Court sustained an indictment against the United Auto Workers for using union dues to sponsor television advertisements supporting the election of certain candidates for Congress. The majority opinion by Justice Frankfurter held that the Federal Corrupt Practices Act is a valid exercise of congressional power, and he cited the act's legislative history to show that Congress had recognized that "money is the chief source of corruption." Frankfurter avoided dealing with the First Amendment issue by declaring it unnecessary to reach a decision; all the Court had to do was decide whether an indictment could be filed for the actions taken. William O. Douglas, joined by Chief Justice Warren and Hugo Black, dissented on the ground that the statute violated the First Amendment's guarantees of speech and assembly.

Although these cases involved strong dissents on First Amendment grounds, the majority of the Court did not seem to equate campaign finance regulation with speech. Rather, the majority opinions emphasized the concern of Congress with maintaining the integrity of the political system by preventing corruption through large donations. In other cases the Court seemed very ready to respect congressional policy choices when they dealt directly with corruption or the possibility of corruption. For example, in *Barry v. United States* (1929), the Court had held that Congress had the power, under Article I, Sections 1 and 5 (judging elections, returns, and qualifications), to compel attendance of witnesses in an investigation of a Senate election in which excessive contributions had been made in the primary. A few years later, the Court ruled that Congress had the power under the Federal Corrupt Practices Act of 1925 to require disclosure of political contributions by a committee that had attempted to influence the selection of presidential electors. In upholding the constitutionality of the law, Justice George Sutherland confirmed the power of Congress under Article I, Section 2, to preserve the purity of federal elections. "To say that Congress is without power to pass appropriate legislation to safeguard such an election from the improper use of money to influence the result," he declared, "is to deny to the nation in a vital particular the power of self-protection." A republican government, Sutherland explained, had to have sufficient power to thwart not only lawless violence but also the corruption associated with the use of money in elections. Significantly, Sutherland implied that Congress, and not the judiciary, had the discretion to choose the means to address that danger (*Burroughs and Cannon v. United States* [1934]).

Looking at all the cases decided by the Court in the half century before *Buckley* that dealt with elections, corruption, and redress of ills, it appears that the justices accepted the rationale of Congress that it had the power to deal with both the actuality and the threat of corruption in the political process. For the most part, the Court took congressional power as a given, and questions of First Amendment rights of speech and assembly, if they arose at all, appeared in dissents or minority concurrences. The Court did not by itself try to define corruption, but rather deferred to the policy choices made by Congress. All that changed with *Buckley v. Valeo* in 1976.

*   *   *

Although we briefly looked at *Buckley* earlier, we now need to examine the case in more detail. Just as the Federal Election Campaign Act (FECA) and its amendments constituted the first serious effort by Congress to control the finances of campaigns, so *Buckley v. Valeo* was the first effort by the Court to reconcile the competing claim by Congress that corruption—both real and potential—in the campaign finance system required a new regulatory system, given the guarantees of speech and association protected by the First Amendment. The case involved eight distinct rulings, each of which would play a role in the law of campaign finance over the next quarter century.

First, five justices voted to sustain the FECA ceilings on individual contributions of $1,000 to any single candidate per election, and an overall limit of $25,000 on all donations by any one contributor. The Court held that these limits did not violate the speech and associational rights of the First Amendment, nor did they discriminate invidiously against nonincumbent or minority party candidates. The justices conceded that "a restriction on the amount of money a person or group can spend on political communication during a campaign necessarily reduces the quantity of expression by restricting the number of issues discussed, the depth of their exploration, and the size of the audience reached." In using the strict scrutiny test, the Court held that the government's desire to limit actual corruption as well as the appearance of corruption constituted the compelling interest needed to limit speech. Indicating its awareness of the Watergate revelations only a few years earlier, the Court noted that the "deeply disturbing examples surfacing after the 1972 election demonstrate that the problem [of corruption] is not an illusory one. Of almost equal concern . . . is the impact of the appearance of corruption stemming from public awareness of the opportunities for abuse inherent in a regime of large individual financial contributions."

In contrast to limits on contributions, the Court found, as we have seen, ceilings on expenditures, by individuals or by groups, to be unconstitutional. Although neutral on its face (i.e., the law did not target any specific content), the law's spending limits nonetheless imposed substantial restraints on the quantity of political speech, the very type of expression at the heart of the electoral process and of the First Amendment. Here the majority found that the governmental interest sufficient to limit contributions—the need to prevent corruption or its appearance—did not meet the requisite standard when applied to campaign expenditures.

The government had argued that limits created a more level playing field, so that those candidates and parties with greater funds would not be able to drown out the message of smaller, poorly funded campaigns. But the Court replied that "the concept that government may restrict the speech of some elements of our society in order to enhance the relative voice of others is wholly foreign to the First Amendment, which was designed to secure 'the widest possible dissemination of information from diverse and antagonistic sources' and 'to assure unfettered interchange of ideas.'"

The Court also discussed the implications of §608(e)(1)—the limitations on private parties spending money for political purposes. The primary effect of this section, the Court noted, restricted the quantity of political speech by individuals, groups, or candidates. Even if facially neutral with regard to ideas, the law limited the very type of political expression protected by the First Amendment. Here the Court inserted the famous footnote 52, which held that such expression, provided it did not constitute actual campaigning, could not be regulated, and the Court provided a list of words that, by their very appearance, would make it a campaign ad—"vote for," "elect," "support," "cast your ballot for," "Smith for Congress," "vote against," "defeat," or "reject." Provided these "magic words" did not appear, the ads would be construed as issue advocacy rather than campaigning, and be exempt from regulation.

The third holding flowed logically from the second—namely, that limits on what a candidate could spend out of his or her own pocket clearly interfered with constitutionally protected freedom. The provision, although trying to level the playing field, nonetheless cast its net too widely. A rich candidate might outspend an opponent because of greater success in fundraising; conversely, the public's perception that a rich candidate had great wealth might stop others from contributing. It made no difference, however, because "the First Amendment simply cannot tolerate [the] restriction upon the freedom of a candidate to speak without legislative limit on behalf of his own candidacy." (Only Justice Marshall dissented from this part of the ruling, noting that in the seven largest states in the 1970 election, eleven of the fifteen senatorial candidates were millionaires; the four who were not millionaires lost their contests. Congress had sufficient reason to believe that this disparity in personal wealth threatened the integrity of the political process.)

Fourth, six members of the Court upheld the disclosure provisions of FECA, which required that every candidate and committee maintain records that included the name and address of every donor who gave more than $10 in a calendar year, and the name, address, occupation, and principal place of business for those who contributed more than $100 in a year. This information had to be submitted in quarterly reports to the Federal Election Commission (FEC). The attack on the provision relied on the Court's decisions in *NAACP v. Alabama ex rel. Patterson* (1958) and in *Gibson v. Florida Legislative Investigation Committee* (1963), in which the Court had turned back efforts by the states to compel branches of the National Association for the Advancement of Colored People to turn over their membership lists to state officials. In both instances the Court had seen the demand as a means of intimidating the civil rights group. The First Amendment protected individuals in their associational rights, and the state had failed to provide a compelling explanation of why it needed these lists. There had to be a "substantial relationship" between a "compelling governmental interest" and the information required; in the Alabama and Florida cases, neither state had been able to show either the substantial relationship or the compelling interest.

Although the "invasion of privacy of belief may be as great when the information sought concerns the giving and spending of money as when it concerns the joining of organizations," Congress had here provided both the substantial relationship and the compelling interest. Disclosure provides the electorate with information as to where candidates received their campaign funds; second, disclosure deters actual corruption as well as the appearance of corruption; and third, the reporting requirements are an essential means of gathering the information needed. Only Chief Justice Burger dissented from this part of the decision, charging that the Court had failed to give traditional standing to an important First Amendment right, that of association, and that even if there were legitimate reasons, the means employed were too broad.

The majority conceded that the reporting requirements might work a hardship on minor parties espousing views different from those of the mainstream, but since that question did not figure in this case, the Court reserved judgment until a later time. That came within a few years, when the Socialist Workers Party claimed that the requirement would serve to chill donations because people would fear having their names associated with a fringe party. In an opinion by Justice Marshall, the Court agreed that the party had made a sufficient showing of a "reasonable probability of threats, harassment, or reprisals," and it could not be constitutionally compelled to disclose donor information (*Brown v. Socialist Workers '74 Campaign Committee* [1982]).

The Court dealt with the FECA-authorized public financing of the presidential election in two separate rulings. Although the act did not actually implement the process, Senator Buckley and others attacked public financing of presidential primaries and campaigns as contrary to several constitutional provisions—the General Welfare Clause, the First Amendment, and the Due Process Clause of the Fifth Amendment—on grounds that it invidiously discriminated against minority parties and their candidates. The Court dismissed all of these challenges, and in a footnote observed that "Congress may engage in public financing of election campaigns and may condition acceptance of public funds on an agreement by the candidate to abide by specified expenditure limitations. Just as a candidate may voluntarily limit the size of the contributions he chooses to accept, he may decide to forego private fundraising and accept public funding." Both Chief Justice Burger and Justice Rehnquist dissented from the public finance provisions, with Rehnquist arguing that public funding "enshrined the Republican and Democratic parties in a permanently preferred position."

The last two parts of the ruling dealt with the mode of choosing members of the FEC. Nearly all of the justices agreed that the principle of separation of powers implicit in the Appointments Clause, by which the president nominated and the Senate confirmed FEC members, had been breached because the FEC would engage in rulemaking and adjudicatory and enforcement powers. However, the Court then granted de facto legitimacy to past rulings by the FEC and stayed the Court's judgment on this matter for thirty days to give Congress the opportunity to take appropriate action and revise the means of appointing and confirming commissioners.

*   *   *

Buckley has been criticized ever since its delivery. The late political scientist and elections expert Frank Sorauf described "the majority opinion in *Buckley* [as] one of the Court's less impressive monuments. It is long and rambling, an obvious pastiche of differing agendas and prose styles. Very likely it is also the longest per curiam opinion in the Court's history." Those who denigrate the decision do so primarily for what they see as the logical inconsistency between legitimizing caps on individual contributions and voiding expenditure limits as conflicting with the core values of the First Amendment protections of speech and assembly.

Critics also charge the Court with failing to provide a consistent rationale to justify the various holdings. Disparate sections of an opinion are permissible, provided that some unifying jurisprudential thesis holds them together. Commentators have been unable to discern what such a rationale might be in *Buckley*. The Court's emphasis on corruption or the appearance of corruption has convinced few people. Brown University political scientist Darrell West claims that in the debate over campaign financing, many people forgot about Watergate and how fundraising abuses lay at the core of the Nixon scandals. The Court's reasoning in *Buckley*, according to West, "in favor of disclosure rules, contributor limits, and voluntary spending caps in the presidential elections was based in large measure on the importance of avoiding either the reality or the perception of corruption in government." The problem, West believes, lies not in *Buckley* but in the "sad irony" that subsequent decisions have rushed to elevate one good—freedom of expression—over every other virtue, allowing those who can provide large amounts of money the very undue influence that the Court decried in *Buckley*.

In contrast, Professor Vincent Blasi of the Columbia Law School and a noted First Amendment scholar, charges that nowhere in the opinion does the Court give serious attention to the broader issues of republican democracy. Americans, he claims, ought not be obsessed with a simple quid pro quo type of corruption but should be concerned about the entire perversion of the campaign finance system that one saw in Watergate. On the contrary, Bradley Smith, a critic of efforts to reform the campaign finance system, and later chair of the FEC, believes the corruption argument not only overblown but wrong. "The constitutional Achilles heel" of *Buckley*, he argues, "is its holding that the alleged anti-corruption interest of the government justifies the burdens that certain campaign finance regulation places on First Amendment rights. Political speech is not free when it is burdened by regulation."

Even if one believed that the Court had paid appropriate attention to congressional fears of corruption, it appeared to have defined corruption quite narrowly, essentially as a quid pro quo, something done because of the exchange of money. Although this might be an intellectually defensible position, it does not necessarily reflect political reality. Whereas elected officials are clearly sensitive to sources of campaign funds, it is not at all clear just how directly a campaign contribution translates into a specific vote for or against a measure. According to Bradley Smith, the Court should have requested a much more encompassing definition of corruption before it could be the "compelling interest" needed to abridge First Amendment rights.

Others believe that corruption is not really the rationale underlying the opinion, but rather the desire to impose equality on the playing field, the same way the Court imposed equality through the apportionment decisions. Some critics believe that because democracy is not a neat and ordered form of government, neither can its politics be entirely clear and well defined. Professor Lillian BeVier of Virginia Law School argues that "neither political equality nor enhancement of democratic dialogue is a permissible legislative goal under the First Amendment." The problem is that the Court (like academic reformers) refused to recognize the realities of the messy but workable system in place; in *Buckley* and its progeny the Court made the mistake of treating the system as an ideal, what it should be, rather than a reality, what it is. Along this line, Harvard Law professor Cass Sunstein likens the *Buckley* decision to the infamous opinion in *Lochner v. New York* (1905). The Court, he charged, assumed that the political marketplace was ideal and just, and therefore should not be tampered with, and then it invalidated a truly democratic reform. Others argue that the Court failed to understand that the political system has many of the characteristics of the marketplace, and as in most markets, simple rules of supply and demand will keep the system running well.

*　*　*

Buckley v. Valeo did not put an end to litigation over campaign finance regulation. Some states tried to devise reform measures that would pass the Court's tests. At the same time the FEC, confronted with that part of the FECA and its amendments that had either passed judicial scrutiny or had not yet been tested, found itself in court repeatedly as it tried to fashion workable rules. In the more than a quarter century between *Buckley* and the time it heard the challenge to BCRA in *McConnell v. Federal Election Commission*, the Supreme Court had several opportunities to revisit the issue of campaign finance regulation and to clarify some of the questions left by *Buckley*. If anything, the situation on the eve of

McConnell was more confusing rather than less in terms of what the First Amendment and the Court required.

As late as 2000 a majority of the Court seemed to maintain the *Buckley* methodology and to draw a distinction between contributions and expenditures, although the growing scandals associated with campaign financing in the 1990s led some of the justices to advocate dropping *Buckley* and adopting a new standard. In *Nixon v. Shrink Missouri Government PAC* (2000), the Court heard a challenge to a 1994 Missouri law imposing limits on contributions to candidates for state office ranging from $250 to $1,000, with the amount to be adjusted in even-numbered years to take into account inflation. In 1998 the amount was adjusted to $1,075 for contributions to candidates for statewide offices. The political action committee (PAC) gave a contribution of $1,025 in 1997 and another $50 in 1998 to Zev David Fredman, a candidate for state auditor, and then announced that it would have given more but for the state law. The PAC and Fredman then brought suit in federal court alleging that the law violated both the First and the Fourteenth Amendment.

The Supreme Court rejected the argument. Writing for a 6–3 majority that relied on *Buckley*, Justice Souter held that state limits may, if consistent with the First Amendment, be placed on political contributions. Although expenditures are protected by the First Amendment, contribution caps will survive if they are closely drawn and reflect a "sufficiently important interest" such as prevention of corruption or its appearance. States are not bound to impose the same dollar limits as the federal government did in FECA, and so long as the limits did not restrict a candidate's ability to run for office, they would be upheld. The challengers had claimed that the state had not produced the type of evidence necessary—that corruption existed or might appear to exist— to warrant imposing limits. To this Souter replied that the statute did not fail for want of such evidence: "The quantum of empirical evidence needed to satisfy heightened judicial scrutiny of legislative judgments will vary up or down with the novelty and plausibility of the justification raised. *Buckley* demonstrates that the dangers of large, corrupt contributions and the suspicion that large contributions are corrupt are neither novel nor implausible." Although the Missouri legislature did not rely on the same sort of evidence referred to in *Buckley*, the record showed that it had taken into account local facts sufficient to warrant concerns over corruption or the appearance of corruption in the state. In effect, *Buckley* remained good law, both for the states and for the federal government, and the contribution/expenditure distinction continued in effect.

What is perhaps most interesting about the Missouri case is that the Court's majority seemed to be lowering the bar for state and federal laws limiting contributions. The Court (1) ratcheted down the level of scrutiny it would apply to contribution limits; (2) expanded the definitions of "corruption" and the "appearance of corruption" to make it easier to sustain contribution caps; (3) lowered the evidentiary burden on the government in terms of what it had to prove to justify fear of corruption; and (4) created a very difficult test for those who would challenge campaign limits as too low. As one scholar noted, the majority "show[ed] dramatic new deference toward contribution limits." In doing so the justices heartened reformers, since if the Court would pay greater deference on the contributions side, then perhaps it might also come around to the same position on limiting expenditures. "The Supreme Court is aware of realities now," wrote Anthony Lewis of the *New York Times*. "It is not in a First Amendment ivory tower, indifferent to the consequences of absolutism."

Three justices dissented, primarily on First Amendment grounds. Justice Kennedy called the *Buckley* contribution/expenditure distinction a "wooden" one that over the years had "adverse, unintended consequences." In particular, Kennedy claimed, *Buckley*

> forced a substantial amount of political speech underground, as contributors and candidates devise ever more elaborate methods of avoiding contribution limits, limits which take no account of rising campaign costs. The preferred method has been to conceal the real purpose of the speech. Soft money may be contributed to political parties in unlimited amounts, and is used often to fund so-called issue advocacy, advertisements that promote or attack a candidate's positions without specifically urging his or her election or defeat. Issue advocacy, like soft money, is unrestricted, while straightforward speech in the form of financial contributions paid to a candidate, speech subject to full disclosure and prompt evaluation by the public, is not. Thus has the Court's decision given us covert speech. This mocks the First Amendment.

Had the legislature imposed such a system, it would be suspect under the First Amendment, but Congress had nothing to do with it; the fault lay with the Court and its decision, one that had "created a misshapen system, one which distorts the meaning of speech." If it were up to him, Kennedy concluded, he would overrule *Buckley*. Justice Thomas, joined by Justice Scalia, also dissented, and in his opinion attacked *Buckley* and its contribution/expenditure distinction as well

Of special interest is Justice Kennedy's observation that all *Buckley* had done was to force contributors to give their money in different and unaccounted ways. Since *Buckley* had upheld the reporting scheme of FECA, it would have been better to have all money coming into a campaign accounted for and open to public scrutiny. Instead, donors could not only evade the limits, but avoid publicity by giving through soft money channels.

Although PACs were neither widespread nor a matter of reformers' concerns at the time of *Buckley*, they soon became so, and the Court heard several cases involving PACs. The FECA recognized the existence of PACs, defined as multicandidate committees, "which received contributions from more than 50 persons and made contributions to five or more candidates for federal office." In these cases the Court also followed the reasoning attached to the contribution/expenditure dichotomy. In *California Medical Association v. Federal Election Commission* (1981), a nonprofit, unincorporated medical association formed a PAC that registered with the FEC, and thus became subject to FECA rules regarding PACs. One of these rules prohibited individuals and unincorporated associations from contributing more than $5,000 per calendar year to any multicandidate committee; a related rule prohibited political committees from knowingly accepting contributions exceeding this limit. The PAC did accept contributions in excess of this limit, and when the FEC announced it would institute a civil suit, the medical association, its PAC, and two individual members filed suit in federal district court seeking to have the relevant portions of the FECA declared unconstitutional, on the grounds that here the money went not to a candidate but to a political committee.

Although the Court could not devise a rationale that won the support of five members, Justice Marshall's plurality opinion (joined by Brennan, White, and Stevens) found *Buckley* to be controlling. Nothing in the law limited the amount the PAC or any of its members could spend to advocate their political views; rather, the law imposed a cap on contributions, and money given to the PAC, for either direct expenditure or passing on to a candidate's own committee, constituted a contribution. Marshall rejected the claim that, because the contribution went to a political committee, rather than to a candidate, the provision did not "further the governmental interest in preventing the actual or apparent corruption of the political process." The provision was necessary to prevent circumvention of the contributions limits upheld in *Buckley*.

A second decision involving a PAC also followed the contribution/expenditure rationale of *Buckley*. A provision of the Presidential Election Campaign Fund Act prohibited PACs from spending more than $1,000 to further the campaign of a presidential candidate who accepted public financing. In *Federal Election Commission v. National Conservative PAC* (1985), the Court struck down this provision on the grounds that efforts to regulate expenditures violated the First Amendment. Justice White, joined by Brennan and Marshall, dissented on grounds that when PACs spent money, they did so as proxies for the contributors, and by treating PACs differently than candidates (a distinction the Court had refused to draw in the California case), the Court was essentially allowing donors to exceed campaign contributions to candidates by routing them through a PAC. Perhaps of even greater interest was Justice Marshall's separate dissent, in which he wrote:

> Although I joined that portion of the *Buckley* per curiam that distinguished contributions from independent expenditures for First Amendment purposes, I now believe the distinction has no constitutional significance. In both cases the regulation is of the same form: It concerns the amount of money that can be spent for political activity. . . . I have come to believe that the limitations on independent expenditures challenged in Buckley and here are justified by the congressional interest in promoting "the reality and appearance of equal access to the political arena," and in eliminating political corruption and the appearance of such corruption.

The Court found that political parties, like individuals, candidates, and PACs, have a right under the First Amendment to make unlimited expenditures on behalf of a candidate. In *Colorado Republican Federal*

Campaign Committee v. Federal Election Commission (1996) (*Colorado I*), the Court considered an FECA provision imposing dollar limits on political party expenditures in connection with the general election campaign for a congressional candidate. Even before a Republican candidate had been selected for the 1986 senatorial election, the Colorado federal Republican committee bought radio time to air advertisements attacking the presumptive Democratic candidate. The Democrats and the FEC charged the Colorado Republicans with violating the FECA by exceeding the allowable party limit.

Once again the Court relied on *Buckley* but, once again, could not muster a rationale on which five justices could agree. Justice Breyer, joined by O'Connor and Souter, invalidated §441a(d)(3) of the FECA on grounds that "the First Amendment prohibits the application of this provision to the kind of expenditure at issue here—an expenditure that the political party has made independently, without coordination with any candidate." Declaring that the issue of unregulated expenditures had long been settled, "we do not see how a Constitution that grants to individuals, candidates, and ordinary political committees the right to make unlimited independent expenditures could deny that same right to political parties." The plurality rejected the government's contention that party expenditures on behalf of a candidate ought to be presumed to have been coordinated with the candidate's campaign, and therefore treated as contributions, which, of course could be regulated.

Justice Kennedy, joined by Chief Justice Rehnquist and Justice Scalia, concurred in part and dissented in part. In essence, these three would have gone further and invalidated the party expenditure limits on their face, whether applied to independent or coordinated party expenditures. Justice Thomas, also joined by Rehnquist and Scalia, would have voided party spending limits in their entirety because the anticorruption rationale at the heart of *Buckley* just did not apply here. "What could it mean," Thomas asked, "for a party to 'corrupt' its candidate or to exercise 'coercive' influence over him? The very aim of a political party is to influence its candidate's stance on issues and, if the candidate takes office or is reelected, his votes. When political parties achieve that aim, it is not corruption; that is successful advocacy of ideas in the political marketplace and representative government in a party system." Only Justices Stevens and Ginsburg dissented, claiming that party expenditure limits met the constitutional test because they served important governmental interests both in avoiding corruption and in "leveling the electoral playing field by constraining the cost of federal campaigns."

Justice Breyer's plurality opinion in *Colorado I* declined to deal with the hypothetical question of what rule would apply if in fact there had been coordination; that issue came back to the Court a few years later in a case labeled *Colorado II.* Breyer, O'Connor, and Souter, the plurality in the first case, were now joined by the two dissenters, Stevens and Ginsburg, to provide a 5–4 majority ruling that limits on a party's coordinated expenditures were constitutional. To reach this conclusion, the five justices rejected a series of assumptions from both sides. They denied the party's contentions that its coordinated spending should be as free from regulation as its independent spending, and that the point of organizing a party is to run candidates, so the coordination is integral to a party structure. The majority also rejected the government's claim that coordinated spending is the same as contributions and should be treated as such, and that if coordinated spending were unlimited it would only aggravate the use of a party as a money funnel to bypass the contribution limits upheld in *Buckley.*

Conceding that each of these arguments appeared "plausible at first blush," the Court rejected them and announced that the limit applied to a party's coordinated expenditures would be subject to "the same scrutiny we have applied to the other political actors, that is, scrutiny appropriate for a contribution limit, enquiring whether the restriction is 'closely drawn' to match what we have recognized as the 'sufficiently important' government interest in combating political corruption."

Although admitting that no recent evidence existed to evaluate unlimited coordinated spending, the Court contended that "the question is whether experience under the present law confirms a serious threat of abuse from the unlimited coordinated spending as the Government contends. It clearly does. Despite years of enforcement of the challenged limits, substantial evidence demonstrates how candidates, donors, and parties test the limits of the current law, and it shows beyond serious doubt how contribution limits would be eroded" if the Court were to strike down the limits on coordinated spending. Moreover, unlike *Buckley* and even *Colorado I,* where the choice was between limiting pure contributions and pure expenditures, here "the choice is between limiting contributions and limiting expenditures whose special value as expenditures is also the source of their power to corrupt. Congress is entitled to its choice."

The majority opinion, even though it claimed to follow *Buckley*, in fact became the first instance in which a majority of the Court strayed from a strict distinction between contributions and expenditures, and despite Souter's effort to differentiate between the *Buckley* test and the problem of coordinated money, critics had for a long time been arguing that the *Buckley* distinction made no sense in the real world of politics. Moreover, all four of the dissenting justices—Rehnquist, Scalia, Kennedy, and Thomas—agreed that they would overrule *Buckley* in part and apply to contribution limits the full strict scrutiny test hitherto applied only to expenditures. Justice Thomas also argued that even if the *Buckley* restrictions made sense in some way when applied to individuals and political committees, they did not make sense when applied to parties, which are inextricably intertwined with candidates.

A third area of campaign finance in which the Court attempted to make sense after *Buckley* concerned the activities of corporations. Federal law had long prohibited contributions from corporate treasuries to federal campaigns. But what about campaigns that did not involve candidates but instead involved referenda? Could a state prohibit a company from advocacy in a referendum where the results might seriously affect its welfare?

Massachusetts had enacted a prohibition against corporations making donations or expenditures in an effort to influence the vote in any referendum, "other than one materially affecting any of the property, business, or assets of the corporation." Moreover, the law specifically excluded any referendum concerning taxation of income, property, or business transactions from being considered as "materially affecting" a corporation. In 1976 the state's ballot included a proposal to authorize a graduated individual income tax. Banks and other financial corporations opposed the measure and went into state court to challenge the validity of the restrictive corporate statute. The Supreme Judicial Court of Massachusetts upheld the measure, ruling that the First Amendment rights of a corporation were limited to issues that materially affected its business, property, or assets, and that the state had it within its power to define certain matters, including taxation, as not materially affecting corporate interests.

The Supreme Court, by a 5–4 vote, reversed this decision in *First National Bank of Boston v. Bellotti* (1978). Justice Lewis Powell wrote that the state court had asked the wrong question. The issue was not whether corporations had First Amendment rights similar to those of natural persons; rather, "the question must be whether [the state law] abridges expression that the First Amendment was meant to protect. We hold that it does." The issue that the banks wanted to talk about—a proposed constitutional amendment—lay at the very heart of First Amendment protection. "It is the type of speech indispensable to decision-making in a democracy. The inherent worth of the speech in terms of its capacity for informing the public does not depend upon the identity of its source, whether corporation, association, union, or individual." Once Powell had found that the type of speech warranted First Amendment protection, the appropriate test would be strict scrutiny, and by this standard the state law failed. If the legislature could tell a bank to mind its own business, then it could say that to any other type of corporation, be it religious, charitable, or civic.

Justice White, in a lengthy dissent joined by Brennan and Marshall, asserted that the majority had committed a fundamental error in failing "to realize that the state regulatory interests [are] themselves derived from the First Amendment," namely, promoting the free marketplace of ideas by preventing domination by wealthy corporations. Although White agreed that corporate speech lay within First Amendment protection, corporate speech was "subject to restrictions which individual expression is not."

Bellotti seemed to open another gap in the wall that Congress and some states had attempted to erect to keep corporate funds out of election campaigns. Even if corporate treasuries could not send money to a candidate, it now appeared that corporations could speak out on political issues of interest to them. So if, for example, two candidates differed over raising or lowering tariffs, a company that would benefit from lower rates could pay for an "issue ad," and voters would not have to go far to guess which candidate agreed with the company's position.

Although the Court had implied in *Bellotti* that restrictions on corporate entities would fail whether applied to businesses or civic associations, in *Federal Election Commission v. National Right to Work Committee* (1982) the Court drew a distinction between the Massachusetts statute and a federal restriction on nonprofit corporations raising funds to contribute to candidate campaigns.

The National Right to Work Committee, a nonprofit corporation without capital stock, established a separate segregated fund to receive and make contributions on behalf of federal candidates. This fund then sent letters to individuals who had previously contributed to the committee, soliciting contributions to the fund. Another lobbying group then filed a complaint with the FEC, asserting that the corporation had solicited contributions from persons who were not stockholders, executive or administrative personnel of the corporation, or their families, in violation of the solicitation restrictions of the FECA. The committee responded that, within the meaning of the FECA, those who received the solicitation letters were "members" of the corporation. The FEC disagreed and the committee filed suit; it lost in district court but then won in the court of appeals, which held that the term "member" had to be given an elastic definition to avoid infringement of First Amendment associational rights.

The Supreme Court reversed this decision in a unanimous opinion by Justice Rehnquist. The Court refused to accept the idea that anyone who had ever made a donation to the committee, or had even been solicited by it, constituted a "member" under the provisions of the FECA. The solicitation letter made no reference to members, and those solicited played no part in the operation or administration of the fund, nor did they have any control over the expenditure of their contributions. In addition, the fund's own articles of incorporation explicitly disclaimed the existence of members. As a result, the FECA prohibition against nonprofits engaging in this type of political activity met all constitutional tests, and the associational rights of the committee were overborne by the governmental interest in "ensuring that substantial aggregations of wealth amassed by the special advantages which go with the corporate form of organization should not be converted into political 'war chests' which could be used to incur political debts from legislators who are aided by the contributions."

A few years later, however, the Court gave nonprofit groups greater leeway in the political arena, holding in a 5–4 opinion that nonprofits could issue pamphlets indicating their position on certain key issues and listing the voting records of candidates, provided they did not actually endorse any specific person. The nonprofit Massachusetts Citizens for Life had prepared a "special election edition" of its newsletter urging citizens to vote "pro-life" in an upcoming primary and reporting the positions of various candidates on pro-life legislation. Although the newsletter carried the pictures of candidates who supported such legislation, the committee explicitly denied endorsing any particular candidates.

Justice Brennan's majority opinion distinguished the pro-life committee's actions from those of the right-to-work group. The latter had attempted to provide money for the use of candidates and thus violated the FECA. But the antiabortion group had simply broadcast its views, and since people joined that group because they shared that viewpoint, it did not have to set up a segregated fund in order to make known its views. Chief Justice Rehnquist, joined by White, Blackmun, and Stevens, dissented and said the Court should defer to the judgment of Congress that corporations of any sort are a distinct category with respect to what type of speech regulation is constitutionally permissible (*Federal Election Commission v. Massachusetts Citizens for Life* [1986]).

Four years later, however, the Court reversed itself and upheld a Michigan statute restricting independent corporate campaign expenditures substantially identical to the federal restriction that had been struck down in *Massachusetts Citizens.* Although the Michigan state law barred corporations from using their treasuries for political purposes, it did allow them to set up segregated funds. The statute exempted expenditures by any television or radio station, or any print media, in regard to either covering a race or even airing an editorial, a clear attempt to avoid First Amendment problems with the press. Justice Marshall's 6–3 opinion in *Austin v. Michigan Chamber of Commerce* (1990) repeated much of the language that the Court had used in *National Right to Work Committee* about the potential abuses of large corporate wealth in the political process. The Michigan act "aims at the corrosive and distorting effects of immense aggregations of wealth that are accumulated with the help of the corporate form and that have little or no correlation to the public's support for the corporation's political ideas." Given this fear of corruption, the state had articulated a sufficiently compelling rationale for restricting corporate involvement in politics. Moreover, because the Michigan Chamber of Commerce was involved in a very wide range of activities, it had a large number of members, many of whom might not share the chamber leadership's political agenda.

Justice Scalia wrote a scathing dissent that began:

> Attention all citizens. To assure the fairness of elections by preventing disproportionate expression of the views of any single powerful group, your Government has decided that the following associations of persons shall be prohibited from speaking or writing in support of any candidate. In permitting Michigan to make private corporations the first object of this Orwellian announcement, the Court today endorses the principle that too much speech is an evil that the democratic majority can proscribe. I dissent because that principle is contrary to our case law and incompatible with the absolutely central truth of the First Amendment: that government cannot be trusted to assure, through censorship, the "fairness" of political debate.

Scalia accused the majority of attempting to overrule or undercut *Buckley*'s rejection of limits on expenditures solely on the basis of resources available to the speaker. Rich corporate bodies, because they had wealth to spend, could be restricted in their speech. He ridiculed the reasoning that the mere potential of harm justifies restrictions on speech. Yet a key element of *Buckley* had been just that. In sustaining the limits on contributions, the Court had relied on Congress's determination that large donations to candidates and political groups indicated either outright corruption or the perception of corruption. In what was certainly the most forceful rejection of this assumption since *Buckley*, Scalia argued that the same strict scrutiny should be applied to contribution caps as well as expenditure caps, and that all speakers, individual as well as corporate, should be treated identically in terms of First Amendment rights.

In another dissent, Justice Kennedy, joined by O'Connor and Scalia, also went back to *Buckley* and charged that the majority had upheld "a direct restriction on the independent expenditure of funds for political speech for the first time in history." The Michigan statute, he believed, failed the strict scrutiny test required by the First Amendment. In

Buckley and *Bellotti*, he claimed, the Court had rejected the argument that expending money to increase the quantity of political speech somehow fosters corruption. "The key to the majority's reasoning appears to be that because some corporate speakers are well supported and can buy press space or broadcast time to express their ideas, government may ban all corporate speech to ensure that it will not dominate political debate," Kennedy asserted. "The argument is flawed in at least two respects. First, the statute is overinclusive because it covers all groups which use the corporate form, including all nonprofit corporations. Second, it assumes that the government has a legitimate interest in equalizing the relative influence of speakers."

By this point one might well wonder how much of the expenditure/contribution rule in *Buckley* had survived. The Court had both negated and upheld limits on expenditures, and although several of the justices had urged doing away with the distinction altogether and applying strict scrutiny to both sides of the equation, that view never commanded a majority of the Court in any given case. The logical inconsistencies of these cases could not be masked. How could a corporation be allowed to engage in political speech on referenda (*Bellotti*) but not support candidates (*Austin*)? Or could they support candidates, if they disclaimed doing so (*Massachusetts Citizens for Life*)? Academics attempting to make sense of this pattern threw their hands up in bewilderment.

Other decisions of the Court in the post-*Buckley* era did little to clarify this confusion. In *Citizens against Rent Control v. Berkeley* (1981), the Court struck down a local ordinance establishing a $250 limit on personal contributions to committees established to support or oppose referenda. Chief Justice Burger's majority opinion found this limit an unconstitutional interference with freedom of association as well as individual and collective rights of expression. *Buckley*, he claimed, did not support contribution limits to committees favoring or opposing ballot measures, although in *Bellotti* the Court had relied on the *Buckley* rationale to strike down state limits on advocacy related to ballot measures. Only Justice White dissented and, repeating his views from *Buckley* and *Bellotti*, argued that the ordinance represented such a negligible intrusion on expression that it ought to be upheld.

*   *   *

In all of these cases the Court had to wrestle with just what *Buckley v. Valeo* meant as applied not only to candidates and their committees but also to PACs, referenda, corporations, and nonprofits. Although a few cases—mostly minor—managed to win over a full Court, in nearly all of them slim majorities tried to make sense out of *Buckley* but confronted strong dissents that called for greater First Amendment analysis that would apply strict scrutiny to both expenditures and contributions.

By the time McCain-Feingold gained congressional approval, constitutional experts could not be sure just how the courts would respond. *Buckley*, according to at least one critic, stood "for the proposition that if [a campaign finance law] is effective, it must be unconstitutional." E. Joshua Rosenkranz, a prominent lawyer who often practiced before the Court, charged that scores of promising reforms that have been enacted into law have fallen to a *Buckley* challenge. Lampooning the Court's distinction between contributions and expenditures, Rosenkranz said that the case stood for the proposition that "a [Ross] Perot or a [Michael] Huffington has an absolute right to buy his way into office. It means that a fat cat has an absolute right to saturate the airwaves with a message advocating for or against a candidate."

One could go on citing one view after another, each one taking a different slant on *Buckley* and its progeny. Law professor Martin Redish probably put it best when, on the eve of the passage of McCain-Feingold, he wrote: "To this point, it would be difficult to declare a clear winner. Indeed, the Supreme Court's decisions on the subject not only have failed to provide a coherent resolution of the competing and complex arguments, they have instead given rise to their own doctrinal and theoretical confusion."

CHAPTER 6

Interlude

Confusion in the District Court

Even before George Bush signed the Bipartisan Campaign Reform Act (BCRA), opponents had lined up to attack it in the courts. The American Civil Liberties Union (ACLU) declared that, although it had long supported campaign finance reform through public funding of races for federal offices, the BCRA, in its view, impinged on traditional First Amendment rights. The act, according to Stephen Shapiro, ACLU legal director, would severely restrict nonprofit, nonpartisan organizations (such as the ACLU itself) "from expressing their views on important public issues in the period immediately preceding an election, a time when those issues are most urgently debated." Within Congress there had been an informal understanding that Senator Mitch McConnell (R-KY) would be the lead plaintiff, and as soon as the president signed the bill, McConnell announced that he would challenge the law in the courts. He welcomed others to join him if they believed that the BCRA deprived them of their constitutional rights: "I look forward to being joined by a strong group of coplaintiffs in the very near future."

McConnell did not have long to wait. Within a few days more than eighty interest groups or individuals announced that they intended to challenge BCRA in the courts. In the end, these eighty-four coalesced into eleven separate lawsuits against the Federal Election Commission (FEC), and all suits were heard and decided as one case, although the emphasis in each suit differed somewhat from others. For example, both the AFL-CIO and the National Rifle Association (NRA) opposed the bill on First Amendment grounds, but differed in both large principles and particulars. Wayne LaPierre, the NRA executive vice president, and James Jay Baker, executive director of the NRA's Institute for Legislative Action, in a joint statement, challenged Congress's efforts to quiet the gun lobby. "The First Amendment," they announced, "does not allow Congress to make laws which deny us the right to speak out on issues." The AFL-CIO was primarily upset over the limits placed on political action committees. The National Association of Broadcasters worried about how much the new law would cost in lost revenues. Soon afterward the Republican National Committee, the California Democratic Party, the California Republican Party, and a variety of local committees and officials joined the suit. The most comprehensive and the lead grouping (twenty-seven litigants) was that associated with Senator McConnell's, and included Representatives Bob Barr (R-GA) and Mike Pence (R-IN).

A formidable army of lawyers represented the various plaintiffs. Altogether, some fifty-five lawyers signed the plaintiff briefs. Although some of them were staff members (usually the general counsel) of specific organizations, others worked for private law firms, and all of them apparently gave their services on a pro bono basis. In the list one could find some of the most important civil liberties attorneys in the country, such as Floyd Abrams of New York and Joel M. Gora of the Brooklyn Law School, who had represented the ACLU in the *Buckley* case. Kathleen M. Sullivan, dean of the Stanford Law School and coauthor of a leading casebook on the First Amendment, had been one of the first to volunteer her services to Senator McConnell. In addition, former solicitor general Kenneth W. Starr, a member of the Washington law firm of Kirkland and Ellis, acted not only for McConnell but also for several of the coplaintiffs.

The FEC argued in favor of the new law, joined by several members of Congress. Although the solicitor general's office would be nominally responsible for defending a federal law in court, in this case it would have the help of some high-powered attorneys and law firms that, like those assisting Senator McConnell, provided their services on a pro bono basis. Because the Justice Department had the responsibility of prosecuting violations under the criminal provisions of the law, it represented the United States. Robert D. McCallum Jr., assistant attorney general, headed a team of ten lawyers from the Department of Justice. Seventeen lawyers, nearly the entire legal department of the FEC, signed the brief, led by general counsel Lawrence H. Norton. In addition, the powerful and politically well-connected Washington law firm of Wilmer, Cutler, and Pickering represented the members of Congress who had intervener status. Although numerous lawyers from the firm worked on the case, only three signed the brief: Roger Witten, Randolph Moss, and former solicitor general Seth P. Waxman.

On April 16, 2002, less than three weeks after the president signed the BCRA, the case was assigned to a three-judge panel consisting of district judge Richard J. Leon, appointed just that year by President George W. Bush; district judge Colleen Kollar-Kotelly, appointed by President Bill Clinton in 1997; and court of appeals judge Karen LeCraft Henderson, named by President George H. W. Bush in 1990. One week later the judges met with lawyers representing both sides in a status conference, in which they heard the parties' proposals on matters of consolidation of suits, intervention, discovery, and the filing of motions. The very next day the court issued a unanimous order outlining a discovery and briefing schedule. Because of the complexity of the issue and the many sections of the law that would be challenged, the court allowed five months for discovery (far longer than normal) and one month for cross-examination of key witnesses and experts. The three judges set November 25 as the deadline for briefs and supporting documents and informed the parties that they would begin hearing oral arguments on December 4, 2002.

* * *

Given the nature of the trial, both sides would try to not only build up the constitutional arguments on their side but also make it appear that unless their views prevailed, dire consequences would be in store for the country's political system. The briefs are full of worst-case scenarios; overblown rhetoric; warnings of slippery slopes should the other side win; and, quite often, reasoning according to horrid possibilities, that is, "If this provision is allowed to stand (or is struck down), then we can expect to see horrible event number 1, then horrible development number 2, et cetera." Nonetheless, picking one's way between the essential constitutional arguments and the surrounding hyperbole, one finds one of the most important public policy debates of the last two decades—to what extent should Congress attempt to control campaign financing related to federal offices, including the political speech that makes up those campaigns, in order to prevent corruption or its appearance?

The BCRA had included a fast-track provision, designed to get the case before the Supreme Court as quickly as possible. Both proponents and opponents of BCRA hoped that the district court would hand down its opinion before the end of January, which would have given the Supreme Court time to hear and decide the appeal before its term ended in June. In fact, during the trial Judge Henderson asked Kenneth Starr, one of McConnell's lawyers, when he thought a decision would be needed so that it could go to the High Court in its current term. He responded late January or early February, and she indicated it could be even sooner than that. By the time the panel released the opinion in May, given the time needed to file for certiorari, prepare briefs and responses, hear arguments, reach a decision, and then write an opinion (and potential dissents), it was clear that the Supreme Court would be unable to take the case before the justices went on their summer hiatus at the beginning of July.

Sometimes a lower court opinion is so well crafted that even if the Supreme Court were to overturn it, the issues would have been clarified, the constitutional questions made evident, and the central questions for the High Court to decide made manifest. There is little positive to be said, however, about the 774-page district court opinion in *McConnell v. Federal Election Commission*. Even recognizing the many complex issues involved in the case, the opinion is so incomprehensible that the three judges had to insert a chart and table of contents to show where each of them stood on particular issues. All the litigants agreed, however, that the decision and the resulting orders were so unhelpful and confusing that a stay should be sought so that the orders would not go into effect until the Supreme Court had heard the case.

* * *

The three judges could agree on little, not even on a single majority opinion. Instead, they issued four opinions—a per curiam opinion and separate opinions from each judge. For decisional purposes, only the per curiam (a memorandum opinion summarizing the findings on which two or more of the judges agreed) matters, but since the three agreed on so little, they could not provide a coherent jurisprudential rationale for the Supreme Court to utilize. Moreover, Judge Henderson refused to sign the per curiam even on those points with which she agreed. The first paragraph of section IA, dealing with part of Title I, provides a sense of the internal dissension on the bench:

> Section 323(a) of BCRA bans national parties from soliciting, receiving, directing, transferring, and spending nonfederal funds (i.e., soft money). Judge Henderson strikes this section down as unconstitutional in its entirety. Judge Leon, for different reasons, files a concurrence, joining with Judge Henderson, except with respect to the ban on national parties from using (i.e., "directing," "transferring," and "spending") nonfederal funds (i.e., soft money) for "federal election activity" of the type defined in Section 301(20)(A)(iii). As to that type of conduct, Judge Leon upholds the constitutionality of Congress's ban on the use of nonfederal funds by national parties for Section 301(20)(A)(iii) communications. Judge Kollar-Kotelly upholds Section 323(a) in its entirety. Accordingly, Judge Leon's decision regarding Section 323(a) controls.

In addition to the 83-page per curiam opinion, Judge Henderson submitted a 166-page opinion, Judge Kollar-Kotelly wrote for 324 pages, and Judge Leon added 191 pages. Each judge found it necessary to include a table of contents as a guide to his or her opinion, but because they agreed on so little, even a careful reader will be unable to find commonality on basic issues. Judge Henderson found BCRA "unconstitutional in virtually all of its particulars; it breaks faith with the fundamental principle—understood by our nation's Founding Generation, inscribed in the First Amendment and repeatedly reaffirmed by the United States Supreme Court—that 'debate on public issues should be uninhibited, robust, and wide open.'" Judge Kollar-Kotelly, on the other hand, after detailing the history of congressional efforts to keep the political process free of corruption, argued that this "thoughtful and careful effort . . . deserves respect." Claiming that her constitutional approach "is rooted in the record of this case and guided by the constitutional boundaries established by the Supreme Court's campaign finance jurisprudence . . . I have only found three of the challenged sections unconstitutional." Like the defenders of the law, Judge Kollar-Kotelly relied heavily on a factual record showing corruption or its appearance, and, far more than Judge Henderson, she indicated her willingness to defer to Congress. Judge Leon also deferred to Congress, but to a far lesser extent than Kollar-Kotelly. Where the government could show that it had a legitimate reason for a rule, and that that rule did not violate First Amendment principles, he would uphold the BCRA.

Judge Leon had the swing vote on almost every issue, and although he frequently joined Judge Henderson in the result, he often differed with her reasoning. Thus he rejected her view that soft money regulation must be subject to strict scrutiny, and agreed with Kollar-Kotelly that such restrictions need be only "closely drawn" to pass constitutional muster, a standard of review less rigorous than strict scrutiny. But, like Henderson, he found that most of BCRA's soft money provisions failed to meet even this lower standard. According to one commentator, Judge Leon took "an unusually creative approach to the judicial role." He "literally rewrote" two key sections of the law in order to make them conform to his constitutional analysis. Congress had provided for a complete ban on national party soft money and, in a more limited way, required state and local parties to use only hard money to pay for specific activities. Leon, and along with him the court, held the complete ban on soft money overbroad, and then in narrowing the allowable uses of the soft money by local parties, upheld that portion of the soft money ban. When it came to the provision on electioneering communication, he struck down the primary definition, then rewrote in effect the backup definition and upheld it. The two main themes of Leon's opinion, and thus of the court, are that (1) Congress has broad authority to regulate the funding of communications by both party and nonparty participants that refer to federal candidates, but (2) otherwise Congress may not restrict party finances.

The district court not only divided deeply in its analysis but also had a great deal of trouble even agreeing on findings of facts. Each of the three judges made different factual findings. Altogether the three sets of factual findings add up to 320 pages, and although some findings were common to at least two of the judges, very rarely did all three agree. As a result, the Supreme Court would derive little if any benefit from the lower court's findings; it would, for all practical purposes, have to review the record from scratch. Even in their opinions, according to one critic, the work of the lower court judges "is distressingly sloppy."

* * *

In all, the district court held ten sections of the Bipartisan Campaign Reform Act of 2002 unconstitutional, but it appeared that no one—plaintiffs or defendants—liked the entire opinion. Both sides tried to put the best face on it by seizing on a section that had gone their way. Senator Feingold, one of the chief sponsors of BCRA, declared that "by and large, the ruling accepts the premise of McCain-Feingold, which is that certain kinds of soft money can be prohibited and that does not violate the First Amendment." Similarly, some of the Republicans who had challenged the law claimed that the decision had gone largely in their favor. "We believe the court has fully vindicated the rights of political parties to participate in state and local elections and to work with state and local parties in furtherance of the mission of the Republican Party," said Bobby R. Burchfield, the Republican National Committee lawyer.

Because the exact impact of the district court's ruling could not easily be ascertained, and because parts of its decision could be overturned when the case reached the Supreme Court, nearly all the parties managed to agree on one thing—actual implementation of the ruling had to be stopped. Under the schedule promulgated by the court, parties had until noon on May 9 to request a stay, and groups ranging from the NRA to the ACLU, to the sponsors of the bill themselves all filed petitions for stays of implementation. Many followed the line articulated by the ACLU in its petition. As long as the current ruling regarding issue advertisements remained in place, "we are without any guidance defining how far these planned ads can go in criticizing the proposed legislation [on civil liberties issues] and members of Congress who support it. We can only assume that the more aggressive we are in our criticism and rhetoric, the more likely our statements will fall within the definition of speech that is now prohibited." Several groups also wondered how the time frame on acceptable or unacceptable issue ads would be determined, since theoretically an ad run eighteen months before an election might very well fall within the ban. Ten days later, the court unanimously granted the stay, pending review by the US Supreme Court.

On June 5, the Supreme Court accepted the case on appeal and in a surprise move set an accelerated schedule for the parties. Initial briefs would have to be filed by 3:00 p.m. on July 8, and reply briefs, by August 21. Instead of the usual one hour of oral argument allotted by the Court to cases before it, this time it would hear four hours of oral argument beginning at 10:00 a.m. on Monday, September 8, 2003. For the first time in decades, the Court would cut short its summer recess. The justices wanted to have a decision in time for the 2004 presidential election.

CHAPTER 7

McConnell v. Federal Election Commission

It would come down to what five members of the Supreme Court would say—whether the Bipartisan Campaign Reform Act (BCRA) and its limits on the activities of political parties violated the Constitution or not. The fact that the justices agreed to meet in September and allotted four hours to oral argument heightened interest in the decision. Although the sponsors of the bill hoped the Court would put its imprimatur on their efforts, and opponents hoped that their constitutional arguments would prevail, cynics took the view that it did not really matter what the Court said. Political campaigns need money the way a car needs gasoline, and one way or another the parties and willing donors would manage to keep the dollars flowing.

The Court's decision, however, would be important for the future. In the years following *Buckley*, the Court's equating of money with speech had seriously hampered reformers, since they believed that except for limits on contributions, all other measures would run afoul of the Court's First Amendment views. If in *McConnell* the Court took a similarly restrictive position, it would be almost impossible to pass any legislation that substantially changed the way Democrats and Republicans financed election campaigns. But if the Court took a more expansive view of congressional power over federal campaigns, then even if BCRA did not work as effectively as its sponsors hoped, reformers might come back and attempt to amend the act and tighten its provisions. Both sides believed that the case would be a watershed event in the history of campaign finance reform.

Because of the complexity of the lower court ruling, there was no clear winner or loser when the sides appealed. Normally, the losing side in the lower court files the appeal and frames the legal questions it wants the Court to review. The winner in the lower court can then respond, usually urging the High Court to affirm the lower court's ruling. In this instance, however, both sides wanted the Supreme Court to reverse different parts of the district court decision and filed a variety of technical motions hoping to get an advantage. Neither side prevailed.

Despite the maneuvering over procedural details, both sides professed pleasure at the speed with which the Supreme Court agreed to hear the case. Floyd Abrams, representing McConnell, said the Court's scheduling meant the case would in all likelihood be settled before the 2004 presidential primaries and caucuses. "It's very important," he said, "to know what the rules of the game are going to be."

*　*　*

Then, in one of its last opinions for the term, the Supreme Court handed down a decision regarding campaign finance law that might—or might not—be a clue as to how it would decide the challenge to BCRA that fall. The existing federal election law (the Federal Election Campaign Act [FECA]) barred corporations from making direct contributions to federal elections but did allow them to establish separate funds—namely, political action committees—that could expend moneys in political campaigns. A nonprofit group, North Carolina Right to Life, and others challenged the applicability of the corporation rule to nonprofit groups, claiming that it violated their First Amendment rights.

The Supreme Court, in *Federal Election Commission v. Beaumont* (2003), held that Congress had sufficient power to regulate the political process to extend that ban to any group without violating the group's constitutional rights. By a vote of 7 to 2, the Court, speaking through Justice Souter, said that the right to free speech does not trump Congress's goal of limiting the corrosive effects of corporate money in politics. The government had argued that permitting nonprofit advocacy groups to ignore the corporate ban would allow their members to circumvent the limits on individual campaign contributions and to do so with little public disclosure about the source of the money. "Any attack on the federal prohibition of direct corporate political contributions goes against the current of a century of congressional efforts," Souter wrote.

All of the justices except Antonin Scalia and Clarence Thomas joined in Souter's opinion, fueling speculation on how the individual justices would align themselves in the upcoming and all-important *McConnell* case. In prior cases, Justices John Paul Stevens, Ruth Bader Ginsburg,

David H. Souter, and Stephen G. Breyer had shown the most sympathy for campaign finance regulation, while Scalia, Thomas, and Anthony Kennedy had been the most skeptical. In the middle, and the key voters in the case, would be Chief Justice William H. Rehnquist, who as an associate justice had supported the limit on campaign contributions in *Buckley*, and Sandra Day O'Connor. Three years earlier they had voted with the liberals to sustain a Missouri law setting limits on campaign contributions, reaffirming that the *Buckley* rationale preventing the appearance of corruption constituted a sufficient rationale for regulation.

For Rehnquist, often characterized as an archconservative, to be considered a potential swing voter showed that the issue of campaign finance reform, on the Court as in Congress, cut across traditional conservative-liberal lines. In prior cases the chief justice had voted to uphold bans on corporate and union contributions, on the grounds that Congress had the power to decide what needed to be done to prevent corruption or its appearance in the world of politics.

At the same time, Rehnquist also balked at laws that hobbled political parties. In 2001 he joined Scalia, Thomas, and Kennedy in dissenting from a 5–4 ruling that upheld federal limitations on amounts political parties could spend in coordination with the campaigns of their federal candidates. He saw no possibility of parties corrupting their own candidates; parties are linked to candidates, he reasoned, and "breaking this link would impose significant costs on speech" (*Colorado II*).

* * *

At ten o'clock on the morning of Monday, September 8, 2003, the clerk of the US Supreme Court ordered all persons in the great courtroom to rise, and—as the nine justices filed in from behind the velvet curtains to take their seats—to come forward if they had business with the Court. Then, after he had intoned the ritual "God save this honorable court," Chief Justice William H. Rehnquist banged his gavel and called the only case on the docket for that special session, *McConnell v. Federal Election Commission*.

Then followed four hours of intense questions and answers, at the end of which even experienced Court watchers could not determine whether five votes existed to uphold the law or strike it down. Uncharacteristically, Justice O'Connor asked few questions and seemed mainly concerned about how to draft a ruling that could strike down parts of the law in a way that would not overturn *Buckley v. Valeo*. As expected, Justice Scalia attacked the law at every opportunity, at one point stopping to read the text of the First Amendment out loud and declaring that "it's a very simple text," the meaning of which ought to be obvious to all. Justice Breyer seemed to support the law, suggesting that its total ban on soft money could be justified on the basis of administrative convenience—not normally a winning argument in First Amendment cases—but that here it would in fact be too difficult to sort out portions that could legally go to state parties.

That in turn prompted the chief justice to comment that he did not find administrative reasons good enough to justify speech restrictions. Such regulations might be acceptable under the tax code, Rehnquist said, but not under the First Amendment. If there was any surprise, it was in Rehnquist's seeming hostility to BCRA and in intimations that perhaps he had been wrong in his earlier votes upholding campaign finance regulations. Under the *Austin* decision, the Court had held that huge corporate treasuries have little correlation to the public's support of the corporation's political views, an idea that had been used as a rationale for parts of BCRA. Rehnquist now seemed to cast doubt on that reasoning, suggesting that the "whole purpose" of the First Amendment was to allow expressions of unpopular views.

Neither side got a free ride during oral argument, and after four hours of intense questioning of the lawyers by the justices, Chief Justice Rehnquist banged his gavel and declared, "The case is submitted." Now the justices would have to sift and weigh the competing constitutional arguments, and in order to achieve at least some of the expedited treatment Congress had requested, they would have to move a good deal faster than the district court. They did, handing down their decision just three months later.

* * *

Because BCRA will be the focus of the cases that came after *McConnell* and leading up to *Citizens United* and *McCutcheon*, it is important to see what the justices decided, and their rationales for doing so.

Unlike many laws, even those with multiple parts, all of which focus on the same object, the BCRA's different titles addressed multiple issues that, despite the relation all bore to campaign finance, rested on different constitutional grounds and needed to be addressed separately. A justice might well vote to uphold the ban on soft money but not the restrictions on electioneering communications. It surprised no one when the Court handed down eight separate opinions, nor when only five justices formed the majority in the vote on some key provisions.

Back when the Court heard *Buckley*, the justices of that era had divided the ruling into sections, each assigned to a different member of the Court. There had been four hours of oral argument on November 10, 1975; the justices met in conference within a day or two, voted, divided up the work, and handed down their joint opinion on January 30, 1976—a rather remarkable eighty-one-day turnaround. A similar division of labor may well have occurred in *McConnell*. Three separate opinions dealing with the major titles, each commanding a majority, constituted the opinion of the Court.

Justices John Paul Stevens and Sandra Day O'Connor coauthored the lead opinion, dealing with BCRA Titles I and II, joined by David Souter, Ruth Bader Ginsburg, and Stephen Breyer.

Chief Justice William Rehnquist wrote the opinion with respect to Titles III and IV, joined by O'Connor, Antonin Scalia, Anthony Kennedy, and Souter, and in part (all except for one provision) by Stevens, Ginsburg, and Breyer, and also in part (except for four provisions) by Clarence Thomas.

Justice Breyer dealt with Title V, joined by Stevens, O'Connor, Souter, and Ginsburg.

Justice Scalia, although concurring in Titles III and IV, dissented with respect to Title I and part of Title II, and concurred in part and dissented in part regarding Title V.

Justice Thomas, joined by Scalia, concurred with various parts of the Rehnquist opinion, dissented in part regarding Title II, and dissented fully from the Court's holding on Titles I and V.

Justice Kennedy, joined by Rehnquist, and in most parts by Scalia and Thomas, dissented as to the holding on Titles I and II.

Chief Justice Rehnquist, joined by Scalia and Kennedy, dissented with respect to Titles I and V.

Justice Stevens, joined by Ginsburg and Breyer, dissented on the ruling on standing regarding one section, and would have upheld §305 on its merits.

Some justices took a more theoretical approach to the problem, setting up First Amendment standards and then asking whether or not BCRA violated them. This view—a First Amendment jurisprudence based on strict scrutiny—had been the theory that Senator McConnell and his allies had pushed in their briefs and arguments in both the district court and High Court, and that Judge Henderson had championed in her lower court opinion. On the other hand, several justices adopted the view of the defenders of BCRA—namely, that real political-world facts indicated that the pre-BCRA regulatory scheme failed to prevent corruption or its appearance, and that the law had been narrowly tailored to address this problem, the position taken by Judge Kollar-Kotelly. Those justices taking this stance also showed a very large deference to Congress and its judgment regarding the severity of the problem of corruption or its appearance in campaign finance, a deference unusual in cases involving the First Amendment.

The lead opinion, coauthored by Justices Stevens and O'Connor, followed this latter approach and upheld most of the provisions in BCRA Titles I and II. With regard to the soft money and related provisions of Title I embedded in different parts of §323, the majority chose not to apply the strict scrutiny standard often associated with the First Amendment, but adopted the less rigorous standard that had been utilized in *Buckley*—namely, whether the regulations had been "closely drawn." Just as in *Buckley*, the Court drew a distinction between campaign contributions and expenditures and held that contribution limits imposed only a marginal restraint on the contributor's right to engage in communication. Beyond that, the majority accepted congressional reasoning: that the government had an important interest in preventing "both the actual corruption threatened by large financial contributions and the eroding of public confidence in the electoral process through the appearance of corruption." Finally, because Congress in its lengthy deliberations had properly relied on *Buckley* and its progeny, the Court had powerful incentives to adhere to stare decisis considerations—that is, letting the rulings in earlier cases guide the Court's current deliberations. The majority saw the issues in the light of *Buckley*, and therefore rejected the plaintiffs' claims that the type of speech and associational burdens imposed by BCRA were substantially different from the burdens imposed earlier by *Buckley.*

Section 323(a), the key provision of Title I, met with approval because the governmental interest in preventing corruption or its appearance in federal races provided sufficient importance to justify contribution limits. This interest is so important that it can support not only restrictions on contributions themselves but also laws designed to prevent the circumvention of these limits. Conceding that it would be difficult to establish explicit quantitative measures of corruption, the Court essentially said Congress did not have to do so: "The idea that large contributions to a national party can corrupt or, at the very least, create the appearance of corruption of federal candidates and officeholders is neither novel nor implausible." Sufficient evidence had been presented to show that the uses of soft money could lead to actual corruption or its appearance, and Congress met First Amendment requirements by closely drawing its restrictions to meet its goal.

Because §323(a) carried such importance, the Court answered each argument that had been brought up against it. It rested upon a sufficient governmental interest and had been narrowly drawn. It was not impermissibly overbroad because it subjected all funds raised to FECA's hard money limits. Because the record showed the close relationship between national parties and state and local parties, Congress could legitimately conclude that party activities connected to a federal election at any level could be regulated in order to prevent corruption and its appearance. By the same token, the ban on national parties soliciting or directing soft money contributions could not be characterized as overbroad; the committees remained free to solicit unlimited amounts of hard money. Although conceivably the ban might adversely affect the speech and associational rights of minor parties, no evidence had been presented to show that this would actually happen, so the Court would not strike down the provision on a facial challenge. Similarly, the claim that BCRA unconstitutionally interfered with the ability of national committees to associate with state and local committees failed to persuade the Court. Nothing in the law prevented them from cooperating, except in regard to the uses of soft money.

The Court also found §323(b), prohibiting state and local parties from using soft money for activities affecting federal elections, to be closely drawn to confront an important objective, and therefore constitutional. This section, perhaps more than any other, highlighted the deference the majority showed to Congress. Looking at the record, the Court pointed out what Congress and everyone knew—close ties and a high level of coordination existed between national parties and their state and local affiliates. Congress thus had justifiable reason to ban the use of soft money by state and local party committees for a variety of purposes that could affect federal elections. Congress had legitimately worried that, given this close connection, soft money could work its way into the political process from the state and local levels upward just as effectively as from the national parties downward:

> Congress both drew a conclusion and made a prediction. Its conclusion, based on the evidence before it, was that the corrupting influence of soft money does not insinuate itself into the political process solely through national party committees. Rather, state committees function as an alternate avenue for precisely the same corrupting forces. Indeed, both candidates and parties already ask donors who have reached the limit on their direct contributions to donate to state committees. There is at least as much evidence as there was in *Buckley* that such donations have been made with the intent—and in at least some cases the effect—of gaining influence over federal officeholders. Section 323(b) thus promotes an important governmental interest by confronting the corrupting influence that soft-money donations to political parties already have.

The plaintiffs, aware that the section might be upheld, had proposed an alternative argument: that even if this provision served legitimate interests, it had not been closely drawn, and therefore unjustifiably burdened associational interests protected by the First Amendment. The Court rejected this argument out of hand, noting that although the rules affected some state campaigns for nonfederal offices, these activities had already been brought under the umbrella of acceptable federal regulation by the Federal Election Commission's pre-BCRA allocation rules. State campaigns already had to be funded in part by hard money because the activities affected federal as well as nonfederal campaigns.

The Court found that the ban on political party committees at any level soliciting funds for, or making direct contributions to, nonprofit groups, §323(d), was not facially invalid. No evidence had been presented to show that a real transgression of associational rights would take place, and Congress had ample reason to draft this provision to prevent circumvention of the soft money rules. Stevens and O'Connor, the chief drafters of this opinion, clearly recognized the validity of the government's insistence that one had to look at the law not in the abstract, but in light of the conditions and practices that made up the real political world.

In a footnote to this section, they pointed out that these groups, although qualifying for nonprofit status, were far from politically neutral. Indeed, the record showed that "many of the targeted tax-exempt organizations engage in sophisticated and effective electioneering activities for the purpose of influencing federal elections, including waging broadcast campaigns promoting or attacking particular candidates and conducting large-scale voter registration and GOTV [get out the vote] drives." They cited in particular an effort in the final weeks of the 2000 presidential campaign, when the NAACP's nonprofit National Voter Fund registered more than two hundred thousand people, promoted a GOTV hotline, ran three newspaper print ads, and made several direct mailings, funded primarily by a $7 million contribution from an anonymous donor.

The Court upheld two other parts of §323—the ban on federal officeholders or candidates from soliciting soft money in connection with a federal election, §323(e); and the ban on state and local candidates or officeholders from using soft money to fund ads promoting or attacking federal candidates, §323(f). Neither provision violated the First Amendment, and both constituted a logical and closely drawn effort by Congress to prevent circumvention of the general ban on soft money.

Several of the plaintiffs argued, "unpersuasively," as the Court described it, that Title I exceeded Congress's Election Clause authority to "make or alter" rules governing federal elections, or that it violated basic principles of federalism by impairing the states' authority to regulate their own elections. The proper test, the majority found, was whether the federal government had commandeered state officials to carry out a federal policy. Title I regulated not state conduct, but that of private entities, candidates, and party committees. Moreover, Title I left states free to impose their own restrictions on state campaign finance procedures.

The Court also dismissed the equal protection argument, in which plaintiffs claimed that political parties had been discriminated against in favor of special interest groups that remained free to raise soft money for voter registration and similar activities. The Court noted that BCRA actually favored the parties by raising the limits on the amount of hard money they could receive for party-building activities. In a passage that clearly showed how the majority favored the arguments of fact over those of theory, and that also indicated the deference paid to Congress, the opinion noted: "Congress is fully entitled to consider the real-world differences between political parties and interest groups when crafting a system of campaign finance regulation."

So far, defenders of BCRA could not have asked for more. A majority of the Supreme Court had reversed those portions of the lower court opinion invalidating parts a, b, and d of the §323 ban on soft money, and had confirmed the lower court's ruling on the constitutionality of parts e and f. They would also be pleased with how the majority treated Title II, with its controversial ban on issue advertisements and the timing of certain types of "electioneering communications." In dealing with Title II, however, although the justices could look at the facts, they could not ignore the vast body of First Amendment jurisprudence that the Court had developed over the previous half century.

Title II dealt with various issues of electioneering speech, including strict reporting requirements, controls on time, and the mandate that sponsors of issue ads identify themselves. The Court upheld the detailed reporting requirements of BCRA as well as its broad definition of what constituted an electioneering communication—"any broadcast, cable, or satellite communication that clearly identifies a candidate for federal office," is targeted to a relevant electorate, and that airs within a specific time period (sixty days before a general election and thirty days before a primary).

The plaintiffs complained that the new law, by failing to draw the *Buckley* distinction between contributions and expenditures, violated their First Amendment right to speech, and especially to this type of speech, political communication. If they avoided *Buckley*'s "magic words" as well as the similar conclusion the Court had drawn in *Federal Election Commission v. Massachusetts Citizens for Life* (*MCFL*) (1986), then issue ads fell outside the limits of congressional power to regulate. The First

Amendment trumped even important considerations regarding campaign rules.

The majority rejected this claim and held that the express advocacy provisions (the magic words of *Buckley* and *MCFL*) had never been a constitutional ruling, but merely part of the Court's statutory interpretation of FECA. In that footnote, and in *MCFL*, the Court had simply tried to fix a potential problem of vagueness and overbreadth in the statute by refining the general idea with some specific suggestions.

The "magic words," so long interpreted by nearly everyone as a hard-and-fast constitutional rule, had been, at least according to five justices, little more than a suggestion on how to refine a vague law and avoid nullifying it. Congress, therefore, had the power to regulate at least some additional types of political speech even if it passed the magic words test.

The majority then had to face the basic First Amendment challenge—namely, that the phrase "electioneering communication" was both overbroad and underinclusive in how it dealt with different types of political speech. To begin with, using their new interpretation of what the *Buckley* magic words test had been, the Court announced that its consideration of the plaintiffs' challenge would be "informed by our earlier conclusion that the distinction between express advocacy and so-called issue advocacy is not constitutionally compelled." Given that assumption, the Court found that the government did, in fact, have the necessary interest to regulate both types of speech, namely, the prevention of corruption or its appearance in the political process.

The five justices engaged in what surely must be considered judicial sleight of hand:

> In light of our precedents, plaintiffs do not contest that the Government has a compelling interest in regulating advertisements that expressly advocate the election or defeat of a candidate for federal office. Nor do they contend that the speech involved in so-called issue advocacy is any more core political speech than are words of express advocacy.... Rather, plaintiffs argue that the justifications that adequately support the regulation of express advocacy do not apply to significant quantities of speech encompassed by the definition of electioneering communications.

This argument fails to the extent that the issue ads broadcast during the thirty- and sixty-day periods preceding federal primary and general elections are the functional equivalent of express advocacy. The justifications for the regulation of express advocacy apply equally to ads aired during those periods if the ads are intended to influence the voters' decisions and have that effect.

In fact, plaintiffs had never conceded any such thing. They operated within the context of *Buckley's* magic words test but had never conceded that issue advocacy fell into the same category. Moreover, the Court failed to deal with true issue advocacy. If the NRA ran an ad that said, "A right to bear arms is protected by the Second Amendment and cannot be abridged by Congress. When you go to vote this fall, consider how valuable this right is to you," that constituted true advocacy of an issue that stood beyond a candidate's effort to get votes. It would be equally as true if the American Association for Retired Persons (AARP) ran an ad that detailed the rising cost of prescription drugs for seniors and then said, "Isn't it about time Congress acted on this issue?" Whether one agrees with the NRA's interpretation of the Second Amendment or the AARP's plan for subsidizing prescription drugs, these are in fact true issue ads and ones that bear directly on the political process. If this is not the core political speech that the Court and scholars have proclaimed to be especially protected by the First Amendment, then what is?

In an important decision affecting nonprofit entities, the Court upheld the district court's ruling that BCRA §204 extended the ban on using general treasury funds to pay for electioneering communications to nonprofit groups, a ruling that followed directly from the *Beaumont* decision earlier in the year.

In one of the few victories for the plaintiffs in this part of the opinion, the Court agreed with the district court's invalidation of §213, requiring political parties to choose between coordinated and independent expenditures in the period after the convention and before the election. This provision, according to the Court, placed an unconstitutional burden on the parties' right to make unlimited expenditures. Even though the amount of speech involved here was relatively small, it was still core political speech, and the government did not have a sufficiently compelling interest in regulating it.

Finally, the Court affirmed the district court's ruling upholding §214, extending to political parties the rule that expenditures controlled by or coordinated with a candidate will be treated as contributions. The Court observed that ever since *Buckley* it had protected truly independent expenditures, but at the same time it had noted that "independent expenditures may well provide little assistance to the candidate's campaign and indeed may prove counterproductive." Thus there was little danger that such expenditures would lead to any form of quid pro quo or other improper commitment from the candidate. This rationale, that wholly independent expenditures posed little danger of corruption, nonetheless could pose problems if there was "a wink or nod" that a certain type of seemingly independent expenditure would be useful to the candidate. This could easily be done through the political party rather than the candidate, but the result would be the same. Nor does the absence of any explicit agreement matter, since there had never been a requirement that coordination between candidates and others be overt or in the form of a contract. Congress had sufficient justification to extend the same strictures that existed on candidates and allegedly independent expenditures to political parties.

In conclusion, the five justices noted:

> Many years ago we observed that "to say that Congress is without power to pass appropriate legislation to safeguard . . . an election from the improper use of money to influence the result is to deny the nation in a vital particular the power of self-protection." We abide by that conviction in considering Congress' most recent effort to confine the ill effects of aggregated wealth on our political system. We are under no illusion that BCRA will be the last congressional statement on the matter. Money, like water, will always find an outlet. What problems will arise, and how Congress will respond, are concerns for another day. In the main we uphold BCRA's two principal, complementary features: the control of soft money and the regulation of electioneering communications.

The paragraph is noteworthy in that it makes no mention of the First Amendment, but rather focuses on the power of Congress to prevent corruption in the electoral process. There is a sense of realpolitik in its rather bleak assumption that no matter what Congress has done in

BCRA, it will not be the last word on reform, since people with money will always find new and innovative ways to get that money into the system, where willing candidates and parties will be eager to accept it. The justices had no idea how soon this prediction would be borne out.

*   *   *

Although the majority opinion regarding Titles I and II did not go unchallenged, other sections of the decision conveyed the views of five or more justices in reference to Titles III, IV, and V.

Chief Justice Rehnquist delivered that part of the opinion dealing with Titles III and IV, and here he had a far larger majority than did the five justices who prevailed on Titles I and II. Justices O'Connor, Scalia, Kennedy, and Souter joined in his entire opinion; and Stevens, Ginsburg, and Breyer joined in all but one section of it. Justice Thomas joined in regard to most of the sections. This is the shortest of all the opinions, with the chief justice allotting at most two paragraphs to most sections, one stating the complaint and the other dismissing it. The Court reaffirmed the district court and dismissed one complaint after another on the grounds that the plaintiffs lacked standing to bring the suit in a facial challenge to the law.

The problems of facially challenging a law manifested themselves almost immediately as the chief justice dealt with §305 of Title III. It required broadcast stations to provide the lowest unit charge to political advertisers beginning forty-five days before a primary and sixty days before a general election, once the candidate promised that there would be no reference to another candidate for the same political office, and that the candidate identified him- or herself at the end of the ad and stated approval of the ad. Senator McConnell claimed that since he intended to run advertisements critical of his opponents in the future, and that he had run them in the past, he had sufficient standing to challenge the law.

"Standing" simply means that a party bringing suit has the right to participate in the litigation. For example, a business owner whose real estate taxes are raised in what he or she considers an unfair manner can challenge the law because he or she could suffer material losses if the tax hike goes into effect. The parent of a child injured in an automobile accident may bring suit on behalf of a daughter who, as a minor, may not be permitted to sue. A person who philosophically opposes the death penalty may not, however, enter a case in which a convicted murderer sentenced to death is appealing the punishment; that person has no direct interest—other than his or her views on capital punishment—and these are insufficient to give him or her standing.

When bringing a facial challenge to a law—that is, a challenge to a law before it goes into effect, on the grounds that it violates some provision of the Constitution—standing is very important. The person bringing the suit must be able to show that he or she, because of his or her position, or holdings, or beliefs (if the law regulates expression), will be directly harmed once the law is implemented. Standing must be specific; a direct nexus must be shown between the person's plans or holdings or beliefs and the operation of the law. To use the death penalty example again, if a state passed a law changing the method of execution from the gas chamber to beheading, a person who opposed capital punishment—no matter how sincere that belief—could not challenge the law; on the contrary, an inmate on death row would certainly have standing to claim that the new method violated the Eighth Amendment ban on cruel or unusual punishment.

The fact that McConnell had run ads critical of his opponents before and planned to do so again did not, in the eyes of the justices, give him the requisite standing. After briefly summarizing how important the Court considered standing under the provisions of Article III of the Constitution, Rehnquist pointed out that Senator McConnell's current term would not expire until January 2009, so that the earliest §305 would apply to him would be in the primary and general election of 2008: "This alleged injury in fact is too remote temporarily to satisfy Article III standing.... Because we hold that the *McConnell* plaintiffs lack standing to challenge §305, we affirm the District Court's dismissal of the challenge to BCRA §305."

Rehnquist made short work of §§304 and 316, the "millionaire provisions" that allowed differential contribution limits for opponents of self-financed wealthy candidates. The Court could find no "cognizable injury that was 'fairly traceable' to BCRA." Moreover, as the district court had noted, none of the plaintiffs was a candidate in an election in which the millionaire provisions would apply, and so the Court affirmed the lower tribunal's dismissal of the complaint.

Standing did not play a role in the McConnell group's challenge to

§311, which required that communications authorized by a candidate or political committee clearly identify the sponsor, and that if the ad had not been authorized by the candidate, and did not announce who paid for it, it lacked authorization. McConnell had claimed that this and all other limits on communication violated the First Amendment. The Court disagreed. It considered that providing this information bore "a sufficient relationship to the important governmental interest of 'shedding the light of publicity' on campaign financing."

The only part of Title III that the Court struck down involved the prohibition against contributions by minors, §318. The Court noted that minors enjoy the protection of the First Amendment, and although the Court had upheld some limits on contributions, as in *Buckley*, as well as a total ban on direct contributions by corporations and unions, it had never approved a total ban on contributions by individuals. To justify such a ban the government would have to show a "sufficiently important interest," and that the remedy had been "closely drawn," in order to avoid an "unnecessary abridgement" of the First Amendment. The government claimed that §318 prevented wealthy parents from using their children as conduits to circumvent federal contribution limits. The government had shown no evidence that this actually occurred, and the Court believed that existing state and federal laws prevented adults from circumventing the limits. Children, therefore, retained the right to make contributions.

In the only challenge to a Title IV provision, the Court dismissed the National Right to Life's argument that the district court had erred in granting intervener-defendant status to Senators McCain and Feingold and others under §403(b) because they lacked standing. The opinion did not really address this issue but neatly sidestepped it. "It is clear," wrote the chief justice, "that the Federal Election Commission has standing, and therefore we need not address the standing of the intervener-defendants, whose position here is identical to the FEC's."

The brevity of the disposition of the Title III provisions reflected the fact that none of them, with the exception of the ban on contributions by minors, really struck at the core political speech guaranteed by the First Amendment. Assuring lowest rate schedules in a specific time period, indexing contribution limits to reflect inflation, and the identification of sponsors of political advertisements could be seen primarily as technical adjustments to laws previously upheld. As to the millionaire provision, the Court followed a long-standing policy of not deciding an issue until ripe—that is, until it had a plaintiff with standing who could show actual injury. Compared with the far more substantive issues in Titles I and II, the Court found Title III matters easy.

* * *

Justice Stephen Breyer wrote that part of the opinion dealing with Title V of BCRA, requiring broadcasters to keep detailed records of political advertisements and requests for time. In upholding the provisions, Breyer was joined by Stevens, O'Connor, Souter, and Ginsburg, the same five who constituted the majority regarding Titles I and II. The *McConnell* plaintiffs, including the National Association of Broadcasters, claimed that §504 imposed onerous administrative burdens that had no justification, and therefore violated the First Amendment. The lower court had accepted this argument and had found §504 facially unconstitutional. The slim five-justice majority, however, disagreed and reversed the district court, holding §504 valid.

Section 504 had three separate provisions. Broadcasters had to keep records of "candidate requests"—that is, requests made by or on behalf of a candidate; "election message requests"—advertisements that referred either to a candidate or to any election for a federal office; and "issue requests," made by anyone in which the content related to a "national legislative issue of public importance," or otherwise relating to a "political matter of national importance."

The Court found no problem in upholding candidate requests, since the Federal Communications Commission (FCC) had required similar records in one form or another since 1938. McConnell and the National Association of Broadcasters called this revised rule "intolerably burdensome and evasive"; Breyer said that the majority could not understand this claim. The FCC had over the years reported on what effort it took for licensees to comply with its rules, and estimated that the candidate request report imposed a burden of no more than six to seven hours of work per year on regular radio and television outlets and less than one hour on cable systems. "That burden means annual costs of a few hundred dollars at most," Breyer wrote, "a microscopic amount compared to the many millions of dollars of revenue broadcasters receive from candidates who wish to advertise." Moreover, the candidate records were not unique; broadcasters had to keep many other types of records to comply with FCC regulations.

With regard to the issue request, the *McConnell* plaintiffs argued that the terms "political matter of national importance" and "national legislative issue of public importance" were unconstitutionally vague or overbroad. The Court, however, found this language no more vague or overbroad than language Congress had used to impose other reporting obligations on broadcasters. (Unlike the print media, which enjoy extensive, in fact almost total, protection from Congress under the Press Clause, the broadcast media, at least constitutionally, have been treated quite differently, with Congress able to impose wide-ranging controls.) The Court admitted that the record keeping might be more burdensome than some FCC requirements, but also less problematic than others. In addition, §504 only required reporting the fact of a request, and the name and address of the person or group making the request; it did not ask for information about the content of the proposed ad. As a result, the Court found no First Amendment bar to §504 in terms of a facial challenge, but once the law went into effect, should there be an actual damage, then plaintiffs remained free to raise a constitutional argument on whether §504, as applied, violated their First Amendment rights.

* * *

The heart of the dissents by Chief Justice Rehnquist and Justices Scalia, Kennedy, and Thomas focused on the majority opinion concerning the Title I ban on soft money, and the Title II ban on certain types of electioneering communication.

As we have seen, the central issue for the majority was defining the type of political corruption that Congress could properly address. Definition mattered, because in *Buckley* the Court had sustained regulations impinging on First Amendment rights in order to curb corruption or the appearance of corruption. Given the recent experience of Watergate, "corruption" and "the appearance of corruption" meant something concrete and brought to mind images of people with cash-stuffed satchels going in and out of the Nixon campaign headquarters. Defenders of BCRA, however, wanted the Court to expand that notion, to look at the subtle but nonetheless corrupting effects that soft money had on the political process.

The four dissenters rejected this view and stood by the notion that corruption had to be overt—the trading of votes for dollars or something close to such a quid pro quo. They found the alleged proof of corruption offered by BCRA defenders insufficient to justify such major inroads on First Amendment rights. The majority rejected that view as "crabbed" and said that it "ignores precedent, common sense, and the realities of political fund-raising exposed by the record in this litigation." Corruption no longer meant a simple trade of votes for dollars, Stevens and O'Connor wrote, but "the manner in which parties have sold access to federal candidates and officeholders that has given rise to the appearance of undue influence. It is not unwarranted for Congress to conclude that the selling of access gives rise to the appearance of corruption."

But the dissents, especially the lead opinion by Justice Anthony Kennedy, which the other three signed in whole or in part, raised serious questions about the First Amendment and the degree to which it could be curtailed by Congress in an effort to cure the political system of alleged corruption. If the majority had deferred to Congress and accepted the fact-based view of the defenders of BCRA, the dissenters proved far less willing to allow Congress, just because it said a problem existed, to interfere with the traditional protections of free speech. Kennedy wasted no time in invoking the First Amendment:

> The First Amendment guarantees our citizens the right to judge for themselves the most effective means for the expression of political views and to decide for themselves which entities to trust as reliable speakers. Significant portions of Titles I and II of the Bipartisan Campaign Reform Act of 2002 constrain that freedom. These new laws force speakers to abandon their own preference for speaking through parties and organizations. And they provide safe harbor to the mainstream press, suggesting that the corporate media alone suffice to alleviate the burdens the Act places on the rights and freedoms of ordinary citizens.

Until this case, Kennedy claimed, the Court had accepted but two principles to determine the validity of campaign finance restrictions. The first had been that of countering corruption, which he defined as an agreement for a quid pro quo between officeholders or candidates on the one hand and donors seeking to influence them on the other.

The second had been the existence of large sums of money in corporate form—namely, companies and unions—and by accepting the corporate form these entities had been blocked from contributions. These two rationales had been the basis for the Court's decisions in *Buckley, Austin,* and *National Right to Work Committee.*

Kennedy and the other dissenters did not want to expand the definitions that the Court had handed down in these cases, all of which required that Congress show that the provisions clearly supported the anticorruption rationale expounded in *Buckley,* and had been closely drawn to do so. "The perception of corruption that the majority now asserts is somehow different from the quid pro quo potential discussed" in those opinions, and the majority, Kennedy charged, had expanded that definition in violation of the clear commands not only of the First Amendment but also of past precedents. Kennedy found these new definitions far too vague and amorphous, so elastic as to allow almost any form of regulation that Congress chose to impose.

Kennedy spent a fair amount of time pointing out the obvious—namely, that the majority had in fact abandoned the quid pro quo basis found in *Buckley.* The majority said that it had done so, and explained why—that new conditions indicated that the old idea no longer sufficed; that instead of an out-and-out trade of votes for dollars, a new problem had arisen, access to the candidate or officeholder only by those who could contribute the large amounts of soft money that evaded FECA limits. Kennedy did not find the majority reasoning persuasive, nor did he accept their so-called commonsense view of modern political reality. "Access in itself," he wrote, "shows only that in a general sense an officeholder favors someone or that someone has influence on the officeholder. There is no basis, in law or in fact, to say favoritism or influence in general is the same as corrupt favoritism or influence in particular." By making that unwarranted conclusion, the majority "dismantles basic First Amendment rules."

Kennedy's dissent reflected, at least in part, the problems that had plagued the lower courts as well as Congress in passing BCRA. There had actually been very few instances of outright corruption; the quid pro quo type of deal had, fortunately, been relatively rare in recent US history. Watergate, which triggered the FECA amendments that eventually led to *Buckley,* had in many ways been a fluke. Although the defenders of BCRA had piled up thousands of pages of anecdotal material, their basic argument had been a sort of, "If there's smoke then there has to be fire," and the fire they attacked involved access to the men and women in office who could enact policies that would affect their interests. Those without money would have no access, and therefore would be shut out of the process.

But did this constitute corruption or its appearance? The BCRA said yes, and it would be wiser to close off the spigot of soft money before the situation reached an actual quid pro quo situation; purchasing access provided enough appearance of corruption. The majority accepted this reasoning, the dissenters did not, and the dissenters had a strong argument in claiming that this new definition of corruption imposed greater limits on the First Amendment than had *Buckley*. Their dissents reflected their bitterness at what they believed to be an abandonment not only of the rules developed in prior decisions but also of basic First Amendment principles.

Justice Kennedy—"This new definition of corruption sweeps away all protections for speech that lie in its path; [the decision] leaves us less free than before."

Justice Scalia—"If the Bill of Rights had intended an exception to the freedom of speech in order to combat this malign proclivity of the officeholder to agree with those who agree with him, and to speak more with his supporters than his opponents, it would surely have said so."

Justice Thomas—"Apparently, winning in the marketplace of ideas is no longer a sign that the ultimate good has been reached by free trade in ideas. It is now evidence of 'corruption.' This conclusion is antithetical to everything for which the First Amendment stands."

The heart of Scalia's dissent consisted of his attack on what he considered three fallacies inherent in the majority opinion: (1) money is not speech, (2) pooling money is not speech, and (3) speech by corporations can be abridged. Scalia made plain what everyone on the Court knew—namely, that in politics money buys expression, whether directly through the purchase of advertisements in one's own name, or less directly by contributions to a campaign or candidate who will then speak out on issues. For the majority, soft money, because of its potential for corruption, deserved less First Amendment protection than did other types of campaign expenditures. For the dissenters, political speech of any kind, made directly or purchased indirectly, constituted the core values protected by the First Amendment. The debate in *McConnell v. Federal Election Commission* was hardly new—it had appeared in the district court opinions, in the briefs before both courts, and in the debate that had gone on in Congress leading up to the passage of McCain-Feingold.

*   *   *

Judge Henderson had complained in the district court that judges had been like ships passing in the night, never touching one another, never actually coming to grips with the key issues. In fact, all three judges had touched on the salient questions, but because they differed so much they had been unable to forge a coherent judicial response to BCRA. That was less true of the Supreme Court. The five who made up the majority agreed that in trying to prevent corruption or its appearance, Congress had the compelling governmental interest to restrict some forms of political speech through campaign finance reform, and that it had done so in an appropriate, closely drawn manner.

The majority also expanded the meaning of corruption beyond the quid pro quo that had been at the heart of *Buckley* and its progeny and accepted the government's contention that soft money purchased access, a new but equally virulent form of corruption. This soft money paid for attack-issue advertisements that, for all practical purposes, rendered the magic words test of *Buckley* obsolete and therefore could be proscribed. The dissenters argued with these conclusions, and in each of the opinions there was a back-and-forth in which the majority responded to some claim by the dissenters, or the dissenters attempted to take apart the basis for the majority conclusion.

These themes that had emerged from the beginning went on to dominate the arguments before and within the Court. On the one hand, those who looked at what they saw as the real world of politics attempted to devise a scheme that, although perhaps circumscribing some First Amendment rights, could be justified because it would purify the political process. It would make election campaigns more honest and open in that they would not be distorted by millions of dollars of soft money and the appearance of attack advertisements that depended on those dollars.

On the other hand stood those who believed that the political process always involved a give-and-take between candidates and those interests seeking to present their case. Although conceding that any deal involving cash for votes should be illegal, they did not see soft money, issue advertisements, or other recent developments in the campaign process as necessarily bad. Certainly they did not view them as sufficient to warrant any limitation on political speech protected by the First Amendment.

In the end, five justices deferred to congressional findings and agreed with the defenders of the law that sufficient evidence existed to warrant the restrictions placed on campaign finance and on political speech. Their opinion emphasized what they saw as real evidence and common sense. Four did not see it that way, and their opinions upheld what had been the Court's devotion to the basic principle that under the First Amendment, political speech in any form is a core value that should not be restricted.

*　*　*

The academic and legal reaction to the decision proved almost unanimously negative. Lillian BeVier of the University of Virginia, a longtime advocate of political speech as the core of the First Amendment, found herself "largely dismayed" by the majority opinion and admitted, "One has, after all, been quite thoroughly vanquished." Robert F. Bauer, a lawyer specializing in election law, lamented the decision as a signal of how little the Court valued another First Amendment right. The decision, he declared, "signals the effective demise of the right of association in campaign finance jurisprudence." James Bopp Jr. and Richard E. Coleson, who represented several socially conservative groups in the case, angrily charged that the Court had shown Congress far too much deference, not in protecting the rights of the unborn but in "protecting incumbent politicians from the people." Other authors also complained that the Court had been too deferential to congressional findings, all to the detriment of core First Amendment values of speech and association

Although one might have expected such criticisms from lawyers on the losing side, the analysis by the distinguished law professor Richard A. Epstein proved equally critical. He denounced the decision as "yet another backward step in the march of constitutional law." Even if one conceded that Congress had the power to enact laws aimed at preventing corruption or its appearance in electoral campaigns, it had done so in a heavy-handed manner that deserved not the acquiescence of the Court but "an instant and merciless repudiation." Although Epstein believed that judges should normally show deference to legislative policy judgments, he argued that courts also had an independent role to play, a role the Supreme Court had completely abandoned in the *McConnell* case. The "dense network of regulations" under BCRA promised full employment for a generation of lawyers, but the bottom line "is less political speech." For that the Court would have to bear much of the blame.

Would BCRA work now that it had the blessing of the highest court in the land? Elizabeth Garrett, director of the University of Southern California's Center for the Study of Law and Politics, thought that the disclosure aspects of the law would probably be fairly effective, but they were the act's least controversial aspects. Moreover, by affirming BCRA's requirements, the Court had put its stamp of approval on other forms of campaign financial disclosure, and these rules "are the most widespread regulation of the campaign finance system, and they are the sole regulation in several electoral arenas," such as state and local elections. Beyond that, Professor Samuel Issacharoff of Columbia University expected few positive results in straightening out the morass that campaign finance had become. If history were any guide, all BCRA would do is "prompt new forms by which money seeks to influence, cajole, inform, capture, and even corrupt." Although the law banned soft money and attempted to limit hard money, in fact the law opened the gates to all sorts of hard money contributions, and in his view hard money could be just as corrosive an influence on the political process as soft.

* * *

Supporters of McCain-Feingold rejoiced. Thomas Mann and Norman Ornstein, two academics who had been involved with the bill from the beginning and who had testified in its defense, believed that the Court had acted properly. They conceded that perhaps they did not understand all of the doctrinal implications of the Court's decision, but what mattered was that they now had a bill with teeth in it. The bill's authors and advocates had won far more than they had expected to, in that the majority had upheld the ban on soft money and all its ancillary provisions, allowed regulation of issue ads, and required the media to keep public records of who asked for and purchased political advertising time. But in their celebration, perhaps they forgot the line in the majority's last paragraph: "Money, like water, will always find an outlet." The truth of that prediction would manifest itself far sooner than anyone had expected.

CHAPTER 8

From *McConnell* to *Citizens United*

In the days following the High Court's decision in the *McConnell* case, one heard the expected joyful statements from the bill's backers and regretful ones from those who had opposed it. The national political parties had already begun their preparations for the 2004 election campaigns to conform their fundraising and campaign expenditure programs to the new law. Although some optimists predicted that a new era in political democracy would be ushered in with the elimination of soft-money and false-issue ads, realists predicted that money—lots of money—would easily find its way into the political system through some other avenue. Senator Mitch McConnell (R-KY) accurately predicted that the law "will not remove one dime from politics. Soft money is not gone, it has just changed its address."

Before long not one but several outlets opened, and campaign money poured through them at a rate equal to or even greater than the floods of soft money in the 1990s. Well before American voters went to the polls in November 2004 to choose between George W. Bush and John Kerry, it became clear that this campaign would be—despite the best efforts of the Bipartisan Campaign Reform Act (BCRA)—the most expensive in the nation's history.

* * *

On the day the decision came down, Democrats, Republicans, and political commentators speculated on just what the new rules would mean. Under BCRA, an individual could give no more than $2,000 to a candidate and no more than $25,000 to a political party in an election cycle. Both parties had three major committees, the national committee that dealt with presidential campaigns, and both a House and a Senate committee. Bob Bauer, a Democratic campaign finance lawyer, told a reporter that in his view, *McConnell* "was not a good decision for the parties," since it would make it much more difficult for them to raise money.

Initially, it appeared that the Democrats, who had relied far more than the GOP on soft money, would be hardest hit by BCRA. The Democrats, according to political scientist and campaign finance scholar Gary Jacobson of the University of California at San Diego, "are going to be in trouble, and unless they could find—and quickly—alternatives to soft money, they are going to be at a major disadvantage." Representative Thomas M. Reynolds (R-NY), chair of the National Republican Congressional Committee, practically crowed in declaring, "Today's ruling breaks the Democrats' back." Even Jim Jordan, former director of the Democratic Senatorial Campaign Committee, conceded the decision is "particularly a blow to the Democratic Party."

In the end, BCRA did not appear to have affected the fundraising abilities of either party, although the deep ideological divisions and high passions of the 2004 presidential campaign may have induced more people to donate than might have done so at other times. Although Democrats, as usual, lagged behind Republicans in overall fundraising, they did not do badly. As of June 30, 2004, a benchmark period for measuring campaign contributions, the Democratic National Party had collected $230 million in hard money, more than double the $102 million it had raised at the same time in 2000. The Republicans also doubled their intake, receiving $381 million, up from $178 million four years earlier. By October the Democratic National Committee, the Republican National Committee, and the various congressional committees tied to the national parties had all exceeded the amounts raised in the 2000 election cycle.

Conditions for both parties were certainly not as bleak as the pessimists had predicted. McCain-Feingold had been on the books for nearly two years by the time the Supreme Court handed down its decision in *McConnell*. During that time party leaders collected millions of dollars in contributions, some of which would be prohibited after the law took effect. But the parties also looked at what other choices they had. Liberal Howard Dean's success on the internet and Richard Viguery's mass mailings for conservative groups showed that although it might take greater effort, money could still be raised. The internet especially offered parties a relatively inexpensive way to advertise as they raised money. Anyone who opened their Web browser from March 2004 onward—that is, after John Kerry secured the Democratic nomination—probably found an appeal, such as, "Buy George W. Bush a one-way ticket back to Crawford." This technique seemed to work very well for Kerry, who raised record amounts of money in the spring quarter, mostly from small contributors. At the same time, mass mailings are also profitable. The executive director of a national rights protection group once explained to me that all he needed was a 2 percent response to bring in more money than it cost for the mailing.

In the immediate aftermath of *McConnell*, one particular type of activist suddenly gained prominence on the political stage. In the past, candidates and parties had valued not only the wealthy individual who could write a six-figure or even seven-figure contribution but also the person, probably well-to-do but not necessarily rich, who could get other people to open their wallets. Under the new law, a campaign volunteer who got twenty-five people to give the maximum individual amount of $2,000 brought in $50,000 to the candidate's coffers, all legitimate "hard money." George W. Bush had early on recognized the value of these people and had created a special club of so-called Rangers, each of whom had raised at least $200,000 for his campaign. In 2004, he expanded this category and created new ones.

Adding further to the confusion, backers of BCRA, flush with their victory in the Court, announced that their next target would be the Federal Election Commission (FEC) itself. Senator Russ Feingold said that he, John McCain, Christopher Shays, and Martin Meehan had, as one of their top priorities, replacing the agency that had proven so ineffective in enforcing campaign finance laws.

Instead of worrying about reconstituting the FEC, McCain and company might well have paid attention to plugging some of the loopholes in the law they had so laboriously crafted. The Supreme Court itself had approved one such activity under the BCRA, noting that certain independent groups, organized under §527 of the tax code, "remain free to raise soft money to fund voter registration, get-out-the-vote activities, mailings, and broadcast advertising." Both Democrats and Republicans recognized the importance of this ruling. Republican lawyer Jan Baran said that *McConnell* "makes the world a safer place for billionaires and 527 organizations. Nonparty interest groups under the current law may raise and spend soft money and the political parties may not." Steve Rosenthal, chief executive of the pro-Democrat Americans Coming Together, one of the most prominent 527 groups, took the decision as a green light for his organization to inform, register, and turn out voters, and by "inform" he meant telling voters "about the failed policies of the Bush administration." Well before the Supreme Court handed down its decision, some of these 527s had started preparing for the 2004 presidential campaign.

While political operatives paid close attention to the fundraising details of McCain-Feingold and the Court's opinion upholding the statute's restrictions, scholars of the Court looked at something entirely different. Senator McConnell and his coplaintiffs attacking the law had mounted what is termed a "facial" challenge, that is, they complained that the law as written would harm them in the future. McConnell, for example, claimed that it would make it much more difficult for him to raise money for his reelection campaign, but he could not present any evidence that he had, in fact, suffered any harm. (The justices knew that he had just been reelected and would not have to run again for several years, so any potential damage would not be evident for a while.)

Courts for the most part do not like facial challenges, the claim that a law, as written, will one day harm them. There are, of course, some areas where a plaintiff can show that the provisions of a new law will definitely have a deleterious—and unconstitutional—effect, but these cases are relatively rare. As a result, when confronted by a facial challenge, unless the plaintiff can show that there will definitely be an immediate harm, the courts will sustain the statute as a matter of judicial deference.

On the other hand, an "as-applied" challenge presents courts with an entirely different issue. The plaintiff is saying that the law has gone into effect, and, as a result, I have suffered a harm. Now the court will look much more closely at the provisions that allegedly created the injury. The Constitution requires that the federal courts can only hear and decide on real cases or controversies. Facial challenges only present potential problems; as-applied suits are real and current. For those who studied the Court, some predicted that when McCain-Feingold faced as-applied challenges, the courts would not be so deferential.

Moreover, a different court would hear these cases. Chief Justice William H. Rehnquist died on September 3, 2005, and John G. Roberts Jr., who had once clerked for Rehnquist, became his successor in the center chair. Then Sandra Day O'Connor, a moderate conservative, retired in late 2005, to be replaced by Samuel A. Alito Jr. While Roberts did not for the most part differ jurisprudentially from Rehnquist, he believed more strongly in the rights of corporations to engage in the political process. Alito was far more conservative than O'Connor, who during her time on the bench had often been the swing vote in 5–4 decisions and had played a key role in upholding McCain-Feingold.

The first as-applied challenge to BCRA came soon enough. Section 203 prohibited any corporation from broadcasting, sixty days before an election, any communication that was targeted to the electorate and that named a federal candidate for elected office. Wisconsin Right to Life broadcast ads such as the following during the sixty days before the 2004 election:

> PASTOR: And who gives this woman to be married to this man?
> BRIDE'S FATHER: Well, as father of the bride, I certainly could. But instead, I'd like to share a few tips on how to properly install drywall. You put the drywall up . . .
> VOICE-OVER: Sometimes it's just not fair to delay an important decision. But in Washington it's happening. A group of senators is using the filibuster delay tactic to block federal judicial nominees from a simple "yes" or "no" vote. So qualified candidates don't get a chance to serve.

> It's politics at work, causing gridlock and backing up some of our courts to a state of emergency.

> Contact Senators Feingold and Kohn and tell them to oppose the filibuster.

> Paid for by Wisconsin Right to Life, which is responsible for the content of this advertising and not authorized by any candidate or candidate's committee.

One of the senators, Russ Feingold, was up for reelection in 2004, and although the ad had clearly been designed to criticize him, it did not specifically call for a vote against him. The committee claimed this was an "issue" ad, and therefore exempt from the sixty-day rule. The FEC disagreed and charged the group with violating §203, and a lower court ruled that the *McConnell* ruling did not allow an "as-applied" challenge to the BCRA. The High Court reversed that ruling and, in *Wisconsin Right to Life v. Federal Election Commission* (2006), sent it back to the lower court with orders to hear the case on its merits.

That same term, the Court heard *Randall v. Sorrell*, a challenge to a Vermont law that placed severe limits on both campaign expenditures and contributions. The Court reiterated the *Buckley* distinction between contributions and expenditures, although many people had thought (or hoped) that with the addition of Roberts and Alito the Court would finally abandon that holding. In a fractured 6–3 decision, it seemed that a majority of the justices were willing to revisit *Buckley* but decided that the Vermont law was not the right vehicle to do so. They voided the expenditure provisions on the basis of *Buckley* and then struck down the contribution limits as being too low. Under the law neither an individual nor a political party could contribute more than $400 to a candidate for statewide office over a two-year election cycle, including primaries. Although the Court had previously upheld donation caps, they had been much higher. As Justice Breyer, who wrote the plurality opinion explained, "We must recognize the existence of some lower bound."

The confusion of the Court can be seen in the six different opinions, what Stevens called "today's cacophony." Breyer sought a middle ground, but it is not clear if Roberts and Alito agreed with his reasoning. Kennedy, Scalia, and Thomas joined in the judgment but not in the reasoning, nor did they agree with each other. Thomas and Scalia repeated their views that all limits on campaign finance violated the First Amendment. Stevens, Souter, and Ginsburg would have upheld the limits, although Stevens wrote that he had become "convinced that *Buckley's* holding on expenditure limits is wrong, and that the time has come to overrule it." Souter and Ginsburg did not want to go that far.

Alito, although joining with Breyer, filed a separate opinion that the Court had not reconsidered its prior rulings because Vermont had not raised a sufficiently direct challenge to the *Buckley* and *McConnell* precedents. To some, it appeared that Alito was inviting exactly such a challenge. The following term he got it.

After the High Court had sent the *Wisconsin Right to Life* case back to the lower court, the group had prevailed, and now the FEC had appealed. Chief Justice Roberts announced the judgment of the Court and had a five-vote majority for the major holdings of his opinion. Restrictions on

TV ads paid for by corporate or union treasuries in the weeks before an election amounted to censorship of core political speech unless those ads explicitly urged a vote for or against a specific candidate. "Where the First Amendment is implicated," he wrote, "the tie goes to the speaker, not the censor." The only ads that could be kept off the air in the thirty days before a primary or sixty days before a general election were those "susceptible of no reasonable interpretation other than an appeal to vote for or against a specified candidate." Legitimate issue ads constituted core political speech and could not be restricted.

Only Alito joined that part of the opinion where Roberts upheld §203 as applied to candidate ads. Scalia, Kennedy, and Thomas preferred to override *McConnell* and strike down §203 as unconstitutional. In dissent, Souter, joined by Stevens, Ginsburg, and Breyer, charged that the majority had unjustifiably overruled the earlier decision. Moreover, the ads could have been run out of a PAC, or they could have omitted Feingold's name. Souter wrote, "What is called a 'ban' on speech is a limit on the financing of electioneering broadcasts by entities that insist on acting as conduits from the campaign war chests of business corporations."

The opinions in this case confound the normal descriptions of Supreme Court justices as "conservative" or "liberal." The five who made up the majority here are normally considered conservative, yet the majority opinion reads as if it could have been written by the American Civil Liberties Union (ACLU), which in fact opposed McCain-Feingold. These justices defended the First Amendment against efforts by Congress to restrict political speech. The dissenters, normally considered liberal (Justice Ginsburg had for many years headed a major ACLU program), upheld congressional power to regulate and limit speech in the name of political integrity.

Federal Election Commission v. Wisconsin Right to Life (2007) dealt only with §203, but it seemed very apparent that other parts of BCRA would be challenged on an as-applied basis and might well lead to voiding some of the law's most important provisions.

Justice Alito, who had seemingly invited more challenges to BCRA, wrote the majority opinion in the next case, *Davis v. Federal Election Commission* (2008), attacking §319(a), part of the so-called millionaire's amendment. The BCRA allowed an opponent in a House race to raise and spend more (in a coordinated campaign) if and when a rich candidate's personal funds exceed $350,000. When that happened, a new asymmetrical regulatory scheme would be triggered. The self-financing candidate remained subject to normal restrictions, but his or her opponent could receive individual contributions at treble the normal limit and could accept coordinated party expenditures without limit. A self-financing candidate, if he or she planned to spend in excess of $350,000, had to make additional financial disclosures to other candidates, their national parties, and the FEC.

Jack Davis ran for the House in 2004 and 2006 and lost both times to an incumbent. He notified the FEC, in compliance with §319(b), that he intended to spend $1 million. After the FEC informed him it had reason to believe he had violated §319 by failing to report personal expenditures during the 2004 campaign, he filed suit for a declaration that §319 is unconstitutional and sought an injunction to prevent the FEC from enforcing it in the 2006 election. The district court ruled that Davis had standing to sue but rejected his claims on the merits and granted the FEC summary judgment. Davis appealed.

The Supreme Court ruled that §319(a) and §319(b) violated the First Amendment. If §319(a)'s elevated contribution limits applied across the board to all candidates, Davis would have no constitutional basis for challenging them. Section 319(a), however, raised the limits only for non-self-financing candidates and only when the self-financing candidate's expenditure of personal funds caused the BCRA threshold to be exceeded. This Court had never upheld the constitutionality of a law that imposed different contribution limits for candidates competing against each other, and it agreed with Davis that this scheme impermissibly burdened his First Amendment right to spend his own money for campaign speech.

In *Buckley*, the Court had soundly rejected a cap on a candidate's expenditure of personal funds to finance campaign speech, holding that a "candidate ... has a First Amendment right to ... vigorously and tirelessly ... advocate his own election," and that a cap on personal expenditures imposed "a substantial," "clear," and "direct" restraint on that right. It found the cap at issue not justified by "the primary governmental interest" in "the prevention of actual and apparent corruption of the political process." *Buckley* is instructive here. While BCRA does not impose a cap on a candidate's expenditure of personal funds, it imposes an unprecedented penalty on any candidate who robustly exercises that First Amendment right, requiring him to choose between the right to engage in unfettered political speech and subjection to discriminatory fundraising limitations. The resulting drag on First Amendment rights is not constitutional simply because it attaches as a consequence of a statutorily imposed choice. Because §319(a) was unconstitutional, §319(b)'s disclosure requirements, which were designed to implement the asymmetrical contribution limits, were as well.

Observers by this point could discern a pattern. Although a majority of the nine justices might have been uncomfortable with the *Buckley* distinction between contributions and expenditures, they were not ready to do away with a distinction that more and more people found unjustified. A person giving a lot of money to a candidate may have had no other motive in mind than to help a person who espoused similar views on important matters. Both the *Buckley* decision and BCRA, on the other hand, viewed the motives of the donor with suspicion, attributing the contribution to a desire to influence the candidate's views or to gain access if he or she was elected. The distinction had been criticized from the time *Buckley* had been decided and had been an underlying assumption of BCRA. After *McConnell*, the first two cases attacking BCRA on an as-applied basis had been successful. Would any part of the law survive?

The next challenge to BCRA came in the lower courts. In January 2005, EMILY's List, a group dedicated to helping pro-choice women candidates, challenged multiple FEC regulations regarding use of federal hard money to pay for activities directed at both state and federal elections. Specifically, EMILY's List challenged an FEC regulation requiring organizations with both a federal political committee and an affiliated 527 organization to use federal hard money (i.e., funds raised in compliance with federal contribution limits) to pay at least 50 percent of its costs related to both federal and nonfederal elections (e.g., administrative expenses). EMILY's List also challenged the FEC's definition of "contribution" to include funds raised in response to solicitations that indicate the money will be used "to support or oppose" the election of federal candidates. Although EMILY's List lost in the district court, it won on appeal. In 2010, the US Court of Appeals for the DC Circuit struck down three challenged FEC regulations, holding that they violated the First Amendment and exceeded the FEC's authority (*EMILY's List v. Federal Election Commission* [2010]).

The three-judge panel (which included Brett Kavanaugh, who wrote the opinion) held that the First Amendment, as interpreted by the Supreme Court, protects the right of citizens to spend unlimited amounts to express their views about policy issues and candidates for public office. It also safeguards the right of citizens to band together and pool their resources as an unincorporated group or a nonprofit organization in order to express their views about policy issues and candidates for public office. The FEC regulations contravene these principles and violate the First Amendment. The Supreme Court did not take the case on appeal.

Here again, one must be very careful when trying to determine First Amendment views on the basis of "conservative" or "liberal." Kavanaugh, who would be appointed to the High Court in 2018 by Donald Trump, is widely viewed as staunchly conservative, yet he, like the conservatives then on the Supreme Court, took the position held by most liberals regarding the protection offered by the First Amendment. Moreover, the very conservative Judge Janice Rogers Brown, in a concurring opinion, opined that the Supreme Court had been wrong in making the *Buckley* dichotomy between contributions and expenditures, and she hoped the day would not be far off when they would correct this error.

* * *

Shortly thereafter, the High Court took a major step in dismantling McCain-Feingold. Section 441b prohibited corporations and unions from using money from their general treasuries to fund "electioneering communications," that is, broadcast advertisements mentioning a candidate in any context, The purpose of this section had been not only to reduce the amount of money candidates had to spend on television ads, but to reduce the influence of television itself in elections.

According to John Nichols and Robert W. McChesney, John Roberts was not only a defender but a champion of corporate influence in politics. *Wisconsin Right to Life* had done away with most restrictions on the airing of so-called issue ads. Roberts wanted a case that would give the Court an opportunity to overturn any remaining rules governing advertising by groups, including corporations. He found what he wanted with a case involving a relatively obscure right-wing group headed by a man who hated Bill and Hillary Clinton.

During the 2004 presidential election, Citizens United, a nonprofit 501(c)(4) organization devoted to conservative causes, filed a complaint with the FEC charging that advertisements for a Michael Moore film were in fact political ads barred by §203. The film, *Fahrenheit 9/11*, was a docudrama criticizing George W. Bush (running for reelection in 2004) and his administration for their handling of the terrorist attacks on September 11, 2001. The FEC dismissed the complaint after finding that the ads for the film did not mention any candidate names.

Citizens United then produced a documentary, *Celsius 41.11* (the temperature at which the brain begins to die), which attacked both Moore's film and the Democratic candidate, John Kerry. The FEC, however, ruled that showing the movie and advertisements for it would violate BCRA because, unlike Michael Moore, Citizens United was not a legitimate filmmaker. In response, David Bossie, the head of Citizens United, decided to make his group a bona fide film company.

Citizens United traces its roots back to Floyd Brown, the creator of the infamous Willie Horton ad in the 1988 presidential campaign. After George H. W. Bush won, Bossie embraced the notoriety of the ad and founded Citizens United. Using the Horton template, Bossie created highly partisan television spots and then ran direct-mail campaigns to fund their broadcast. In 1991, to take one example, the organization produced commercials in support of Clarence Thomas's nomination to the Supreme Court. The ads consisted mainly of disparaging the character of members of the Senate Judiciary Committee.

Although Citizens United engaged in a number of attacks on Bill Clinton during his presidency, it maintained a relatively low profile during George W. Bush's terms, except for its efforts to counter the Moore film and to get its own film into circulation. At the time, Citizens United had a total budget of $12 million a year, most of which came from individual donations, but a very small amount, roughly 2 percent, came from for-profit companies. It would be this minuscule contribution from corporate treasuries that would allow the Court to decide as it did.

After Bossie decided to turn the organization into a film studio, over the next few years it produced several movies, all with conservative themes, and many of them narrated by Newt and Callista Gingrich.

They included *Fire from the Heartland*, starring Michelle Bachmann; *The Gift of Life*, against abortion rights; and *Rediscovering God in America*, charging that the decline of the nation resulted from efforts to drive God out of the public square. Some of these found a small audience, but then Bossie found the subject he wanted most.

In 2007, the two leading candidates for the Democratic presidential nomination were Barack Obama and Hillary Clinton. Bossie had hated Mrs. Clinton from the previous decade, when her husband had been president. He now made *Hillary: The Movie*, a pastiche of newsreel footage, eerie music, and interviews with rabid partisans who accused Senator Clinton of all sorts of bad things—she's power-hungry, will lie to get what she wants, and other charges in a similar vein. About the only positive comment was that she did not look bad in a pantsuit.

Bossie wanted the movie to come out in late 2007, so that it would ruin Clinton during the 2008 primary season. Bossie also hoped that it would help the conservative cause and make money. He offered a cable company a million dollars to make *Hillary* available for free to its viewers, and then tried to get it accepted for video on demand. But all depended on how the FEC would classify the film. If the agency concluded that *Hillary* was a work of entertainment or journalism, like *Fahrenheit 9/11*, then Bossie could show it any way he wanted and at any time. But if the FEC determined it to be an "electioneering communication," then it would fall under §203 and could not be shown within thirty days of a primary and sixty days before a general election.

Bossie hired Jim Bopp, a well-known lawyer with extensive contacts within the conservative community, and Bopp went straight to the FEC to get a ruling. It surprised no one that the commission declared the film an "electioneering communication," for that was indeed what it was. Bopp and Bossie decided to fight this ruling and went to the US District Court for the District of Columbia. The three-judge panel dismissed Citizens United's request for an injunction against the FEC, so that it could air the movie while the trial was in progress. On July 18, 2008, the judges awarded summary judgment to the FEC and held that *Hillary: The Movie* had no other purpose than to inform the electorate that Clinton was unfit for office, that she would make the United States and the world a horrible place, and people should not vote for her. Under the special rules of BCRA, Citizens United appealed directly to the Supreme Court, which granted cert on November 14, 2008.

Although Bopp had a good reputation among conservatives and had been the winning lawyer in the *Wisconsin Right to Life* case, Bossie felt uneasy about him and began making phone calls to well-placed conservative politicians and activists. They all told him the same thing—get rid of Bopp and hire former solicitor general Ted Olson. It was Olson who stood up in court at oral argument on March 24, 2009.

Olson, an experienced member of the elite Supreme Court bar, understood that normally it takes a great deal of effort to get the justices to rule on a constitutional basis, since that often requires overturning a precedent. It would be far easier if he could convince them they did not have to touch any constitutional issues; all Citizens United needed to win was for the Court to agree that BCRA did not apply to documentaries or nonprofit organizations. He began, however, with a paean to the First Amendment and charged that the most precious of freedoms was being smothered by "the most complicated, expensive, and incomprehensible regulatory regimes ever invented by the administrative state." But all the Court needed to do was recognize that Congress had never intended BCRA to apply to small nonprofits like Citizens United.

Olson's modest approach seemingly disappointed Antonin Scalia. "So you're making a statutory argument now? You're saying this [film] isn't covered by [BCRA]." That's right, Olson agreed. He wanted the Court to decide the case on the narrowest possible statutory ground and thus avoid the bigger constitutional issues. Scalia seemed dissatisfied.

Malcolm Stewart, the deputy solicitor general, rose to defend the FEC's decision. Stewart had joined that office in 1993, had argued more than forty cases before the High Court, and had an enviable record of wins and awards. He was certainly experienced enough that he should have recognized the danger in a question posed by Samuel Alito, who considered McCain-Feingold broadly written, too broadly in fact. This case dealt with film, Alito noted, limiting it to broadcast and cable media. But could the law limit a corporation from "providing the same thing in a book? Would the Constitution permit the restriction of all of those as well?"

Yes, Stewart responded. Such restriction "could have been applied to additional media as well." Suddenly all of the justices were paying attention. "That's pretty incredible," Alito said, and asked if a campaign biography could be banned. Stewart, recognizing the error he had made, tried to backtrack. "I'm not saying it could be banned. I'm saying Congress could prohibit the use of corporate treasury funds and could require a corporation to publish it using its PAC."

Kennedy, who had always stood with the conservatives in matters of campaign finance, jumped in. Suppose an advocacy organization published a book. "Your position is that under the Constitution, the advertising for this book or the sale for the book itself could be prohibited within the sixty- and thirty-day periods."

"Yes," Stewart responded.

According to Jeffrey Toobin, neither Alito nor Kennedy had the instinct for the jugular, but Chief Justice John Roberts did, and he proceeded to push Stewart down the slippery slope. What if the book had one name, "one use of the candidate's name, it would be covered, correct?"

"That's correct," was the response. The chief justice pushed on. "It's a 500-page book, and at the end it says, and so vote for X, the government could ban that?"

"Well, if it says vote for X," Stewart replied, "it would be express advocacy and it would be covered by the preexisting Federal Election Campaign Act."

With that answer, Stewart—and through him the government—had taken a ridiculous position, namely, that the government could make it a criminal act to publish a five-hundred-page book if at the end it had one line that included a candidate's name. Did McCain-Feingold really authorize that? Could Congress even ban a book? Alito's question could have been answered any number of ways besides claiming that the government could restrict publications. How did Stewart, an experienced and highly competent appellate litigator, dig himself such a hole?

At the conference, after a 5–4 vote, the chief justice assigned the case to himself. From available evidence it appeared that he was willing to decide the case along the narrow lines that Ted Olson had proposed, a statutory interpretation that said BCRA did not apply to nonprofit organizations. Roberts's first draft did just that, and then Kennedy entered a concurrence that said the Court should have declared McCain-Feingold's restrictions unconstitutional. Moreover, Kennedy would have reversed the 1990 *Austin* decision, and even the century-old Tillman Act that prohibited corporate donations to campaigns. Scalia, Thomas, and Alito rallied to Kennedy's side, and Roberts withdrew his draft and assigned the opinion to Kennedy.

When Kennedy circulated his revised draft, the four liberals hit the ceiling. David Souter, who had already announced his retirement at the end of the term, wrote a blistering dissent that essentially accused the chief justice and the conservatives of manipulating decisions so as to get the results they wanted. He pointed out that the chief justice himself, in an earlier case that term, had berated the defendant's lawyer for raising an issue that had not been addressed in the briefs, and now he was joining in Kennedy's opinion that did just that.

Roberts understood that with the Court split as it was, there could be strong disagreement on any case. But Souter's opinion went far beyond that and attacked the fairness of the conservative justices and their willingness to discard precedent and rules whenever it suited their convenience. So Roberts came up with a face-saving (for him) idea. He would withdraw the majority opinion and put Citizens United down for reargument in the fall. On June 29, 2009, the last day of the term, the Court surprised everyone by announcing that the case had been restored to the docket. Moreover, the parties were told to file new briefs addressing a single issue: "For the proper disposition of this case, should the Court overrule either or both *Austin v. Michigan Chamber of Commerce*, 494 U.S. 652 (1990), and the part of *McConnell v. Federal Election Comm'n*, 540 U.S. 93 (2003), which addresses the facial validity of Section 203 of the Bipartisan Campaign Reform Act of 2002, 2 U.S.C. §441b?"

The Court rarely orders reargument; the last time it had done so was during the Burger years. Moreover, as court watchers knew, the order meant not that the Court was considering overruling the cases it cited, but that it in fact already had the votes to do so. The conservatives were so eager to do this that they did not want to wait until the traditional opening of the fall term—the first Monday in October—but set oral argument for September 9, 2009.

The case was Elena Kagan's first opportunity to appear before the Supreme Court as solicitor general, a position that President Obama had named her to only a few months earlier. She and her team knew they had a hopeless case, and despite the best efforts of the liberal members of the Court, the final vote was a foregone conclusion.

Roberts assigned the opinion to Kennedy, who during his tenure had shown a strong aversion to campaign finance limits. He had dissented in both *Austin* and *McConnell*, and his draft concurrence in *Citizens United* the previous spring had led the Court not only to reschedule the case but to issue a question calling the holdings in the prior cases into doubt. The fact that some 2 percent of Citizens United's budget came from corporate donors gave Kennedy and his allies the opportunity they wanted to tackle the government's restrictions on corporate money in elections, restrictions that dated back to the Tillman Act of 1907. Kennedy jumped right into it:

> The holding of *McConnell* rested to a large extent on an earlier case, *Austin*. *Austin* had held that political speech may be banned based on the speaker's corporate identity. In this case we are asked to reconsider *Austin* and, in effect, *McConnell*. . . . We hold that stare decisis does not compel the continued acceptance of *Austin*. The Government may regulate corporate political speech through disclaimer and disclosure requirements, but it may not suppress that speech altogether.

Kennedy went over the various troubles Citizens United had in trying to show *Hillary: The Movie*, and also various proposals put forth by both sides on how the case could be decided on narrower statutory grounds. The Court declined to do so because that would require "intricate case-by-case determinations to verify whether political speech is banned, especially if we are convinced that, in the end, this corporation has a constitutional right to speak on this subject." The Court could not decide the case on narrower grounds "without chilling political speech, speech that is central to the meaning and purpose of the First Amendment."

He then went into an extensive analysis of how the regulations promulgated by the FEC in accordance with McCain-Feingold had created an impossible maze into which corporations and other groups wandered at their peril. To show that the Court was not suddenly granting speech rights to corporations, he cited more than twenty cases that had extended First Amendment protection to corporations. "If the First Amendment has any force," he said, "it prohibits Congress from fining or jailing citizens, or associations of citizens, for simply engaging in political speech." He rejected outright the government claim that because corporations control so much wealth, allowing them to participate in the campaign process would have a distorting effect. To accept this rationale, he charged, "would permit Government to ban political speech simply because the speaker is an association that has taken on the corporate form."

Malcolm Stewart's stumbling answer that the FEC could also restrict the sale or advertising of books also came in for Kennedy's scorn. "This troubling assertion of brooding governmental power," he declared, "cannot be reconciled with the confidence and stability in civic discourse that the First Amendment must secure." Untrammeled political speech is indispensable in a democracy, "and this is no less true because the speech comes from a corporation rather than from an individual." Any governmental attempt to command how a person may get his or her information is censorship. "This is unlawful. The First Amendment confirms the freedom to think for ourselves."

At the core of the case stood a BCRA provision that set aside a brief period of time, before both primaries and general elections, when corporations could not fund political commercials. Kennedy saw this as out-and-out censorship: "By taking the right to speak from some and giving it to others, the Government deprives the disadvantaged person or class of the right to use speech to strive to establish worth, standing, and respect for the speaker's voice." The government, Kennedy declared, "may not by these means deprive the public of the right and privilege to determine for itself what speech and speakers are worthy of consideration. The First Amendment protects speech and speaker, and the ideas that flow from each."

One by one Kennedy went down the reasons put forth by the government to sustain not only *Austin* but also portions of McCain-Feingold and found them all wanting. The fear of corruption, which Kennedy implicitly defined as a quid pro quo, found no basis in the evidence. The argument for stare decisis also failed, since neither party could defend *Austin*, which, he claimed, contravened the Court's earlier holdings in *Buckley* and *Bellotti*. *Austin*, he declared, is now overruled, as is that part of *McConnell* banning corporate expenditures in political campaigns. Only the BCRA's disclaimers and disclosure requirements passed constitutional muster. Within the Court, Kennedy had a reputation for having "a thing" about the First Amendment; his opinion certainly reflected that.

Citizens United not only won its case but in doing so got the Court to overturn a century's worth of precedent in which Congress had attempted to keep corporate and union money out of campaigns. This upset many people, not least of whom were the so-called liberal bloc on the court, John Paul Stevens, Ruth Bader Ginsburg, Stephen Breyer, and Sonia Sotomayor. For Stevens, now nearing ninety, Kennedy's opinion embodied all that he found wrong in the Roberts Court. The case should have been, in his view, resolved simply by ruling whether McCain-Feingold applied to films like *Hillary: The Movie* or to nonprofits like Citizens United. Instead, the majority had transgressed a "cardinal" principle: "If it is not necessary to decide more, it is necessary not to decide more." Here Stevens was quoting from a line that Roberts had often used while on the DC Circuit, and threw it back in his face.

Stevens's dissent was his swan song; he retired from the Court later in the year to be replaced by Elena Kagan. It ran ninety pages, far more than the majority opinion, and he questioned every one of Kennedy's premises, starting with what he saw as Kennedy's contempt for stare decisis and precedent. As for Kennedy's charges of censorship and banning of speech, Stevens said this was a simple case of corporate-funded commercials before an election. The corporation could run as many commercials as it wanted at other times, and employees of the firm could form a political action committee that could run ads at any time.

Stevens took particular aim at Kennedy's assumption that corporations and human beings had identical rights under the First Amendment: "The Framers took it as a given that corporations could be comprehensively regulated in the service of public welfare. Unlike our colleagues, they had little trouble distinguishing corporations from human beings, and when they constitutionalized the right to free speech in the First Amendment, it was the free speech of individual Americans that they had in mind." It was an impressive dissent, but Anthony Kennedy had the five votes.

Both Chief Justice Roberts and Justice Antonin Scalia entered concurring opinions responding to Stevens. Roberts spoke to Stevens's arguments that the Court should have applied the doctrine of constitutional avoidance or decided the case on narrower grounds, and that stare decisis should have prevented the Court from overturning *Austin*. Scalia argued that the original textual meaning of the First Amendment applied to the question of independent spending by corporations.

In fact, it is impossible that in 1791 the Framers considered the First Amendment to have covered both natural persons and corporations, because the corporate form itself was rare in America until the middle of the nineteenth century. In addition, the few early corporations were, for the most part, created for a single purpose, such as building a road or a canal. Nonetheless, as Adam Winkler has convincingly shown in his book *We the Corporations* (2018), businesses since the founding of the nation have fought in courts for civil liberties equal to those of human beings, and usually won.

Winkler points out, however, that despite Stevens's dissent, Kennedy did not invoke the idea of corporate personhood, an idea that first made its appearance in the Supreme Court in 1886 in *Santa Clara County v. Southern Pacific Railroad Co.* Rather, Kennedy went back to an earlier idea that corporations are no more than associations of people and, as such, have the same rights as those people because it is actually the people—the stockholders—who are speaking through their voluntary association. Corporations assume the rights of the corporation's members.

Moreover, the majority's reasoning did not rely on the legal fiction that corporations are persons, but rather on traditional First Amendment arguments. The key question, according to Kennedy, was whether Congress had the power to limit this kind of political speech. The First Amendment says that Congress shall make no law "abridging the freedom of speech." It does not say "the freedom of speech of persons." The Court was trying to decide what Congress could or could not do, not about who got the benefit of those actions. And Congress, the Court ruled, had no power to limit political speech, no matter whether the speaker was a person or an organization.

*   *   *

Although they should have expected it, especially after the bitter infighting within the Court, the justices seemed surprised at the public backlash against *Citizens United*, and from all parts of the political spectrum. Polls showed that eight in ten Americans opposed the decision. Among

Democrats 85 percent said *Citizens United* had been wrongly decided, as did 76 percent of Republicans and 81 percent of independents. Even five years later an overwhelming majority of Americans, 78 percent, believed the ruling should be overturned. Hillary Clinton and Bernie Sanders, the two main contestants for the 2016 Democratic nomination, both said that overturning *Citizens United* would be a litmus test for their Supreme Court nominees.

Not all comment was negative. Joel Gora, one of the lawyers who had represented the ACLU in the *Buckley* case, noted:

> Of course, only time will tell what the real impact of the *Citizens United* decision will be, either doctrinally, practically, or politically. But, whatever results, to me the case is a landmark of political freedom. It has already changed the campaign finance conversation away from limits and towards issues like disclosure, public subsidies, plus further deregulation of the limits on political funding. The decision will lead to increased political speech, a more informed electorate, and a more robust economy. A win, win, win situation.

Not everyone agreed, and the justices were certainly unprepared for the reaction from the White House. Just a few weeks before the decision came down on January 21, 2010, Robert Bauer took over as the new White House counsel. Bauer had been in private practice for more than three decades, during which he had helped nearly every major Democratic candidate find their way through the complexities of campaign finance law. When Obama was elected to the Senate in 2004, he chose Bauer as his personal attorney. In the White House, Obama had initially named Greg Craig as counsel, but constant bickering between Craig and chief of staff Rahm Emanuel led to Craig leaving in the fall of 2009.

Unlike Craig, Bauer understood campaign finance law and immediately saw *Citizens United* as an invitation to chaos. Candidates and political parties faced real scrutiny from their constituents and from the media, especially over the sources of the money they received for campaigning as well as how they spent it. Kennedy's majority opinion authorized independent outlays by companies and committees that could remain generally unknown. The case did uphold disclosure requirements, and so campaigns and committees would have to reveal where their money came from. But the required filings with the FEC often took place weeks or months afterward, and donors had multiple—and legal—ways to camouflage their identities. *Citizens United* allowed unlimited amounts of money to go to little-known organizations that could spend it on commercials just before an election. Then by the time the FEC filings took place, the election would be over, and public interest would be minimal. Also, while it was true the decision allowed unions as well as corporations to spend, Bauer knew that unions had been losing membership and influence for years. They could now spend unlimited amounts of money—which they did not have.

Like Bauer, David Axelrod, Obama's chief political adviser, was infuriated by the decision, and the two of them convinced the president that in his State of the Union speech, to be given six days after the Court handed down *Citizens United*, he should address the issue. All three knew that some of the justices would be there, and not even Franklin Roosevelt, at the height of his battle with the Supreme Court in the 1930s, had publicly criticized the Court for its decision. But Obama, who had taught constitutional law, thought the decision terribly wrong, and he decided to do so. According to at least one scholar, the Obama White House saw the conservative majority on the Court as just another group of Republicans, deserving no greater deference than Republican members of the Senate or House.

Six justices attended the State of the Union address on January 27, 2010, and they sat in the front rows where the president could hardly be unaware of them. "It's time to require lobbyists to disclose each contact they make on behalf of a client with my Administration or Congress," said Obama. "And it's time to put strict limits on the contributions that lobbyists give to candidates for public office." He then looked out to the justices and said, "With all due deference to separation of powers, last week the Supreme Court reversed a century of law that I believe will open the floodgates for special interests—including foreign corporations—to spend without limit in our elections." All the Democrats rose in a standing ovation, and then Obama continued, "I don't think American elections should be bankrolled by America's most powerful interests or, worse, by foreign entities." After more applause from the Democrats, Obama asked Congress—both Democrats and Republicans—to pass a bill that would fix these problems.

Because the media had, as usual, been given an advance copy of the speech, the television producer knew when a reference to the Court would come and had his camera trained on the justices. When Obama said that foreign corporations could spend without limit, Samuel Alito shook his head and mouthed, "Not true." He shook his head again when Obama made another reference to foreign influence. The other members of the Court—Roberts, Kennedy, Ginsburg, Breyer, and Sotomayor—sat without any expression on their faces. Behind Alito, Senator Charles Schumer (D-NY), one of the Senate leaders, was nodding his head as enthusiastically as Alito was shaking his.

Who was right? Did the decision, as Obama charged, open the way for foreign corporations to put money into American elections, or, as Alito believed, did it not? Kennedy's opinion skirted the issue, and the majority opinion explicitly said: "We need not reach the question whether the Government has a compelling interest in preventing foreign individuals or associations from influencing our Nation's political process." So technically Alito was right, but Obama had chosen his words carefully. "I believe [the decision] will open the floodgates" of foreign money. During oral argument, in response to a question from Justice Ginsburg, Ted Olson had responded that the Constitution required the government to treat American and foreign corporations the same way, and he believed both should be allowed to spend money on American political campaigns. Since the decision claimed that no special risk existed of corporations corrupting the political system, it would seem that the majority would have reached the same decision if the case had been about foreign corporations. One must wonder how the Court would have treated foreign corporations if such a case came up after the 2016 election.

On one thing Obama was surely correct—the decision would open "the floodgates" to corporate political spending and allow the wealthiest people in America to exert even greater influence in the next election cycle. In fact, spending in the 2012 election rose dramatically. Corporations, following *Citizens United*, not only could use general treasury moneys to fund independent expenditures in favor of or against specific candidates but also could give unlimited amounts to super PACs, a special type of political action committee that could accept unlimited contributions from both individuals and corporations as long as they did not coordinate their expenditures with the campaign of any federal candidate, that is, those running for the House, the Senate, or the White House. Corporations publicly gave more than $70 million to super PACs in 2012; the Chevron Corporation alone gave $2.5 million to House Speaker John Boehner's Congressional Leadership Fund. Some commentators claimed that the corporations would have given even more if super PAC donations did not have to be disclosed.

Corporations, as one lobbyist explained, prefer nondisclosure, given the chance that a political donation to a particular super PAC would offend customers with different views. As a result, many companies gave their donations to political advocacy groups that were not required to publicly name their contributors. Nonprofit 501(c) organizations, trade associations, and so-called 527 committees accounted for most of the $300 million in "dark," or undisclosed, money that flowed into the 2012 races from corporate sources, or a little less than one-third of all the money spent in that cycle. (Recall Senator McConnell's comment that "soft" money wasn't gone; it would just find a new home.)

Investigative reporters were later able to reveal that the Prudential Insurance Company, Dow Chemical, and Merck Pharmaceuticals each gave more than $1 million to the US Chamber of Commerce to fund political activities. Qualcomm, a maker of computer chips, was forced to disclose its political spending as part of a lawsuit settlement; it turned out the company had given $2.8 million in dark money in 2012, far more than its disclosed donations. In Montana, the Western Tradition Partnership, which funneled money to Republican campaigns, solicited corporate funds by emphasizing the lack of publicity: "Corporate contributions are completely legal under this program. There's no limit on how much you can give. It's confidential. . . . No politician, no bureaucrat, no radical environmentalist will ever know."

The Center for Public Integrity, a nonpartisan campaign finance watchdog group, estimated that in 2012 there was nearly $1 billion in new political spending from corporations, unions, and individuals, all traceable to *Citizens United*. Moreover, that number is for federal races, where the data are easier to come by. Most analysts believe that contributions and spending also increased at the state and local levels. Adam Winkler suggests that since historically the spending for offices such as mayor, judges, district attorneys, and the like has been low, corporations could have a large impact with far smaller contributions than those given to federal races.

Although advocates of campaign finance reform in general, and of McCain-Feingold in particular, bemoaned *Citizens United* as crippling BCRA, the Supreme Court was not yet finished dismantling the act.

CHAPTER 9

Meet Mr. McCutcheon

The Supreme Court handed down its decision in *Citizens United* on January 21, 2010, and it had immediate repercussions in lower court cases. Speech.NOW.org had filed suit in the US District Court for the District of Columbia, challenging provisions of the Federal Election Campaign Act (FECA) that had been either subsumed or left in place by McCain-Feingold.

SpeechNOW is a nonprofit organization (527) that had been formed by individuals wishing to pool shared resources so they could make larger independent political expenditures, primarily issue advocacy advertisements uncoordinated with any candidate campaigns. These ads carefully avoided endorsing or opposing any specific candidates. SpeechNOW solicited contributions only from individuals and accepted no money from corporations, and individual plaintiffs involved in the suit wanted to contribute more than was allowed under federal law.

The organization sought an advisory opinion from the Federal Election Commission (FEC) as to whether it would have to register as a political committee under FECA in order to accept individual contributions for the purpose of making independent expenditures for issue advocacy ads. The FEC opinion held that because of SpeechNOW's interest in influencing federal elections, FECA contribution limits applied, and SpeechNOW had to register as a political committee once it had raised more than $1,000 in contributions each year.

In February 2008, SpeechNOW and several individuals filed suit in the district court challenging the FEC's interpretation of FECA political committee registration requirements, contribution limits, and disclosure requirements. The district court in July denied SpeechNOW's request for an injunction, holding that "sufficiently important government interests support limits on contributions to political committees, including groups like SpeechNOW who intend to spend all their money on independent expenditures."

SpeechNOW appealed the case to the US Court of Appeals for the District of Columbia Circuit. The appeals court ruled in March 2010 (after waiting to see what the decision would be in *Citizens United*) that limits on what individuals could give, and the amount SpeechNOW could receive, were unconstitutional. Contribution limits to an independent expenditure-only group violate "the First Amendment by preventing [individuals] from donating to SpeechNOW in excess of the limits and by prohibiting SpeechNOW from accepting donations in excess of the limits." The court noted that limits on contributions directly to candidates remained constitutional.

The court, however, upheld FECA's disclosure and reporting requirements, which meant that SpeechNOW had to register as a political committee. While such requirements placed some burden on First Amendment rights, the burden is minimal "given the relative simplicity with which SpeechNOW intends to operate." The government declined to appeal the decision, but SpeechNOW asked the Supreme Court to review the disclosure and reporting requirements that would now be required if it had to register as a political committee. The High Court denied cert on November 1, 2010.

Another lower court case, *Republican National Committee v. Federal Election Commission* (2010), involved an as-applied challenge to McCain-Feingold. Prior to its passage, there had been practically no limits on so-called soft money, funds that did not go directly to a candidate (hard money) and could be used to fund issue advertisements (provided no candidate names were mentioned), state and local campaigns, and get-out-the-vote activities. In the Bipartisan Campaign Reform Act (BCRA), Congress had tried to close the loophole that would allow almost unrestricted donations to go to a political party and thus bypass the per-individual hard money restrictions. The act placed limits on how much a political party could receive annually from a donor regardless of how the party intended to use the money. It also limited how state and local parties used contributions in circumstances that could impact federal elections, such as certain get-out-the-vote or issue advocacy campaigns.

In *McConnell* the High Court had upheld the law against a facial challenge. Now the Republican National Committee (RNC), as well as the

California Republican Party and several local GOP groups, brought an as-applied suit, claiming the soft money restrictions were unconstitutional. The plaintiffs claimed that they sought to raise unlimited soft money only for state and local activities that had little or no connection to federal elections. In essence, they promised not to provide any benefits to soft money donors beyond those afforded to hard money donors who contributed the legal maximums.

The three-judge panel upheld the restrictions and noted that although the Republican groups portrayed their complaint in an as-applied manner, many of them had already been addressed and rejected in *McConnell*. They agreed with the RNC that *Citizens United* undercut any theory that large contributions to political parties could be corrupting simply because they facilitated access to or created gratitude from the candidates. Access and gratitude alone did not rise to the level of quid pro quo corruption. The panel, which spoke through Judge Brett Kavanaugh, relied on another justification that had been expressed in *McConnell*—the "close relationship between federal officeholders and the national parties," which could give the impression of corruption. In other words, because of this relationship, large donations to the party could give the same impression as large donations to the candidates. Since *Citizens United* did not address the soft money issue, the lower court believed itself still bound by *McConnell*.

Kavanaugh's opinion nonetheless showed hostility to the Supreme Court's reasoning in *McConnell*. It questioned the theory that such limits could be justified simply by the close connection between candidates and parties, but as Kavanaugh noted more than once in the opinion, the panel's hands were tied by the Supreme Court, and he essentially called for the High Court to take the case and reassess those views, especially after *Citizens United*. However, when the RNC appealed, the Court denied cert, with Justices Scalia, Kennedy, and Thomas voting to take the case.

* * *

In his State of the Union address, President Obama not only had attacked the *Citizens United* decision but also asked Congress to pass new legislation covering campaign finance. On April 29, 2010, Representative Chris Van Hollen (D-MD) introduced H.R. 5175, also known as the

DISCLOSE Act (Democracy Is Strengthened by Casting Light on Spending in Elections Act), while Charles Schumer (D-NY) sponsored the measure in the Senate.

* * *

The DISCLOSE Act included a number of steps to ensure that the public would know the amount of and the source of so-called dark money. Organizations spending money in federal elections, including super PACs and certain nonprofit 527 groups would have to promptly disclose donors who had given $10,000 or more in any election cycle. Introduced in a Democratic-controlled Congress, the DISCLOSE Act passed the House in June 2010. However, both the Senate and the House spent nearly all their time and energy that session enacting the Affordable Care Act. When the Republicans took over control of Congress in January 2011, they had no interest in the DISCLOSE Act.

Eight years later, after the Democrats regained control of the House of Representatives in the 2018 midterm elections, Representative Adam Schiff (D-CA) introduced a constitutional amendment to void *Citizens United* and increase regulation of campaign contributions and expenditures. The decision, according to Schiff, "overturned decades of legal precedent and has enabled billions in dark money to pour into our elections." While amending the Constitution is "an extraordinary step, it is the only way to safeguard our democratic process.... This amendment will restore power to everyday citizens."

The Schiff amendment would allow Congress and the states wide leeway to enact content-neutral limitations on contributions and independent expenditures, and also would allow but not require public financing of campaigns. It would also overturn the *Davis* decision, by allowing Congress and the states the power to "restrict the influence of private wealth by offsetting campaign spending or independent expenditures with increased public spending."

The proposal would probably not have been able to muster the necessary two-thirds vote in the House, and certainly not in the Republican-controlled Senate. It drew little attention in any case because the House, led by Schiff, began inquiries into the possible impeachment of Donald Trump.

In the term following that of *Citizens United*, the High Court handed down another opinion on campaign finance reform, this one a state measure from Arizona. In 1998 the state's voters had approved a ballot measure known as the Clean Elections Act, which established public financing for statewide office campaigns, such as those for governor. Candidates who chose to participate in the new system had to collect a specific number of five-dollar donations in order to be eligible for the state funds. Under the law, if a participating candidate was outspent by a nonparticipating opponent, the government would give the participating candidate additional funds to match the amount raised in private funds by his or her opponent, in an amount up to three times the original government subsidy. Two candidates who utilized the Clean Elections system were Democrat Janet Napolitano, elected governor in 2002 (and later to be Obama's secretary of homeland security), and Republican Jan Brewer, elected governor in 2010.

After the Supreme Court struck down BCRA's so-called millionaire's amendment in *Davis v. Federal Election Commission* (2008), the Arizona Free Enterprise Club's Freedom Club PAC challenged the Clean Elections Commission in August 2008. In *Davis* the Court ruled that BCRA's goal of leveling the playing field did not justify a system in which "the vigorous exercise of the right to use personal funds to finance campaign speech produces fundraising advantages for opponents in the competitive context of electoral politics." The Freedom Club PAC claimed that the Arizona system had the same goal—leveling the playing field—and thus suffered the same constitutional defects.

On January 20, 1910 (the day before the High Court handed down *Citizens United*), Judge Roslyn Silver of the US District Court for the District of Arizona, struck down the matching funds provision of the Clean Elections law as unconstitutional. Although Judge Silver agreed with the plaintiffs that the matching funds provision could not stand under *Davis*, she termed that decision "illogical . . . an ipse dixit unsupported by the slightest veneer of reasoning to hide the obvious judicial fiat by which it is reached." Silver suspended her order while the Arizona Clean Elections Commission appealed to the Court of Appeals for the Ninth Circuit. In a remarkably quick turnaround, the court on April 12, 2010 reversed, holding that the state's matching funds provision was analytically distinct from BCRA's millionaire's amendment.

The Supreme Court granted cert, heard oral arguments on March 28,

2011, and three months later reversed the Ninth Circuit. Just as it had in *Davis*, it ruled that schemes to "level the playing field" violated the Constitution. Chief Justice Roberts wrote for the five-person majority that included Scalia, Thomas, Kennedy, and Alito, while Justices Ginsburg, Breyer, and Sotomayor joined Justice Kagan's dissent. Roberts agreed that the Arizona plan was in fact different from that provision of McCain-Feingold struck down in *Davis*. But, he continued, those differences actually impinged on free speech even more than did the federal law. Politics is a highly competitive process, and neither the state nor the federal government can do anything to tip the balance, even under the guise of leveling the playing field (*Arizona Free Enterprise Club's Freedom Club PAC v. Bennett*).

It should be noted that not all efforts to avoid corruption in the political process met the same fate. In 2011, Judge Brett Kavanaugh, then a member of the Court of Appeals for the District of Columbia, wrote an opinion upholding federal laws banning persons who are not citizens of the United States from contributing to political parties or PACs, or making expenditures expressly advocating for or against specific candidates. The plaintiffs argued that even though they were not citizens, the law (codified at 2 U.S.C. §441e[a]) violated their First Amendment rights. Under a number of Supreme Court precedents, Kavanaugh wrote, "the government (federal, state, and local) may exclude foreign citizens from activities that are part of democratic self-government in the United States." The court then dismissed the case, and the Supreme Court issued a memorandum opinion affirming the judgment (*Bluman v. Federal Election Commission*).

In New York, the Court of Appeals for the Second Circuit early in 2012 upheld New York City's political campaign and lobby laws that (1) limited campaign contributions by individuals and companies that have business dealings with the city; (2) exclude such contributions from matching with public funds under the public financing scheme; and (3) expanded the prohibition on corporate contributions to include partnerships and limited liability corporations. The long list of plaintiffs included "New York City voters, aspiring candidates for local office, a business owner, lobbyists and individuals associated with lobbyists, limited liability companies, and political parties."

The city's administrative rules regarding campaigns and campaign financing had been redrawn after a series of scandals, and then in 1998 voters had approved charter amendments designed to lessen even further any political influence that could be exercised by individuals and companies doing business with the city. Judge Paul A. Crotty painstakingly went through a series of investigations, scandals, and responses to indicate that the city had more than enough evidence to justify its efforts to limit the "pay-for-play" donations from city contractors (*Ognibene v. Parkes* [2010]).

Later in 2012 the Supreme Court showed that it had meant what it had said in *Citizens United*, when it summarily reversed the decision by the Montana Supreme Court in *American Tradition Partnership, Inc. v. Bullock*.

In a 1912 ballot initiative, the citizens of Montana had passed the Montana Corrupt Practices Act in response to the undue influence of corporations on state elections. At the time, a number of "copper barons" controlled most of the political process through quid pro quo financial transactions with politicians. In response, the state restricted the amount of money that corporations and individuals could donate to campaigns. After the *Citizens United* ruling, the American Tradition Partnership challenged the 1912 law, which prohibited independent expenditures to influence political campaigns by corporations. In October 2010 District Judge Jeffrey Sherlock ruled the Montana law unconstitutional. Judge Sherlock said he agreed with US district judge Paul Magnuson, who had overturned a similar ban in Minnesota. Magnuson had written that *Citizens United* "is unequivocal: The government may not prohibit independent and indirect corporate expenditures on political speech." Montana attorney general Steve Bullock, a Democrat who had been elected to that office in 2008, argued on behalf of the state that the Corrupt Practices Act should remain in place, and appealed the decision to the Montana Supreme Court.

Aware that no matter how it ruled, there would be an appeal to the US Supreme Court, the majority opinion included a great deal of historical evidence to document the "corrupting influence of campaign contributions on elections." *Citizens United* focused primarily on the free speech limitations of BCRA, whereas the Montana court focused on the historical precedent for allowing campaign finance restrictions. In particular, the Montana court called the Supreme Court's declaration that corporations have the same constitutional rights as individual citizens "utter nonsense." The abundant historical precedent allowed the majority to argue that their ruling was consistent with the original intent of the First Amendment.

Additionally, the Montana court called *Citizens United* a "crabbed view of corruption" and argued that prior to Montana's campaign finance laws "the state of Montana and its government were operating under a mere shell of legal authority." The majority criticized *Citizens United* as being unrealistic about the corrupting influence of unlimited secret money, and the court cited a litany of evidence to prove the direct correlation between independent expenditures and political corruption. Although the opinion did in fact blatantly contradict *Citizens United*, the Montana court claimed that the state law had major differences with McCain-Feingold and therefore should be allowed to stand.

James Nelson, who was one of the two dissenters, agreed with the majority opinion and called the reasoning of *Citizens United* "smoke and mirrors," but he did not believe that the Montana court had the authority to contradict the Supreme Court. According to Nelson, when the highest court makes a constitutional ruling, all other courts must follow it.

That was essentially the gist of the High Court's per curiam decision, which it used without holding any oral argument: "The question presented in this case is whether the holding of *Citizens United* applies to the Montana state law. There can be no serious doubt that it does. See U.S. Const., Art. VI, cl. 2. Montana's arguments in support of the judgment below either were already rejected in *Citizens United*, or fail to meaningfully distinguish that case. . . . The judgment of the Supreme Court of Montana is reversed."

Justice Breyer, joined by his fellow dissenters in *Citizens United*, believed that this would have been a good opportunity to reconsider that case: "Given the history and political landscape in Montana, that court concluded that the State had a compelling interest in limiting independent expenditures by corporations. Thus, Montana's experience, like considerable experience elsewhere since the Court's decision in *Citizens United*, casts grave doubt on the Court's supposition that independent expenditures do not corrupt or appear to do so."

Justice Ginsburg, joined by Breyer, urged the Court to reconsider *Citizens United*. "Montana's experience, and experience elsewhere since this Court's decision in *Citizens United* make it exceedingly difficult to maintain that independent expenditures by corporations 'do not give rise to corruption or the appearance of corruption.'"

This was the first time in more than forty years that the High Court had summarily reversed a state supreme court with four strongly dissenting justices and with practically no factual justification. There had been some question as to whether the ruling in *Citizens United* applied equally to state election law, and in this case—with absolutely no analysis as to whether conditions differed in state elections—the majority essentially put another nail in the coffin of campaign finance reform.

Following *Citizens United*, the state of Iowa changed its campaign finance laws to allow for independent expenditures by corporations and unions but left intact the ban on direct contributions to candidates and political committees by corporations. Unions, however, were permitted to make such contributions. The Iowa Right to Life Committee Inc. (IRTL), an antiabortion group, challenged the ban as well as several other provisions of different campaign finance laws and reporting requirements, saying they violated the free speech and equal protection of the law provisions of the Constitution. IRTL objected to being categorized as a "political committee" and the necessary reporting that required, and especially to the state ban on direct corporate contributions to candidates. The district court held that IRTL lacked standing to challenge several provisions, and found the others constitutional (*Iowa Right to Life Committee v. Smithson* [2010]).

IRTL appealed to the Court of Appeals for the Eighth Circuit, which on July 19, 2013, handed down a lengthy decision that agreed with the lower court that IRTL lacked standing to challenge some of the provisions, found a few of the minor provisions unconstitutional, but upheld the main portions relating to bans on corporate expenditures to candidates (*Iowa Right to Life Committee v. Tooker* [2013]). Both sides appealed to the Supreme Court, but the High Court had its hands full with another case that had far more far-reaching implications.

*   *   *

Shaun McCutcheon is the founder and CEO of Coalmont Electrical Development in Alabama. An electrical engineer, he is rich but is not among the superrich. As he himself put it, "I do not come from a political family, and I do not come from a rich family." A self-made man, he believes in supporting charities and causes he believes in by giving them generous donations. This had not been a problem with nonpolitical groups, but it proved so when he wanted to support political campaigns; if he gave as much as he wanted to, he could wind up in prison for five years. McCutcheon went to the FEC, which confirmed that if he gave beyond the legal limits, he would be breaking the law. So he went to court, arguing that federal campaign restrictions abridged his First Amendment rights.

McCutcheon's case spotlighted the inherent contradiction in campaign finance law that had bedeviled the courts and the political system ever since *Buckley v. Valeo* in 1976. In that case, the Court drew a distinction between expenditures by candidates, which could not be restricted because that constituted political speech protected by the First Amendment, and contributions to candidates and parties, which the Court said did not constitute speech and so could be regulated. It was, in the opinion of many, a ludicrous distinction at the time, but although the more conservative justices who came onto the bench starting in the Reagan years often criticized the *Buckley* distinction, they never seemed to have the five votes to overturn it.

Now the courts would be getting a case that highlighted *Buckley*'s irrationality. McCutcheon wanted to speak up, and do so by donating to candidates and political causes he supported, and not only by giving them more than federal law allowed for one candidate; he wanted to give to a number of candidates, so that his total contribution would also exceed the law. There was never any doubt in McCutcheon's mind that giving money to support candidates and causes was a form of speech, and restrictions on what he could do with his own money violated the First Amendment. As he told a reporter, "If the government tells you that you can't spend your money where you want, there should be a real, real good reason." He did not think that the law provided that reason.

In terms of specifics, McCain-Feingold limits an individual to $48,000 in contributions to candidates and $74,600 to party committees or PACs, or a total of $123,200 in an election cycle. McCutcheon wanted to donate to twenty-seven candidates but could not do so because of BCRA limits, so he wrote a number of checks in $1,776 increments and contributed $33,088 to fifteen candidates during the 2012 election cycle. He wanted to give more—$75,000 to party committees and $21,312 to other candidates. During the 2013–2014 cycle, he wanted to give more than $60,000 to candidates, as well as $75,000 to three Republican national party committees. If he had done so, he would have easily exceeded federal limits. McCutcheon decided to fight the law in court at a time when a number of conservative lawyers and activists believed the time was ripe to launch a challenge.

Under terms of McCain-Feingold, challenges to the law are heard in federal district court and can then be appealed directly to the US Supreme Court. A three-judge court sitting in the District of Columbia in September 2012 ruled against McCutcheon's challenge and, in a perfect declaration of judicial restraint, declared, "It is not the judicial role to parse legislative judgment about what limits to impose." However, Judge Janice Rogers Brown conceded that "the constitutional line between political speech and political contributions grows increasingly difficult to discern." McCutcheon appealed to the Supreme Court, which in February 2013 granted cert in *McCutcheon v. Federal Election Commission*, with oral arguments set for the following October. While no one knew how the nine justices would vote, the fact that at least four were willing to hear the case gave backers of campaign finance laws great concern. Jeffrey Toobin wrote in the *New Yorker*: "Think the Supreme Court's decision in *Citizens United* was bad? A worse one may be on the horizon." The president of Democracy 21, Fred Wertheimer, warned: "As damaging as *Citizens United* has been to our political system, the Supreme Court would make a bad situation far worse if it strikes down the overall contribution limits."

Over the summer, in preparation for the October oral argument, not only the two principals, McCutcheon and the FEC, submitted briefs laying out their arguments, but so did others, including the RNC, Senator Mitch McConnell, and a combined amicus brief representing more than a dozen liberal groups, including Common Cause, People for the American Way, the League of Women Voters, and the American Federation of Teachers. Notably absent, however, was anything from the oldest defender of the First Amendment, the American Civil Liberties Union (ACLU).

Between 1976, when it entered an amicus brief in *Buckley*, and 2010, when it submitted one in *Citizens United*, the ACLU filed briefs in every campaign finance case that reached the Supreme Court and also took part in some challenges to state laws. In every single one, the ACLU opposed the laws as violations of the First Amendment protection of free speech.

Then, on April 19, 2010, just three months after the Court handed down its decision in *Citizens United*, the ACLU issued a press release announcing a change in its policy. At a meeting the day before the national board voted 36–30 to reaffirm that limits on spending by individuals or organizations for the purpose of advocating causes or candidates impinge on the liberty protected by the First Amendment. However, the board was now prepared to accept spending limits that are part of voluntary public financing plans, provided candidates had a "true choice" as to whether to participate and if the plans provided sufficient and equitable funding. The board also agreed that the organization would accept "reasonable limits" on campaign contributions. The revised policy "acknowledges that very large contributions to candidates may lead to undue influence of corruption and, at a minimum, have the appearance of impropriety and undermine public confidence in the electoral system's integrity."

What happened? It would seem that the *Citizens United* decision, with implications of massive amounts of corporate money flowing into political campaigns, may have been the trigger. But the decision had a long history. In 2007 a special committee had been formed to study the ACLU's campaign finance policy and had reported back to the national board several times before the April 2010 vote. The committee had heard testimony from a panel of First Amendment scholars and lawyers, and there had been extensive debate and discussion.

In fact, the board had been debating the issue for more than forty years, and it had shown up on the board's agenda twenty-two times since 1970. The new policy was the result, according to the press release, of more than four decades of study and discussion. The ACLU was now ready to accept contribution as well as expenditure limits provided that they "be fair, reasonable, understandable, and not unduly burdensome. It must also ensure integrity and inclusivity, encourage participation and protect rights of association."

The close vote indicated how divided the board was over the issue. Burt Neuborne, the former ACLU legal director, said the rigid First Amendment position had become problematic: "I believe the ACLU's adamant opposition to limits on massive campaign spending by the super rich gets the constitutional issues wrong." As what he termed "the corrosive effects on democracy" of unrestrained campaign spending became clear, he changed his mind and began opposing the ACLU position.

On the opposite side, Nadine Strossen, a past ACLU president and professor at New York Law School, believes that the former policy provided the benefits of "added free speech, and added voices, and added opinions." For her, the type of campaign reform measures endorsed by Neuborne are a kind of "Incumbents Protection Act," that just make it harder for challengers to mount effective campaigns. She notes that *Citizens United* "unshackled all corporations, including nonprofit corporations, such as the ACLU, which itself was mentioned expressly in the Supreme Court's decision, along with the Sierra Club, and the National Rifle Association, as well as unions. All of us will be able to speak more and all of us will be able to receive more information."

Interestingly, the press release, dated April 19, 2010, is the next to the last posting on the ACLU's website under campaign finance reform. The last one, dated December 22, 2016, involved a New York Civil Liberties Union challenge to New York State's Ethics Reform Law and had less to do with finance than the problems it would cause issue advocacy groups, like the ACLU, in getting the message out. There are no postings on campaign finance after that date, and the ACLU did not file an amicus brief in McCutcheon.

*　*　*

At ten o'clock on October 8, 2013, the marshal of the Court called on the audience to rise and pay attention as the justices filed in through the velvet curtains. A few minutes later Chief Justice John Roberts called Case 12-536 and invited the lawyer for McCutcheon, his former law clerk Erin Murphy, to begin. For the next hour the justices barraged Murphy and Solicitor General Donald Verrilli with questions. While the reporters who covered the argument seemed to agree that a majority of justices leaned toward McCutcheon, there was more than a little confusion. Usually the factual record is developed in the lower court, so that the justices have that information as background to the legal arguments presented in the briefs and orally. But that had not been the case here. In the district court McCutcheon had sought a preliminary injunction to stop the FEC from enforcing limits, while the FEC moved for a motion to dismiss. The lack of a record, normally an important part of the case, can be seen in some of the comments from the bench:

SCALIA: This campaign finance law is so intricate that I can't figure it out. It might have been nice to have, you know, the lower court tell me what the law is.

SOTOMAYOR: I'm a little confused, okay? I'm confused because we're talking in the abstract. This decision was based on a motion to dismiss. And there is a huge colloquy about what happens and doesn't happen. We don't have a record below.

BREYER: Justice Sotomayor is saying: I don't know. And I don't know, either, because there's been no hearing, there's been no evidence presented. There is nothing but dismissal.

While it is true that the Court did not have the benefit of a record, that does not mean that the justices did not have an understanding of campaign finance law. In the ten years following *McConnell*, they had been hearing one case after another, all attacking BCRA, and in every case they had ruled provisions of the act unconstitutional as an infringement of the First Amendment. What they had finally come face-to-face with involved not simply a challenge to BCRA's limits on campaign contributions but the dichotomy laid down four decades earlier in *Buckley*, that campaign expenditures constituted speech and therefore could not be regulated, while contributions could be controlled because they were not speech.

The justices met in conference the next day and determined what to do about the case—decide it and assign opinions, dismiss it until a proper record could be constructed, or perhaps set it for reargument with specific questions, as they had done in *Citizens United*. No one would know until the Court announced its decision, which, as it turned out, would not be for several months.

One month later the US Court of Appeals gave Shaun McCutcheon something to cheer about. It struck down a New York State law limiting the amount of contributions to independent committees to $150,000 per year. According to a spokesman for the New York Progress and Protection PAC, McCutcheon had promised to give the group at least $200,000 to aid its fight for local conservative candidates, including

Joseph J. Lhota, the Republican candidate for mayor who lost to Bill de Blasio. "I am very pleased," McCutcheon told a reporter, "that another court has decided to rule in favor of free speech" (*New York Progress and Protection PAC v. Walsh* [2013]).

On April 2, 2014, Chief Justice Roberts announced the Court's opinion. Roberts authored the plurality opinion, joined by Scalia, Kennedy, and Alito, with Clarence Thomas concurring in most of it. Justice Stephen Breyer dissented, joined by Ginsburg, Kagan, and Sotomayor. In short, Shaun McCutcheon won; Roberts declared the aggregate contributions limit unconstitutional, and McCutcheon could now give away as much of his money as he pleased. The chief justice began his opinion by declaring, "There is no right more basic in our democracy than the right to participate in electing our political leaders." He then constructed his arguments around four basic propositions.

First, the decision did not require the Court to revisit *Buckley*. McCutcheon had only challenged the aggregate contribution ceiling, and this did not require a reexamination of the contribution-expenditure distinction, nor of the base contribution limits on how much could be given to a single candidate or committee within an election cycle. Here Thomas departed from the majority and in his concurrence boldly argued for the unconstitutionality of all contribution limits, in effect doing away with the dichotomy.

Second, the Court did not consider *Buckley* as a binding precedent on the question of aggregate contributions. The *Buckley* Court had upheld the FECA cap but had done so in a cursory manner, admitting that the question "had not been separately addressed at length by the parties." In the end, the issue had merited only a three-sentence paragraph in a 139-page opinion. The Court would not be bound by those three sentences in the face of the strong argument presented by McCutcheon.

Third, despite the dissent's efforts to develop a broad definition of political corruption, the only one that merited consideration was quid pro quo corruption, and "the Government may not seek to limit the appearance of mere influence or access." The distinction between quid pro quo corruption and influence "may seem vague at times, but the distinction must be respected in order to safeguard basic First Amendment rights."

Fourth, the decision reversed the district court's judgment that the aggregate limit served a "loophole closing" function to stem corruption.

But, "if there is no corruption concern in giving nine candidates up to $5,200 each, there is no risk that additional candidates will be corrupted by donations of up to $5,200." The danger is that a rich donor might channel a great deal of money to one candidate or PAC, and that problem is averted by the base cap.

In conclusion, the chief justice conceded that the government's desire to reduce the amount of money in politics might be attractive to many people, but "money in politics may at times seem repugnant to some, but so too does much of what the First Amendment vigorously protects. If the First Amendment protects flag burning, funeral protests, and Nazi parades—despite the profound offense such spectacles cause—it surely protects political campaign speech despite popular opposition." The aggregate contribution limits "intrude without justification on a citizen's ability to exercise 'the most fundamental First Amendment activities.'"

Justice Thomas concurred in the result but chastised his conservative brethren for not going far enough and scrapping *Buckley* entirely. The case represented "yet another missed opportunity to right the course of our campaign finance jurisprudence." At least two of the amici briefs had urged this course, those of the Republican National Committee and the Cato Institute, but only Thomas seemed receptive to their message. "The Court's decision in *Buckley v. Valeo* denigrates core First Amendment speech and should be overruled."

It is likely that Roberts, Scalia, Kennedy, and Alito agreed with Thomas, but there are reasons why they chose not to go that far. Although they expected criticism after *Citizens United*, they probably did not expect it to be so vehement, or to have the president of the United States attack it in his State of the Union address. *McCutcheon* went far enough, and they did not want another firestorm if they eviscerated *Buckley*. Moreover, it has been Chief Justice Roberts's style to chip away at decisions he does not like rather than trying to kill them off completely. He does have a good sense of institutionalism and knows that the Court's credibility would be undermined if it went too far too often. In many ways, however, there really is not that much left of *Buckley*.

Justice Breyer also built his dissent around four propositions. First, he charged the majority with abdicating judicial restraint. In complex matters like campaign finance, the judgment should be left to the elected branches, and not be determined by justices' preferences. In his eyes,

McCutcheon was a brazen case of judicial activism, exactly the sort of decision that conservatives had railed against ever since the Warren years.

Second, the majority had ignored one of the basic requirements for judging, namely, knowing the facts. Breyer over the years has been very much a judge who relies on the record. He fully agrees with Louis Brandeis's famous comment that "knowledge is essential to understanding, and understanding should precede judging." Here there was no record from the lower court, but the majority had plowed ahead anyway, totally oblivious to the "importance of protecting the political integrity of our governmental institutions." The two cases—*Citizens United* and *McCutcheon*—left Congress with no power to deal with the "grave proven problems of democratic legitimacy" that campaign finance presented.

Third, all of the justices except Thomas seemed concerned about the corruption that money could introduce into the political system, but they disagreed with its nature. For the majority, the only type of corruption that could be addressed was the quid pro quo, where money sought and received specific rewards. Breyer considered this far too narrow a definition and agreed with the authors of BCRA that purchasing access by itself could corrupt the political process.

Fourth, Breyer charged that the decision would drastically change the political process by allowing wealthy donors to give enormous sums to elect the candidates of their choice. He summed this up in comments he made when reading his dissent: "If the Court in *Citizens United* opened a door, today's decision may well open a floodgate.... Where enough money calls the tune, the general public will not be heard."

As might be expected, foes of McCain-Feingold rejoiced in the *McCutcheon* decision, while BCRA supporters shed copious tears. Reince Priebus, chair of the Republican National Committee, which had been one of the appellants in the case, called the decision "an important first step toward restoring the voice of candidates and party committees and a vindication for all those who support robust, transparent political discourse.... When free speech is allowed to flourish, our democracy is stronger." The Cato Institute people were happy, but not that enthusiastic, since only Justice Thomas had embraced the position in their amicus brief that *Buckley* should be totally discarded. James Bopp, the lawyer who first brought Shaun McCutcheon's case to court, practically crowed: "This is a great triumph for the First Amendment."

On the other side, Fred Wertheimer, president of Democracy 21, charged the majority with overturning forty years of national policy and thirty-eight years of judicial precedent: "The Supreme Court has turned our representative system of government into a sandbox for America's billionaires and millionaires to play in." Burt Neuborne, a New York University law professor who had argued many cases for the ACLU, lamented that "American democracy is trapped in a sealed box built by the Supreme Court. . . . Five justices are slowly but surely pumping the air out of the box." Dean Erwin Chemerinsky of the University of California at Irvine Law School was a bit more measured in his criticism, but he believed the decision would result in "many more challenges and many more rulings invalidating campaign finance laws of all types."

Ronald Collins and David Skover, in their book on the case, say that it is always hard to peer into a crystal ball to see exactly what the decision portends for the future. But, they add, "it is safe to note that the Roberts Court has yet to see a campaign finance law it liked in the six signed opinions it issued prior to *McCutcheon.* . . . Now that number was seven."

*   *   *

McCutcheon came down on April 2, 2014, and three days later the High Court denied cert in the *Iowa Right to Life* case, leaving intact the state ban on corporate contributions in Iowa elections. Why it did so is unclear, since only in rare cases do we get an explanation of why cert is denied. The reporter for Reuters wrote that the Court had "ducked" the new case after its highly controversial decision only a few days earlier on campaign finance. However, when the Montana law had come up, the 5–4 majority issued a brief memorandum opinion that said under the Supremacy Clause, Supreme Court decisions applied to the states as well as to the federal government. Yet here it left intact a state law that seemingly ran counter to *Citizens United.*

A year later the Court heard another kind of campaign finance case. Once again the justices split 5–4, but with a different lineup.

During her candidacy for county court judge in Hillsborough County, Florida, Lanell Williams-Yulee personally solicited campaign contributions. She stated that she served as the "community Public Defender"— although her title was "assistant public defender"—and inaccurately stated in the media that there was no incumbent in the judicial race.

The Florida Bar filed a complaint against Williams-Yulee and alleged that her actions during the campaign violated the bar's rules regulating campaigns. A referee was appointed who suggested that Williams-Yulee receive a public reprimand. Williams-Yulee appealed the referee's finding, and the Supreme Court of Florida held that she violated bar rules for directly soliciting funds for her judicial campaign. Williams-Yulee appealed and claimed that the Florida Bar rule prohibiting a candidate from personal solicitation of funds violated the First Amendment protection of freedom of speech.

Over the years, it should be noted, some of the justices had gone on record as being personally opposed to the election of state judges. In *Caperton v. A. T. Massey Coal Co.* (2009), a coal company had lost a suit and plaintiffs had been awarded $50 million in damages. Knowing that the West Virginia Supreme Court of Appeals would hear the case, Don Blankenship, Massey's chair, gave $3 million to support the candidacy of Brent Benjamin, who won a seat on the court by less than fifty thousand votes. When the court heard the case, Benjamin did not recuse, and voted to reverse the $50 million award. Although the Supreme Court did not find or accuse Benjamin of wrongdoing, it reversed the West Virginia high court on the grounds that such a massive donation had the appearance of judicial corruption and could not be allowed.

The question posed by the Florida case, *Williams-Yulee v. Florida Bar* (2015), seemed simple: Does a rule of judicial conduct that prohibits candidates for judicial office from personally soliciting campaign funds violate the First Amendment? Chief Justice Roberts, for a 5–4 majority, said it did not. The Court held that rules limiting speech have typically been subjected to strict First Amendment scrutiny because such speech often deals with issues of public concern, precisely the subject matter the First Amendment was meant to protect. Therefore, the government may restrict the speech of a judicial candidate only when the restriction is narrowly tailored to serve a compelling state interest. The restriction in this case served the compelling state interest of preserving public confidence in the integrity of the judiciary and was sufficiently narrowly tailored to that interest.

Justice Ruth Bader Ginsburg wrote an opinion concurring in the result but dissenting in part of the reasoning. She argued that there was no need to apply an exacting standard of scrutiny to a state's endeavor to distinguish between political and judicial elections. Therefore, states should be granted broad latitude to regulate judicial elections, particularly with respect to campaign finance issues, as vast amounts of spending in judicial elections threaten the appearance and reality of an independent judiciary.

Justice Antonin Scalia dissented from both the result and the reasoning and argued that the First Amendment protects all speech unless widespread and long-standing tradition permits its regulation, which was not the case here. Because the rule in question presumptively violated the First Amendment, the Court could only uphold it if it was narrowly tailored to serve a compelling state interest. In this case, there is no evidence that banning personal requests for contributions in a judicial election increased public faith in judicial integrity, and the rule bans much more speech than would be narrowly tailored to serve such an interest. Justice Clarence Thomas joined in Scalia's dissent, while Anthony Kennedy and Samuel Alito dissented separately.

Although there are still some provisions of the Bipartisan Campaign Reform Act (BCRA) that have not been attacked, it is unlikely that the Court will hear any challenges that would gut major portions of the law the way *Citizens United* and *McCutcheon* did. The courts do not seem to have a problem with reporting requirements, although it is possible for donors to give large sums of money to certain types of organizations that do not have to report either the names of their contributors or the amounts involved. (However, in a recent case in the DC Circuit, the court allowed the identity of an original donor to remain sealed while the merits of the case are tried.)

As for the *Buckley* distinction between contributions and expenditures, the Court did not *formally* undo that dichotomy, although Justice Thomas urged his colleagues to do so. In *McCutcheon* the Court heard an attack on the aggregate limits of how much a single person could donate; there was no hint of any corruption, especially of the quid pro quo type that the chief justice said is the only kind that counts, so the Court evaded having to overturn *Buckley*. But, as Ronald Collins notes, the "contribution-expenditures dichotomy lives on at least in form, [but] as a practical matter *Buckley* was significantly undermined."

In November 2019, the Court, after granting certiorari, sent *Thompson v. Hebdon* back to the Ninth Circuit for a rehearing. The case involved an Alaska law that limited the amount an individual could contribute to a candidate for state office or to a PAC to $500 per year. A group of donors argued that the restrictions violated their First Amendment rights. Both the district court in 2016 and the Court of Appeals for the Ninth Circuit in 2018 upheld the restrictions, the latter saying that neither *Citizens United* nor *McCutcheon* prevented a state from enacting limits to protect the integrity of the political process. The Supreme Court granted cert, and then in a per curiam decision essentially told the lower courts that they had completely misinterpreted the holdings of both cases, and that in rehearing they needed to follow the guidelines set down in *Randall v. Sorrel* (2006), and not those of *Iowa Right to Life Committee v. Tooker* (2014). Either way, I do not think it will make much difference anywhere else in the country. Given the polarization in American politics at the moment, it is difficult to envision any sort of bipartisan effort to pass new campaign finance laws to protect the integrity of the political system. If, however, control of enough state houses changes hands in the next election cycle, there may be some creative efforts to enact campaign finance laws for the purpose of protecting the integrity of the political system, at least on the state level.

The fact remains, however, that in the wake of the Court's decision emasculating McCain-Feingold, 39 percent of the American people felt that our campaign finance system needed fundamental changes, and an additional 46 percent believed the system should be rebuilt completely. This sentiment certainly led the newly elected Democratic majority in the House of Representatives to introduce, as its first order of business, H.R. 1, formally known as the "For the People Act." The bill, with 225 cosponsors, aimed to expand voting rights, eliminate gerrymandering, strengthen ethics rules, and most important from our point of view, limit the influence of private donors in politics.

The bill, which passed the House on a strict party line vote, 234–193, would have introduced voluntary public financing for campaigns, matching small donations at a 6:1 ratio. It would also impose stricter reporting rules requiring candidates, parties, and PACs to disclose the amount of and source of so-called dark money. The Federal Election Commission would be restructured to have an odd number of members in an effort to eliminate gridlock in that agency. Finally, it supported a constitutional amendment to overturn *Citizens United*, so that longtime restrictions on corporations and unions could be reimposed. The bill, of course, had no chance of passage in the Senate so long as the Republicans held a majority, and were led by Mitch McConnell (R-KY), a fervent opponent of any and all efforts at campaign finance reform.

In this book I have tried to show that the whole issue of campaign finance reform is not a simple question of good and bad. Those who support restrictions on money from corporations and large donors do so in the name of political integrity, and even if the current Court accepts only a quid pro quo definition of corruption, advocates of BCRA and other measures are legitimately worried about other types of corruption, such as purchasing access or influencing votes on particular issues. Certainly, the record of the National Rifle Association is a worst-case example of how legislators have been cowed into opposing any and all gun controls.

On the other hand, opponents of measures such as BCRA base their argument on traditional First Amendment grounds. One might well recall the words of Louis Brandeis in *Whitney v. California* (1927): "If there be time to expose through discussion the falsehood and fallacies, to avert the evil by the processes of education, the remedy to be applied is more speech, not enforced silence." At the heart of the Speech Clause is political speech, and it may take several forms, as Chief Justice Roberts pointed out, including wearing protest armbands and burning the flag, as well as protecting political speech exercised through monetary contributions.

Whether we like it or not, in politics money is speech, and the simplest way to see this is that without funds, candidates for office cannot afford the expenses entailed in modern campaigns. That was the rationale in *Buckley*, but where the Court went wrong, in my opinion, is that contributing to a campaign is also a form of speech. Shaun McCutcheon had money, but he did not have the desire to hold an elected office. He did, however, have strong views, and he expressed his ideas in a perfectly legitimate way—he gave money to candidates whose positions reflected his. Those donations were McCutcheon's speech, a fact recognized by the Court even if it did not follow Justice Thomas's call to do away with the *Buckley* dichotomy.

Justice O'Connor in her *McConnell* opinion declared that "money, like water, will always find an outlet." One could take this several ways. One is that there will always be money in politics, there always has been, and it is a fact of political life we should acknowledge. As Senator McConnell suggested, soft money is not gone; it just has a different address. No matter how we try to protect the integrity of the political system, we cannot do it by trying to cut off the funding needed by candidates.

Early on I quoted my friend Robert Post's Tanner Lectures at Harvard, in which he said that in thirty years of teaching he had been unable to make sense of the Court's campaign finance decisions: "The need for political speech appears self-evident, but so also does the need for electoral integrity. Each seems indispensable, and yet in cases like *Citizens United* they appear incompatible." While sharply criticizing both *Buckley* and *Citizens United,* Post's proposal of a "managerial authority" to protect the "electoral integrity" of the political process seems to me as fraught with difficulties as the current situation.

In the past, legislators have been moved to enact reform legislation only after a scandal exposed the worst side of campaign financing. In the history of campaign finance reform, that seems to be the pattern, and the only time that an effort is made to rein in excesses. The decisions of the Roberts Court eviscerating McCain-Feingold call into question whether even scandal could now bring forth legislation to protect the integrity of the electoral system.

Federal Election Campaign Act of 1971

Although Congress did not actually finish passage of the bill until January 1972, it continues to be known as the act of 1971.

General

- Broadened definitions of *contribution* and *expenditure* as applied to a political campaign, but exempted monetary loans made in accordance with applicable banking laws.
- Prohibited the promise of employment or other political benefits by any candidate in exchange for support.
- Exempted communications, nonpartisan registration, and get-out-the-vote campaigns by corporations aimed at their stockholders or by unions aimed at their members.
- Exempted from the contribution and expenditure limits separate funds to be used by a corporation or a union solely for political purposes.

Contribution Limits

- Imposed a ceiling on contributions by any candidate or members of his or her immediate family to his or her own campaign of $50,000 for president or vice president; $35,000 for senators; and $25,000 for representatives.

Spending Limits

- Restricted the total amount that could be spent by federal candidates for advertising in communications media to ten cents per eligible voter or $50,000, whichever was greater. The number would be determined annually by the US Bureau of the Census.

- Defined *communications media* to include radio, television, newspapers, magazines, billboards, and automatic telephone equipment.
- Of this spending limit, no more than 60 percent could be spent on radio and television.
- During the presidential primary season, candidates for their party's nomination would also be subject to the ten-cents-per-voter limit.
- Provided that the broadcast and nonbroadcast spending limits be increased in proportion to the annual increases in the Consumer Price Index over the base year of 1970.

Disclosure and Enforcement

- Required all political committees that anticipated receiving more than $1,000 during a calendar year to file an organizational statement listing the principal officers, scope of activities, names of the candidates it supported, and such other information required by law.
- Named the appropriate federal officers to oversee this registration as the clerk of the House for House candidates, the secretary of the Senate for Senate candidates, and the controller general for presidential candidates.
- Required each committee to report any individual expenditures of more than $100 and any expenditures aggregating more than $100 during a calendar year.
- Required each committee to report all contributions in excess of $100, with the name and address of the contributor and the date of the contribution.
- Required the supervisory officers to prepare annual reports based on the committee submissions and to make them available to the public.
- Required the reporting of the names, addresses, and occupations of any lender or endorser of any loan in excess of $100.
- Required any person who made any contribution in excess of $100, other than through a political committee or directly to the candidate, to report that to the supervisory officers.

- Prohibited any contribution to a candidate or a committee by one person in the name of another.
- Required that all reports filed with the federal government also be filed with the secretary of state in the state in which the committee operated or the election was held.

———

Miscellaneous

- Prohibited radio and television stations from charging political candidates a rate more than the lowest unit cost for the same advertising time available to commercial advertisers. This provision would apply only in the forty-five days prior to a primary and in the sixty days prior to a general election.
- Provided that any amounts spent by an agent of the candidate and fees paid to an agent for services would be considered part of the expenses covered by the overall limits.
- No radio or television station could charge for advertising unless it received written consent from the candidate and unless the candidate certified that these charges would not exceed the legal expenditure limits.

1974 Amendments to FECA

Federal Election Commission

- Created a six-member commission, consisting of three Democrats and three Republicans, to enforce and monitor the law.
- The president, the Speaker of the House, and the president pro tem of the Senate would each appoint two members, one from each party, all subject to confirmation by both houses of Congress.
- The secretary of the Senate and the clerk of the House, as the designated record keepers under the 1971 FECA, would serve as ex officio members, primarily to provide access to the records in their custodial care.
- The commissioners would serve staggered six-year terms, with a rotating one-year chair.

Contribution Limits

- Set a limit of $1,000 per person for each primary, runoff, or general election, with a limit of $25,000 per year to all candidates for federal office.
- Set a limit of $5,000 per organization, political committee, or national or state party organization for each election, but no limit on the aggregate amount they could spend in a campaign or the amount they could contribute to party organizations supporting federal candidates.
- Set limits on what candidates and their families could spend out of their own pockets—$50,000 for president or vice president, $35,000 for a Senate seat, and $25,000 for a House seat.
- Set a limit of $1,000 on independent expenditures by private persons on behalf of a candidate.

- Barred cash contributions of more than $100 and foreign contributions.

Spending Limits

- Presidential primaries—$10 million total per candidate for all primaries. In a state presidential primary, a candidate may spend no more than twice what a Senate candidate in that state would be allowed to spend.
- Presidential general elections—$20 million per candidate.
- Presidential nominating conventions—$2 million for each major political party, with lesser amounts for the minor parties.
- Senate primaries—$100,000 or 8¢ per eligible voter, whichever is greater.
- Senate general elections—$150,000 or 12 per eligible voter, whichever is higher.
- House primaries and general elections—$70,000 in each.
- National party spending—$10,000 per candidate in House general election; $20,000 or 2¢ per eligible voter, whichever is greater, for each candidate in Senate general elections; and 2¢ per voter (approximately $2.9 million) in presidential general elections. These expenditures would be above the candidate's individual spending limits.
- For those states where a House seat covers the whole state the House candidate would have the same spending limit as the Senate candidate.
- Repealed the media spending limitations in the 1971 FECA.
- Exempted expenditures of up to $500 for food and beverages, invitations, unreimbursed travel expenses by volunteers, and spending on "slate cards" and sample ballots.
- Exempted fundraising costs of up to 20 percent of the candidate spending limits. Thus, the spending limit for House candidates would be effectively raised from $70,000 to $84,000, and for candidates in presidential primaries from $10 million to $12 million.
- Provided that spending limits be increased in proportion to annual increases in the Consumer Price Index.

Public Financing

- Presidential general elections—voluntary public financing. Major party candidates would automatically qualify for full funding before the campaign. Minor party and independent candidates would be eligible to receive a proportion of full fundraising based on past or current votes received. If a candidate opted for full public funding, no private contributions would be permitted.
- Presidential nominating conventions—optional public funding. Major parties automatically would qualify. Minor parties would be eligible for lesser amounts based on their proportion of votes received in a past election.
- Presidential primaries—matching public funds of up to $5 million per candidate after meeting fundraising requirement of $100,000 raised in amounts of at least $5,000 in each of twenty states or more. Only the first $250 of individual private contributions would be matched. The matching funds were to be divided among the candidates as quickly as possible. In allocating the money, the order in which the candidates qualified would be taken into account. Only private gifts raised after January 1, 1975, would qualify for the 1976 general elections. No federal payments would be made before January 1976.
- Provided that all federal money for public funding of campaigns would come from the Presidential Election Campaign Fund. Money received from the federal income tax dollar checkoff automatically would be appropriated to the fund.

Disclosures and Enforcements

- Each candidate has to establish one central campaign committee through which all contributions and expenditures on behalf of that candidate must be reported. In addition, each committee has to designate specific bank depositories for campaign funds.
- Full reports of contributions and expenditures must be filed with the Federal Election Commission ten days before and thirty days after every election, and within ten days of the close of each quarter, unless the committee expended less than $1,000 in that quarter.

In nonelection years, the committee must also file a year-end report.

- Contributions of $1,000 or more, received within fifteen days before an election, must be reported to the FEC within forty-eight hours.
- Prohibited contributions made in the name of another.
- Loans would be treated as contributions, and all loans had to have a cosigner or guarantor for each $1,000 of outstanding debt.
- Any organization that took any action or spent any money or committed any act for the purpose of influencing an election (including but not limited to the publication of voting records) must file a report as a political committee.
- Every person who spent or contributed more than $100, other than through or to a candidate or political committee, must report that sum.
- Permitted government contractors, unions, and corporations to maintain separate and segregated political funds.
- Provided that the FEC would receive campaign reports, make rules and regulations (subject to review by Congress within thirty days), maintain a cumulative index of reports (both filed and not filed), make regular and special reports to Congress and to the president, and serve as an election information clearinghouse.
- The FEC received the power to render advisory opinions, conduct audits and investigations, subpoena witnesses and information, and go to court to seek civil injunctions.
- Criminal cases would be referred by the FEC to the Justice Department for prosecution.
- Increased existing fines for violation of the law to $50,000.
- Provided that a candidate for federal office who failed to file reports could be prohibited for the term of that office plus one year.

———

Miscellaneous

- Set January 1, 1975, as the effective date for the act, except that there would be immediate preemption of state laws.
- Removed Hatch Act restrictions on voluntary activities by state and local employees in federal campaigns if not prohibited by state law.

- Prohibited solicitation of campaign funds through the use of franked mail.
- Preempted state election laws for federal candidates.
- Permitted use of excess campaign funds to defray expenses of holding federal office or for other lawful purposes.

1976 Amendments to FECA

Federal Election Commission

- Reorganized the FEC as a six-person panel, all members of which were to be appointed by the president and confirmed by the Senate.
- Prohibited members of the FEC from engaging in any outside business activities, and gave them one year from the time they joined the commission to end such business interests.
- Gave Congress the power to veto individual sections of any regulation proposed by the panel.

Contribution Limits

- An individual could give no more than $5,000 a year to a political action committee and $20,000 to the national committee of a political party; this amplified but did not negate the 1974 provision that set a $1,000-per-election limit on individual contributions to a candidate and an aggregate limit for individuals of $25,000 a year.
- Limited a multicandidate committee to giving no more than $15,000 a year to the national committee; the 1974 limit of $5,000 per election, per candidate remained in effect.
- The Democratic and Republican senatorial campaign committees could give no more than $17,500 a year to a candidate.
- Permitted campaign committees organized to back a single candidate to offer "occasional, isolated, and incidental support" to another candidate; the 1974 law had not permitted any support by such a committee to anyone else.
- Attempted to stop the proliferation of political action committees by membership groups, corporations, and unions. All political action committees established by a company or an international union

would be treated as a single committee for purposes of campaign limits, namely, $5,000 to the same candidate in any election.

Spending Limits

- Presidential and vice presidential candidates could not spend more than $50,000 of their own or their families' money on their campaigns if they accepted public financing.
- Exempted from the spending limits payments by a candidate or a national committee for the legal and accounting services required to comply with the campaign law, but required that such expenditures still be reported.

Public Financing

- Presidential candidates who received federal matching funds and then withdrew from the prenomination campaign had to return unspent federal money.
- Cut off federal funds to any candidate who received less than 10 percent of the vote in two consecutive presidential primaries in which he or she had entered.
- Set out procedures by which an individual who became ineligible for matching federal funds could have eligibility restored through an FEC finding.

Disclosure and Enforcement

- Gave the FEC exclusive power to prosecute civil violations of the law and transferred to the commission jurisdiction over violations formerly in the criminal code, in effect giving it full jurisdiction over all types of violations of federal campaign election law.
- Required approval of four members of the FEC to issue regulations or advisory opinions or to initiate civil actions and investigations.
- Labor unions, corporations, and membership organizations had to

report expenditures of $2,000 or more per election that had been used to communicate with their members or stockholders urging them to support or oppose particular candidates. Expenditures on issues would not have to be reported.

- Candidates and political committees had to keep records of contributions of $50 or more; the 1974 law had set the amount at $10.

- Candidates and political committees could waive the requirement for quarterly finance reports in a nonelection year if less than $5,000 had been raised or spent; the 1974 limit had been $1,000. Annual reports would still have to be filed.

- Political committees and individuals making an independent expenditure of more than $100 to advocate the election or defeat of a candidate had to file a report with the FEC, and the committee or individual state, under penalty of perjury, had to verify that the expenditure had not been made in collusion with a candidate.

- Independent expenditures of $1,000 or more made within fifteen days of an election had to be reported within twenty-four hours.

- The FEC could issue advisory opinions relating only to specific factual situations, and such advisories could not be used to spell out commission policy. Such opinions had precedential value only for future situations where the factual situation was for all intents and purposes the same as the original.

- The FEC could initiate investigations only after it received a properly verified complaint or had reason to believe, based on information that came to it in the normal course of its business, that a violation had occurred or would occur in the near future. It could not launch an investigation based on anonymous complaints.

- The commission had to make an effort at reconciliation on allegations of campaign law violations before going to court. Violations of criminal law would still be referred to the Department of Justice, and the attorney general had to report back to the FEC within sixty days what action, if any, he or she had taken, and then every thirty days thereafter until the matter had been fully resolved, either through trial or dismissal.

- If an individual knowingly violated the campaign law for a sum of money greater than $1,000, he or she would be liable under a criminal provision for a one-year jail sentence and a fine of up to $25,000, or three times the amount of the contribution or expenditure involved, whichever was greater.

- Civil penalties could be imposed for violation of the law in fines of $5,000 or an amount equal to the contributions or expenditures involved, whichever was greater. For violations knowingly committed, in addition to the criminal penalties there could be civil fines of $10,000 or an amount equal to twice the amount involved, whichever was greater. The civil fines could be imposed either by courts or by the FEC as part of a conciliation agreement.

Miscellaneous

- The law placed greater limits on the fundraising abilities of corporate and union political action committees. Companies could seek contributions only from stockholders or from executive and administrative personnel and their families. Unions could solicit only from union members and their families. Twice a year, however, corporate and union PACs could seek contributions through mailings from all persons not included in this restriction. Such contributions would have to be anonymous and be received by a third party that would keep records, but would transfer the funds to the PACs without identifying the donors.
- Trade association PACs could solicit contributions from stockholders, executive and administrative personnel, and their families of member companies.
- Union PACs could use the same method to solicit campaign contributions as corporate PACs, and would then have to reimburse the company at cost for mailings and other related expenses.

1979 Amendments to FECA

Disclosure

- Candidates for federal office had to file finance reports if more than $5,000 was either received in contributions or expended. The earlier law required reports no matter the amount raised or spent.
- Local party organizations were excused from filing reports for certain voluntary activities, such as get-out-the-vote and voter registration drives, if the amount expended on these activities came to less than $5,000 a year. However, if expenditures on activities outside this area amounted to more than $1,000, a report had to be filed. Previously a report had to be filed when the costs for any types of expenditures exceeded $1,000.
- An individual could spend up to $1,000 on behalf of a candidate or $2,000 for a political party in the form of so-called voluntary expenses, such as use of his or her home, food, or personal travel, without it being counted as a reportable donation.
- Political committees would no longer have to have a chairperson, but would continue to have to have a named treasurer.
- Ten days, instead of the previous five, would now be allowed for a person who received a contribution of $50 or more on behalf of a candidate's committee to forward it to the treasurer of that committee.
- Committee treasurers had to preserve financial records for at least three years. Previously the FEC could set the time that records had to be kept.
- A candidate's campaign committee had to have the name of the candidate in its title, and a political action committee had to have the name of its affiliated organization in its title.
- The law reduced the amount of information that political action committees needed to provide in order to register from eleven to six categories. An important category the law removed was the requirement

that political action committees name the candidates they supported. In effect this merely cured a problem of duplication, since the committees still had to report the names of candidates to which they contributed money.

- The law reduced the total number of mandatory reports candidates and committees had to file from twenty-four to nine and set the dates for these reports on a schedule that gave the officials responsible for preparing reports a little more time to do so.

- Presidential campaign committees had to file monthly reports, plus pre- and postelection reports during an election year if they had received contributions of more than $100,000. Committees receiving less than this amount would file quarterly reports. During a nonelection year the committees could choose whether to file monthly or quarterly reports.

- Political committees not directly affiliated with a candidate had to file either monthly reports or a minimum of nine reports during a two-year election cycle.

- The FEC had to be notified within forty-eight hours of contributions of $1,000 or more made between twenty days and forty-eight hours before the election. Previously the window had been fifteen days and forty-eight hours.

- Names of all contributors of $200 or more had to be reported; previously the amount had been $100.

- All expenses above $200 had to be itemized; the previous threshold had been $100.

- Independent expenditures of $250 or more had to be reported; the previous amount had been $100.

Federal Election Commission

- The law established a "best effort" standard by which the FEC would determine if a candidate or a committee had complied with the law. Committees had complained about the difficulty of meeting all of the minutiae in the law and regulations, and this provision made compliance rest upon the spirit of the effort rather than complete attainment of all requirements.

{ *Appendix D* }

- Extended the right to ask for an advisory opinion to any person who had a question about a specific campaign transaction; previously only officeholders, candidates, and committees could make such a request.
- Required the FEC to issue advisory opinions within sixty days of the request rather than the previous "reasonable time." If a request were made within sixty days of an election, the FEC had to respond in twenty days.
- Within five days of receiving a complaint about an election law violation, the FEC had to notify any person or committee accused of the violation. The accused then had fifteen days to respond.
- Four of the six members of the FEC had to vote that there was "reason to believe" that a violation of the law had occurred in order for an investigation to begin, at which point the accused would be notified that an investigation was in process.
- If four members believed that probable cause existed that a violation had taken place, the FEC would be required to try to resolve the matter by conciliation within ninety days. Approval of the conciliation agreement required assent by four of the six members.
- The FEC would no longer serve a clearinghouse function on information on all elections, but only those for federal office.
- The FEC would no longer conduct random audits of committees but would initiate an audit only after four members of the commission voted that evidence existed that a specific committee had not complied substantially with federal election law.
- The secretaries of state had to keep copies of FEC reports on file for public examination for two years; previously they had to keep reports on House candidates on file for five years, and reports on Senate and presidential candidates for ten years.
- The law provided for an expedited procedure by which the Senate as well as the House could veto proposed FEC regulations.

Enforcement

- Extended the basic substance of both the civil and criminal provisions of the earlier law.
- Allowed PACs to include ten pseudonyms on each report to protect

against the illegal use of names of contributors. The true identity of the ten would be provided to the FEC but not made public.

- The law prohibited the use of FEC reports, particularly names of contributors, for commercial solicitation, but the names of PACs listed with the FEC could be used to solicit campaign contributions.

Political Parties

- State and local party groups could buy, without limit, buttons, bumper stickers, yard signs, and the like for voluntary activities.
- State and local party groups could conduct voter registration and get-out-the-vote drives on behalf of presidential tickets without any financial limit.

Public Financing

- The amount given to the Democratic Party and the Republican Party to help finance their nominating conventions was raised from $2 million to $3 million.

Miscellaneous

- Buttons and printed materials could promote one candidate and make passing reference to another candidate without that being considered a contribution to the second candidate. In commercial advertisements, whether in print or broadcast media, such references could not be made unless reported as a contribution to the second candidate.
- Leftover campaign funds (but not federal matching dollars) could be given to other political committees or to charities.
- Leftover campaign funds could not be converted to personal use, except by members of Congress at the time of the law's enactment.
- Members of Congress, candidates for Congress, and federal em-

ployees could not solicit campaign contributions from other federal employees; an inadvertent solicitation would not be a violation.

- Congressional employees could make voluntary contributions to members of Congress other than their own immediate employers.
- The law continued the ban on solicitation or receipt of campaign contributions in a federal building. It would not be a violation, however, if contributions received at a federal building (such as a check sent to a senator at her office) were forwarded within seven days to the appropriate political committee, and if instructions for sending contributions did not indicate that they should be sent to a federal office.

Bipartisan Campaign Reform Act of 2002

Title I: Reduction of Special Interest Influence

BAN ON SOFT MONEY

- National parties and congressional committees may only raise and spend hard money received from individuals and political action committees (PACs).
- Labor unions and corporations may not contribute to campaigns.
- State parties have to use hard money contributions to pay for get-out-the-vote and voter registration drives in the 120 days preceding an election.
- State parties must also use hard money to pay for any activities designed to influence a federal election during an election year (even-numbered years).
- A $10,000 individual contribution is made for specified state activities.
- Candidates may not raise soft money for get-out-the-vote, voter registration, or other federal election activities.

CONTRIBUTION LIMITS

- Individual limits for contributions to candidates are raised from $1,000 to $2,000, with primary and general elections considered two separate elections.
- Individual aggregate limits are raised from $25,000 to $37,500 per year.
- An individual may give $25,000 (up from $20,000) of the annual aggregate to national political party committees, and $10,000 (up from $5,000) to state party committees.
- National party committees may give $35,000 (up from $17,500) to a party Senate campaign.

- These numbers are to be indexed for inflation in odd-numbered years and are to remain in effect for the entire two-year election cycle.

- National party committees (and any of their subordinate committees), as well as certain other types of political committees, must file reports with the Federal Election Commission (FEC) regarding the amount and sources of the moneys raised and expended during federal election activity.
- So-called building funds, originally permitted to manage soft money expenditures, are abolished.

Title II: Noncandidate Campaign Expenditures

ELECTIONEERING COMMUNICATIONS DISCLOSURE

- Every organization not otherwise banned from making electioneering communications must report any expenditure of $10,000 or greater on broadcast electioneering communications.
- Such a communication is defined as any broadcast, cable, or satellite communication that clearly refers to an identified candidate; is run within sixty days of a general election or thirty days of a primary, convention, or caucus; and is designed to influence the electorate for that office.
- Should these previous provisions be struck down by the courts, then a secondary definition would come into play regarding advertisements that promoted, supported, attacked, or opposed a candidate. If a communication at any time during the election year is "suggestive of no plausible meaning other than an exhortation to vote for or against a specific candidate," then it is an electioneering communication and subject to the other provisions of the law.
- Within twenty-four hours of such a communication, a report must be filed with the FEC that details the name of the person buying the airtime, the treasurer's name, organization contact information, the election, and the name(s) of the candidate(s) identified in the

advertisement as well as the names and addresses of all donors contributing more than $1,000 and all disbursements over $200.

COORDINATED COMMUNICATIONS AS CONTRIBUTIONS

- Electioneering communications made in coordination with a candidate or party committee are regarded as contributions to the candidate or committee, and subject to all hard money requirements and limits.

RESTRICTIONS ON CORPORATIONS AND LABOR UNIONS

- Corporations and labor unions are prohibited from running or indirectly financing electioneering communications identifying or targeting a federal candidate within sixty days of a general election. However, a corporate or union PAC may pay for such activities with hard money.
- Nonprofit corporations exempt under §§501(c)(4) and 527 of the Internal Revenue Code may not run targeted communications.
- A targeted communication is a broadcast, cable, or satellite communication run within sixty days of a general election or thirty days of a primary, featuring the name or likeness of a candidate whose audience consists primarily of the residents of the state associated with the candidate identified in the advertisement.

INDEPENDENT EXPENDITURE DEFINITION

- An independent expenditure expressly advocates the election or defeat of a clearly identified candidate and cannot be coordinated with candidates or their campaign committees.

DISCLOSURE SCHEDULE FOR INDEPENDENT EXPENDITURE GROUPS

- Sponsors of independent expenditures who spend more than $10,000 at any time during an election cycle must disclose details of that expenditure within forty-eight hours to the FEC. During the last twenty days before an election, independent expenditures exceeding $1,000 must be disclosed to the FEC within twenty-four hours.
- Each time these limits are exceeded within these time frames, the sponsor must file a new report to the FEC within forty-eight or twenty-four hours.

- Parties must choose to make either independent expenditures or co-ordinated expenditures on behalf of congressional candidates, but may not do both.

PARTY AND CANDIDATE COORDINATION

- Coordination between a party and a candidate occurs when payment is made in cooperation with, at the suggestion of, or per an understanding with a candidate, a candidate's agent or campaign, or party.
- The FEC is instructed to expand its current definition of coordination, taking into account factors such as republication of campaign materials, use of a common vendor, common employees, substantial discussion between an advertiser and a candidate or party, and coordination of corporate or union internal communications on get-out-the-vote, voter registration, or electioneering communications.

———

Title III: Miscellaneous

PERSONAL USE OF CAMPAIGN FUNDS

- Candidates are prohibited from using campaign funds for personal use.

FUNDRAISING ON FEDERAL PROPERTY

- Fundraising on federal property, including the White House and the Capitol, is prohibited.

FOREIGN DONATIONS

- Candidates and parties may not receive donations from persons who are not citizens or permanent legal residents.

MILLIONAIRE OPPONENT

- In order to address the growing number of millionaires using their own personal wealth to seek federal office, the contribution limits for Senate candidates facing self-financing candidates are increased on a sliding scale.
- A threshold is established of $150,000 plus the number of eligible voters in the state times 4¢.

- If the personal spending of a wealthy candidate, minus that of the opponent, exceeds that threshold by a factor of two or three, the limit on individual contributions for the non-self-financing candidate is increased 300 percent to $6,000.
- If the threshold is exceeded by four to twenty times, the limit on individual contributions is increased 600 percent to $12,000.
- If the threshold is exceeded by a factor greater than 10, the limit on individual contributions is raised sixfold, and the limit on all party-coordinated expenditures is removed.

TELEVISION MEDIA RATES

- Broadcast stations may not raise rates for campaign advertisements.
- Stations currently required to charge candidates their lowest unit cost may no longer bump campaign advertisements in favor of commercial ads paying a higher rate.
- In order to receive the lowest unit cost, candidates must certify to the stations that they will include in their ads an audio statement that the candidate and/or sponsor takes responsibility for the content of the ad. If the candidate makes this statement, he or she must identify him- or herself.
- A television ad must also include a picture of the sponsoring candidate.
- Parties may also avail themselves of the lowest unit cost rate if they follow the conditions in this section.

FEC SOFTWARE FOR DISCLOSURE

- The FEC is to develop standards for vendors to follow in developing software for campaign finance reporting that is user-friendly, transmits instantaneously, and is posted on the internet immediately. Candidates for the presidency and for the House of Representatives will be required to file electronically beginning in 2001.

POLITICAL AD DISCOUNT FOR PARTIES IS CONDITIONED ON COORDINATED SPENDING-LIMIT DONATIONS TO PRESIDENTIAL INAUGURAL COMMITTEES

- All contributions to presidential inaugural committees have to be reported and posted on the FEC website. Foreign nationals or persons born overseas who are not US citizens may not contribute to inaugural committees.

PUBLIC FINANCING STUDY

- The FEC is required to complete within one year after passage of the law a study of public financing of campaigns, as currently implemented in states such as Arizona and Maine.

CLARITY ON ELECTION-RELATED ADVERTISING DISCLAIMERS

- Existing requirements on sponsorship statements, to let viewers know who is paying for political advertisements, are extended to include all electioneering communications sponsored by political committees, parties, candidate committees, and PACs.
- The disclaimer must include the sponsor's name, website, or street address, and must be legible. Candidate-run television advertisements must include a picture of the candidate.

INCREASE IN PENALTIES FOR FECA VIOLATIONS

- For any violation where the sum involved is $25,000 or less, a person may be fined or imprisoned for no more than one year, or both. Where the sum is greater than $25,000, a person may be fined or imprisoned for no more than five years, or both.

STATUTE OF LIMITATIONS FOR FECA VIOLATIONS

- The statute of limitations for election law violations is extended from three to five years.

SENTENCING GUIDELINES FOR FECA VIOLATIONS

- The US Sentencing Commission is directed to develop and/or amend FECA violation guidelines based on aggravating or mitigating circumstances, and make legislative recommendations to Congress within ninety days of the passage of BCRA.
- Penalties are to be enhanced for violations involving foreign money, large numbers of transactions, large dollar amounts, use of governmental funds, intent to achieve a benefit from government, and involvement of candidates and/or campaign officials.

- The civil penalty is increased to 300 percent of the amount involved in the violation, up to a maximum of 1,000 percent of $50,000. The criminal penalty is increased to at least 300 percent of the amount involved, up to a maximum of 1,000 percent or $50,000, and up to two years' imprisonment.

Title IV: Severability; Effective Date

SEVERABILITY

- If the Supreme Court invalidates any part of BCRA, the remainder of the bill remains in force.

EFFECTIVE DATE

- This act will go into effect thirty days after enactment.

EXPEDITED COURT REVIEW

- Any constitutional challenges to this law will be heard in the federal district court for the District of Columbia, and any appeals from its decision will go directly to the US Supreme Court. The courts are also to expedite any challenges "to the greatest possible extent."

Title V: Additional Disclosure Provisions

FEC INTERNET POSTINGS OF DISCLOSURE

- Electronically filed disclosure notices must be posted by the FEC on its website within twenty-four hours of receipt; paper disclosures must be filed within forty-eight hours. All PACs, candidates, and campaign committees that raise over $50,000 must henceforth file all disclosure reports electronically.

FEC WEBSITE "CLEARINGHOUSE"

- The FEC is to create a centralized website of all reports filed under FECA, and any other "election-related information" disclosed to other agencies, such as the Internal Revenue Service (IRS) and the Federal Communications Commission (FCC).

DISCLOSURE SCHEDULE FOR PARTIES AND CANDIDATES

- Candidates must file monthly disclosure reports during the election year, and national party committees must file monthly reports at all times.

POLITICAL ADVERTISER DISCLOSURE TO TELEVISION AND RADIO STATIONS

- Radio and television stations must make available to the public information on political advertising. The FCC already requires such records to be kept, but now they are to be public and must include the name of the person buying the airtime, contract information, a list of the sponsoring organization's executives and directors, the rate charged, the class of the time sold, and the date and times such ads ran on the air.

CHRONOLOGY

1883	Pendleton Act
1897	Nebraska, Missouri, Tennessee, and Florida ban corporate contributions
1905	Armstrong Committee exposes insurance scandals
1907	Tillman Act, first federal effort to reform campaign financing
1910	Publicity Act
1921	*United States v. Newberry*
1923	Teapot Dome Scandal
1925	Federal Corrupt Practices Act
1939	Hatch Act
1940	Hatch Act Amendments limiting certain types of contributions
1943	War Labor Disputes Act limited union contributions
1944	Establishment of first political action committees by labor
1947	Taft-Hartley Act made permanent ban on labor union contributions
1960	Kennedy-Nixon television debates
1961	President Kennedy appoints Heard Commission to investigate campaign financing
1966	Long Act authorizes limited federal funding of presidential campaigns
1971	Federal Election Campaign Act (FECA)
1971	Revenue Act implements federal funding of presidential campaigns
1972	*United States v. Brewster*
1973–1974	Watergate scandals; President Nixon resigns in August 1974
1974	FECA Amendments
1974	Federal Election Commission established as a congressional agency
1976	*Buckley v. Valeo*
1977	Federal Election Commission reestablished with presidential appointments
1979	Additional FECA amendments, which allowed "soft money"
1987	Byrd-Boren bill to limit PAC moneys
1990	*Austin v. Michigan Chamber of Commerce*
1990	Keating savings and loan scandal
1996	Bill Clinton and Al Gore find ways around campaign finance laws
2002	Bipartisan Campaign Reform Act (McCain-Feingold)

LIST OF CASES

American Tradition Partnership, Inc. v. Bullock, 567 U.S. 516 (2012)

Arizona Freedom Enterprise Club's Freedom Club PAC v. Bennett, 564 U.S. 721 (2011)

Austin v. Michigan Chamber of Commerce, 494 U.S. 652 (1990)

Barry v. United States, 279 U.S. 597 (1929)

Bluman v. Federal Election Commission, 800 F. Supp. 2d 281 (D.C. Cir. 2011) (aff. 565 U.S. 1104 (2012)

Brown v. Socialist Workers '74 Campaign Committee, 459 U.S. 87 (1982)

Buckley v. Valeo, 424 U.S. 1 (1976)

Buckley v. Valeo, 519 F.2d 821 (D.C. Cir. 1975)

Burroughs and Cannon v. United States, 290 U.S. 534 (1934)

Bush v. Gore, 531 U.S. 98 (2000)

California Medical Association v. Federal Election Commission, 453 U.S. 182 (1981)

Caperton v. A. T. Massey Coal Co., 556 U.S. 868 (2009)

Citizens against Rent Control v. Berkeley, 454 U.S. 290 (1981)

Citizens United v. Federal Election Commission, 558 U.S. 310 (2010)

Colorado Republican Federal Campaign Committee v. Federal Election Commission, 518 U.S. 604 (1996) (*Colorado I*)

Common Cause v. Democratic National Committee et al., 333 F. Supp. 803 (D.D.C. 1971)

Common Cause v. Federal Election Commission, 692 F. Supp. 1391 (D.D.C. 1987)

Davis v. Federal Election Commission, 554 U.S. 724 (2008)

Doe v. Reed, 561 U.S. 186 (2010)

EMILY's List v. Federal Election Commission, 581 F.3d 1 (D.C. Cir. 2010)

Federal Election Commission v. Beaumont, 539 U.S. 146 (2003)

Federal Election Commission v. Colorado Republican Federal Campaign Committee, 533 U.S. 431 (2001) (*Colorado II*)

Federal Election Commission v. Massachusetts Citizens for Life, 479 U.S. 238 (1986)

Federal Election Commission v. National Conservative PAC, 470 U.S. 480 (1985)

Federal Election Commission v. National Right to Work Committee, 459 U.S. 197 (1982)

Federal Election Commission v. Wisconsin Right to Life, 541 U.S. 449 (2007)

First National Bank of Boston v. Attorney General, 371 Mass. 773 (1977)

First National Bank of Boston v. Bellotti, 435 U.S. 765 (1978)

Gibson v. Florida Legislative Investigating Committee, 372 U.S. 539 (1963)

Iowa Right to Life Committee v. Smithson, 750 F. Supp. 2d 1020 (S.D. Iowa 2010)

Iowa Right to Life Committee v. Tooker, 717 F.3d 576 (8th Cir. 2013); cert. denied, 134 S.Ct. 1787 (2014)

Lochner v. New York, 198 U.S. 45 (1905)

McConnell v. Federal Election Commission, 251 F. Supp. 2d 176 (D.D.C. 2003)

McConnell v. Federal Election Commission, 540 U.S. 93 (2003)

McCutcheon v. Federal Election Commission, 572 U.S. 185 (2014)

NAACP v. Alabama ex rel. Patterson, 357 U.S. 449 (1958)

New York Progress and Protection PAC v. Walsh, 733 F.3d 483 (2d Cir. 2013)

Nixon v. Shrink Missouri Government PAC, 528 U.S. 377 (2000)

Ognibene v. Parkes, 671 F.3d 174 (2nd Cir. 2011)

Pipefitters Local Union No. 562 v. United States, 407 U.S. 385 (1972)

Randall v. Sorrell, 548 U.S. 230 (2006)

Republican National Committee v. Federal Election Commission, 561 U.S. 1040 (2010)

Santa Clara County v. Southern Pacific Railroad Co., 118 U.S. 394 (1886)

SpeechNOW.org v. Federal Election Commission, 599 F.3d 686 (D.C. Cir. 2010)

Susan B. Anthony List v. Driehaus, 573 U.S. 149 (2014)

Thompson v, Dauphinais, 217 F. Supp. 3d 1023 (Alaska 2016)

Thompson v. Hebdon, 589 U.S. __ (2019)

Thompson v. Hebdon, 909 F. 3d 1027 (9th Cir. 2018)

United States v. Brewster, 408 U.S. 501 (1972)

United States v. Classic, 313 U.S. 299 (1941)

United States v. Congress of Industrial Organizations, 335 U.S. 106 (1948)

United States v. International Union of United Automobile, Aircraft, and Agricultural Implement Workers of America, 352 U.S. 567 (1957)

United States v. National Committee for Impeachment, 469 F.2d 1135 (2nd Cir. 1972)

United States v. Newberry, 256 U.S. 232 (1921)

Whitney v. California, 274 U.S. 357 (1927)

Williams-Yulee v. Florida Bar, 135 S.Ct. 1056 (2015)

Wisconsin Right to Life v. Federal Election Commission, 546 U.S. 410 (2006)

BIBLIOGRAPHIC ESSAY

There are literally hundreds of books and law review articles on campaign finance and efforts to reform it, and the topic has been reported in the popular press as well, both in news stories and as opinion pieces. What follows, therefore, should be understood as a skimming of the surface, pointing to books and articles that can get the reader, if she so wishes, deeper into the topic.

For the early years of campaigning and how Americans in the early national period financed elections, see the older but still useful Richard P. McCormick, *The Second American Party System: Party Formation in the Jacksonian Era* (Chapel Hill: University of North Carolina Press, 1966), and George Thayer, *Who Shakes the Money Tree? American Campaign Financing from 1789 to the Present* (New York: Simon & Schuster, 1971). For the Pendleton Act, which in many ways was the first effort at campaign finance reform, see Ari H. Hoogenboom, *Outlawing the Spoils: A History of the Civil Service Reform Movement, 1865–1883* (Champaign: University of Illinois Press, 1961).

Good overviews of mid-twentieth-century reform efforts are Robert E. Mutch, *Campaigns, Congress, and the Courts: The Making of Federal Campaign Finance Law* (Westport, CT: Praeger, 1988); Frank J. Sorauf, *Money in American Elections* (Boston: Little, Brown, 1988); and Jeffrey H. Birnbaum, *The Money Men: The Real Story of Fund-raising's Influence on Political Power in America* (New York: Crown, 2000). For a typical negative view of efforts to reform campaign financing, see Bradley A. Smith, *Unfree Speech: The Folly of Campaign Finance Reform* (Princeton, NJ: Princeton University Press, 2001). Frank J. Sorauf, *Inside Campaign Finance: Myths and Realities* (New Haven, CT: Yale University Press, 1992), is also useful. Although we tend to associate the abuses of big money in presidential campaigns, we should recall that all of the various laws have also been directed at House and Senate races. For this, see Robert K. Goidel, Donald A. Gross, and Todd G. Shields, *Money Matters: Consequences of Campaign Finance Reform in U.S. House Elections* (Lanham, MD: Rowman and Littlefield, 1999).

One of the best-known scholars of the subject was Herbert E.

Alexander, whose *Financing Politics: Money, Elections, and Political Reform* went through many editions; see the fourth edition (Washington, DC: CQ Press, 1992). Alexander also did a number of studies on the financing of specific elections, such as *Financing the 1964 Election* (Washington, DC: Citizens Research Foundation, 1966), and wrote the prescient article "The Political Process after the Bipartisan Campaign Finance Reform Act of 2002," 2 *Election Law Journal* 47 (2003).

For the Tillman Act, see Francis Butler Simkins, *Pitchfork Ben Tillman: South Carolinian* (Baton Rouge: Louisiana State University Press, 1944); for the next series of scandals, Burl Noggle, *Teapot Dome: Oil and Politics in the 1920s* (Baton Rouge: Louisiana State University Press, 1962), remains the best source. To see how difficult it was to find actual records of money spent in elections, even when required by law, see one of the earliest studies of the subject, Louise Overacker, *Money in Elections* (New York: Macmillan, 1932), as well as her *Presidential Campaign Funds* (Boston: Boston University Press, 1946). See also Paula C. Baker, *Curbing Campaign Cash: Henry Ford, Truman Newberry, and the Politics of Progressive Reform* (Lawrence: University Press of Kansas, 2012), and Robert E. Mutch, "The First Federal Campaign Finance Bills," in *Money and Politics*, ed. Paula Baker (University Park: Pennsylvania State University Press, 2002).

The literature on Watergate is immense, but in most of the studies there is little on the efforts to reform campaign finance. Readers interested in Watergate can start with Bob Woodward and Carl Bernstein, *All the President's Men* (New York: Simon & Schuster, 1974), and Stanley I. Kutler, *The Wars of Watergate* (New York: Alfred A. Knopf, 1990). Two works that do look at the effect on campaign finance are Ralph K. Winter Jr., *Watergate and the Law: Political Campaigns and Presidential Power* (Washington, DC: American Enterprise Institute, 1974), and J. Anthony Lukas, *Nightmare* (New York: Viking, 1976), which examine the Ervin Committee's little-noticed efforts at the time to look into some of the activities of the Committee to Re-elect the President.

Although the federal election laws were strengthened in 1974, they did not always produce the results that Congress had intended. For this, see Steven M. Gillon, *That's Not What We Meant to Do: Reform and Its Unintended Consequences in Twentieth-Century America* (New York: Norton, 2000).

Buckley v. Valeo, for better or worse, is the real starting point of the

Supreme Court trying to figure out the proper balance between freedom of speech and the integrity of the political system. See the various essays in Christopher H. Banks and John C. Green, eds., *Superintending Democracy: The Courts and the Political Process* (Akron, OH: University of Akron Press, 2001), especially those by Joel M. Gora, who was the attorney for the ACLU in *Buckley*, and by Christopher Banks. Two articles on the case that specifically address the free speech aspects are Nelson W. Polsby, "*Buckley v. Valeo:* The Special Nature of Political Speech," 1976 *Supreme Court Review* 1, and Kathleen M. Sullivan, "Political Money and Freedom of Speech," 30 *University of California Davis Law Review* 663 (1997). See also Anthony Corrado, "Money and Politics: A History of Campaign Finance Law," in *Campaign Finance Reform: A Sourcebook*, ed. Anthony Corrado, Trevor Potter, Thomas E. Mann, and David Ortiz (Washington, DC: Brookings Institution, 1997).

Much of the background leading up to McCain-Feingold involved the soaring amount of money raised and spent by campaigns at all levels. Although the Federal Election Commission is legally required to keep track and issue reports, these publications are, to say the least, usually incomprehensible. For the late 1980s through the 2008 election, see Herbert E. Alexander and Monica Bauer, *Financing the 1988 Election* (Boulder, CO: Westview Press, 1991); Herbert E. Alexander and Anthony Corrado, *Financing the 1992 Election* (Armonk, NY: M. E. Sharpe, 1995); John C. Green, ed., *Financing the 1996 Election* (Armonk, NY: M. E. Sharpe, 1999); David B. Magleby, ed., *Outside Money: Soft Money and Issue Advocacy in the 1998 Congressional Elections* (Lanham, MD: Rowman and Littlefield, 2000); David B. Magleby, ed., *Financing the 2000 Election* (Washington, DC: Brookings Institution, 2002); David B. Magleby, ed., *The Other Campaign: Soft Money and Issue Advocacy in the 2000 Congressional Elections* (Lanham, MD: Rowman and Littlefield, 2003); and David B. Magleby and Anthony Corrado, eds., *Financing the 2008 Election* (Washington, DC: Brookings Institution, 2011).

McCain-Feingold is explicated in the text, but the comments on it are plentiful. Right after its passage the American Enterprise Institute, the Brookings Institution, and the Campaign and Media Legal Center jointly sponsored the panel "The Future of Campaign Finance Reform," www .brookings.org/comm/transcripts/20020301.htm. The Public Citizen also analyzed the measure, www.citizen.org/campaign/legislation

/bcralaw/index.cfm. James Bopp Jr., one of the leading lawyers for the anti-BCRA forces, seemed to have been writing his brief even as the bill went through Congress and, together with Richard E. Coleson, published it as a law review article, "The First Amendment Needs No Reform: Protecting Liberty from Campaign Finance 'Reformers,'" 2002 *Catholic University Law Review* 51. John Samples thought the law would do little good; *The Fallacy of Campaign Finance Reform* (Chicago: University of Chicago Press, 2006).

The depositions gathered for the *McConnell* case and other materials by expert witnesses as well as members of Congress are collected in edited form in Anthony Corrado, Thomas E. Mann, and Trevor Potter, eds., *Inside the Campaign Finance Battle: Testimony on the New Reform* (Washington, DC: Brookings Institution, 2003). The Pew Foundation underwrote many of the studies submitted to the Court in favor of the legislation; these may be accessed at www.pewtrusts.com, using the search function for connections to "Campaign Finance Reform."

The lengthy and in some places tortured opinions of the three-judge district court are discussed in Robert F. Bauer, "A Glimpse into the Future? Judge Kollar-Kotelly's View of Congressional Authority to Regulate Political Money," 6 *University of Pennsylvania Journal of Constitutional Law* 95 (2003), and Richard Briffault, "What Did They Do and What Does It Mean?," *id.* at 58. Both Bauer and Trevor Potter believe the court had gotten "a bad rap" that it did not deserve. Potter, "McCain-Feingold and the D.C. District Court," 6 *Journal of Constitutional Law* 88 (2003).

As could be expected, the High Court's *McConnell* decision generated a great deal of comment on both sides. For an overview, see my essay in Melvin I. Urofsky, ed., *The Public Debate over Controversial Supreme Court Decisions* (Washington, DC: CQ Press, 2006), 377–386. The response in law journals was extensive; the following are some of the initial offerings: Lillian R. BeVier, "*McConnell v. FEC*: Not Senator Buckley's First Amendment"; Robert F. Bauer, "*McConnell*, Parties, and the Decline of the Right of Association"; Samuel Issacharoff, "Throwing in the Towel: The Constitutional Morass of Campaign Finance"; and Richard Epstein, "*McConnell v. Federal Election Commission*: A Deadly Dose of Double Deference"; all of which appeared with other articles in a symposium in 3 *Election Law Journal* (2004). See also Richard L. Hasen, "*Buckley* Is

Dead, Long Live *Buckley:* The New Campaign Finance Incoherence of *McConnell v. FEC,*" 153 *University of Pennsylvania Law Review* 31 (2004).

Citizens United, as might be expected, triggered an avalanche of comments. One place to start is Thomas O. Mason and Sophie A. James, eds., *Campaign Finance and the Citizens United Supreme Court Case* (Hauppauge, NY: Nova Science Publishers, 2011), which has some congressional testimony, analysis, as well as the text of the opinion itself. Robert C. Post of the Yale Law School gave the Tanner Lectures at Harvard in 2013; those two lectures, as well as the comments of a panel, are gathered in *Citizens Divided: Campaign Finance Reform and the Constitution* (Cambridge, MA: Harvard University Press, 2014), in which Post tried to suss out a meaning for democracy. Where Post is calm and balanced, Richard L. Hasen is not in *Plutocrats United: Campaign Money, the Supreme Court, and the Distortion of American Elections* (New Haven, CT: Yale University Press, 2016). Also in this vein is Lawrence Lessig, *Republic, Lost: How Money Corrupts Congress—and a Plan to Stop It* (New York: Twelve, 2011).

There are either biographies or works about several of the justices who sat on the Court from *McConnell* to *McCutcheon,* but the key figure here is the chief justice, John G. Roberts Jr. CNN legal analyst Joan Biskupic has written *The Chief: The Life and Turbulent Times of Chief Justice John Roberts* (New York: Basic Books, 2019). Also of interest here is Jeffrey Toobin, *The Oath: The Obama White House and the Supreme Court* (New York: Doubleday, 2012).

Nearly every law review in the country had one or more articles on the case. The following is just a limited sample: Richard Epstein, "*Citizens United v. FEC:* The Constitutional Right That Big Corporations Should Have But Do Not Want," 34 *Harvard Journal of Law and Policy* 639 (2011); Richard L. Hasen, "*Citizens United* and the Illusion of Coherence," 109 *Michigan Law Review* 581 (2011); Robert L. Kerr, "Naturalizing the Artificial Citizen: Repeating *Lochner*'s Error in *Citizens United v. FEC,*" 15 *Communication Law and Policy* 311 (2010); and Justin Levitt, "Confronting the Impact of *Citizens United,*" 29 *Yale Journal of Law and Policy Review* 217 (2010). A good share of the criticism over the case involved granting rights to corporations akin to those that the Bill of Rights provides for natural citizens, that is, humans. However, as Adam Winkler has convincingly shown, the courts since the days of the early republic have been treating businesses, and later on corporations, as if they did in fact have rights.

Adam Winkler; see *We the Corporations: How American Businesses Won Their Civil Rights* (New York: Liveright/Norton, 2018).

Following *Citizens United* the American Civil Liberties Union by a narrow vote accepted the need for some limits on campaign contributions. The information on the ACLU's position from *Buckley* forward can be found on www.aclu.org; see especially the press release dated April 18, 2010. The decision upset many people, including longtime civil liberties activist Burt Neuborne; see his "Why the ACLU Is Wrong about *Citizens United*," *Nation*, March 21, 2012.

Everything one might want to know about the *McCutcheon* case is in Ronald Collins and David Skover, *When Money Speaks: The* McCutcheon *Decision, Campaign Finance Laws and the First Amendment* (Chicago: SCOTUS Books-in-Brief, 2014). See also Bradley A. Smith, "*McCutcheon v. FEC*: An Unlikely Blockbuster," 9 *New York University Journal of Law and Liberty* 48 (2015); and Sarah C. Haan, "The CEO and the Hydraulics of Campaign Finance Deregulation," 109 *Northwestern University Law Review* 27 (2014).